# FOR
## *the*
# PEOPLE

# FOR

## *the*

# PEOPLE

*A Story of Justice and Power*

# LARRY KRASNER

ONE WORLD

NEW YORK

*For the People* is a work of nonfiction. Some names and
identifying details have been changed.

Published in the United States by One World, an imprint of Random House,
a division of Penguin Random House LLC, New York.

ONE WORLD and colophon are registered trademarks of
Penguin Random House LLC.

LIBRARY OF CONGRESS CATALOGING-IN-PUBLICATION DATA
Names: Krasner, Larry, 1961– author.
Title: For the people : a story of justice and power / Larry Krasner.
Description: First edition. | New York : One World, 2021
Identifiers: LCCN 2020056778 (print) | LCCN 2020056779 (ebook) |
ISBN 9780593132920 (hardcover) | ISBN 9780593132937 (ebook)
Subjects: LCSH: Krasner, Larry, 1961– | Criminal defense lawyers—Pennsylvania—
Philadelphia—Biography. | Public prosecutors—Pennsylvania—Philadelphia—
Biography. | Criminal justice, Administration of—Pennsylvania—Philadelphia. |
Philadelphia (Pa.)—Politics and government
Classification: LCC KF373.K69 A3 2021 (print) | LCC KF373.K69 (ebook) |
DDC 340.092 ⌊B⌋—dc23
LC record available at https://lccn.loc.gov/2020056778

Printed in the United States of America on acid-free paper

oneworldlit.com

246897531

First Edition

Book design by Caroline Cunningham

*For Lisa, whose blue-gray eyes somehow see the future.*

# CONTENTS

# FOR
*the*
# PEOPLE

# INTRODUCTION

*Shine a light*
*Through the eyes of the ones left behind*
　　　　　—ELTON JOHN, "Philadelphia Freedom"

I am now the elected district attorney of the city and county of Philadelphia, Pennsylvania—one of the largest cities in the United States. Philadelphia is a diverse and wonderfully quirky city, known for Brotherly Love (and Sisterly Affection more recently), Ben Franklin, police corruption and brutality, the U.S. Constitution, cheesesteaks and soft pretzels, Questlove and the Roots, rabid sports fans, patronage, its successive waves of immigration, big-city ward politics, the Declaration of Independence, high poverty, high home ownership, a working-class attitude, affordability, a great restaurant scene, and its magnetic attraction for millennials. It's also known for bombing itself.

But this book is not about my time as DA. It's about the little story of how I got there—and the bigger story of how an outsider movement for criminal justice reform took power and then took office. Before I was sworn in, my long life's work as a lawyer was in criminal defense and civil rights—as far from the work of a traditional prosecutor as a lawyer could be. Back in that life, I joined with other Philly outsiders to push for justice against the insiders in the all-powerful Office of the District Attorney, the institution I now run. But our work as outsiders didn't accomplish a whole lot—at least not enough—before our movement did the uncomfortable thing: We took back power. We outsiders went inside and took over the institution we had fought against all our lives.

Philadelphia is rightly famous for its national parks, historical sites, statuary, and artifacts dedicated to the ideals of freedom and governmental restraint. Independence Mall, in the center of the city, includes the antique Independence Hall, where the Declaration of Independence and U.S. Constitution were drafted in all their deeply flawed glory. The little brick house where Betsy Ross sewed the first American flag from hemp is nearby. Independence Hall looks out at the National Constitution Center, a modern museum across a blocks-long grassy expanse. The tourist-friendly Liberty Bell Center sits on that grassy mall, adjacent to the museum's most recent and smallest addition: its guilty conscience, the slave memorial that roofs over the archaeological remains of General Washington's slaves' quarters. In Mount Vernon, Washington owned 316 slaves. As president in Philadelphia, he owned nine. They were: Oney Judge, Christopher Sheels, Hercules, Austin, Richmond, Paris, Giles, Moll, and Joe. The stone corners of the slaves' tight lodgings are underground, nearly hidden, visible only from ground level through glass. You have to look down to see them.

There are other good reasons to look down in Philly. The many legacies of slavery are also nearly hidden here. Unrestrained government still tramples freedom in the city, this time through its criminal justice system, but it can be hard to see. Consider, for example, that 27 percent of Pennsylvania's state prisoners in 2017 had been sentenced in only one of the state's sixty-seven counties: Philadelphia. Those incarcerated Philadelphians are hidden in prisons that dot the state's rural and suburban counties, stretching west until they run out at the Ohio border.

Sometimes the system hides in plain sight: In Philly you can't walk down a city block without passing someone currently on county probation or parole. You just don't know who it is. When I was running, Philadelphia's county supervision rate (the rate of people currently on probation and parole) was one in twenty-three, higher than in any other big city in America. Among African Americans, the rate was one in fourteen. For African American men in Philly, that rate was even higher. Philly's rate of county supervision was twelve times higher than the supervision rate in New York City, a two-hour drive north. In comparison, the rate of adults on probation or parole was one in fifty-five in the United States, the most carceral country in the world. Philly's rate was more than twice the national rate.

When I ran for DA, what was visible for decades in Philadelphia was an outsized police department the city could ill afford. Philadelphia—currently the country's sixth largest city—had the fourth largest police department, with more than six thousand uniformed personnel. Despite a thirty-year downward trend in crime nationally and locally, and despite being the poorest of the ten largest cities in the United States, the city continued to fund cops at the expense of desperately needed resources for public education; treatment for mental illness, addiction, and trauma; and economic development—all the things that we know actually prevent crime. Yet this generously funded police department had not reduced Philadelphia's rates of violent crime compared to other jurisdictions. The national and local downward trend in crime was real, but so was the fact that even during decades of declining crime, Philly chronically had higher violent crime rates than jurisdictions with smaller police departments.

The city's war on the freedom of its own citizens was also evident in the fact that, until recently, Philadelphia had sentenced more juveniles to life without any possibility of parole than any other city in the world. Sometimes Philly had sentenced those juveniles to death. Philadelphia remained the only northeastern U.S. city where the death penalty was even available—and it had a history of being one of the most prolific producers of death-row residents in the country.

Pennsylvania lawmakers hadn't helped their biggest city to reclaim its history as a cradle of freedom. Its legislators had increased the number of criminal offenses to nearly 1,500—a 500 percent increase from the 1970s, when there were 282 Pennsylvania crimes that worked just fine. Add to that Pennsylvania lawmakers' mad love for mandatory sentencing laws and high sentencing guidelines, and here was what you got: While the rest of the country had increased the number of people in prisons and jails an alarming 500 percent during the period of mass incarceration starting in the 1980s, Pennsylvania had increased its numbers more than 700 percent by 2017, with Philadelphia being its primary driver. Pennsylvania has outpaced the rest of the most incarcerating country in the world.

Many upstate Pennsylvania legislators' unrelenting urge for incarceration was pragmatic: Mass incarceration benefited their rural, exurban, and suburban county economies by feeding their primary industry, public state prisons, once coal and steel were gone. Mass incarceration increased highway funds (never mind that incarcerated people didn't drive) and other federal funding where state prisons were situated because inmate populations were counted in the local census. Mass incarceration also built political power through gerrymandering by counting people in jails as residents even though they couldn't vote. It advanced the careers of politicians who posed as good economic stewards for their counties, talking tough on crime, which affected their counties far less than Philadelphia and Pittsburgh. Meanwhile, these counties, where the coal and steel industries had disappeared, switched to mining the bodies of urban Pennsylvanians—people from somewhere else, whose racial, cultural, and economic differences made locking them up that much easier—and hid them in their state prisons. But my thirty years as a lawyer told me that even lawmakers' powers were slow and limited compared to the power a local chief prosecutor wielded. Legislators had little control over chief prosecutors' decision making—their discretion to decide how to handle their cases.

By the time I ran for Philly's chief prosecutor in 2017, I already knew that chief prosecutors hold the power to make life-changing decisions within their jurisdictions. They unilaterally decide whether or not to use the law to try to kill people, take their freedom, take their clean records and good reputations, take their future employability and their livelihoods, take their ability to form and provide for families, take them away from their families, and take their peace of mind and their money. Chief prosecutors have the latitude to offer favorable or unfavorable deals for guilty pleas on heavy or light charges, to offer diversion programs that avoid convictions, to drop cases, to try cases the right way or the wrong way, and to present honest or untruthful witnesses. They can decide to be impartial or use victims as political pawns, to hide evidence or provide it, to recklessly or purposefully convict the innocent, to leave wrongfully convicted people stuck in jail or help exonerate them, to over-incarcerate or de-carcerate, to try to be even-handed or discriminate, to wisely steward society's resources toward prevention and rehabilitation or burn up so much money on punishment that there's nothing left for anything else. It's a lot of power. And thirty years in courthouses had taught me the sad truth that most chief prosecutors have abused it.

When I ran my long-shot campaign to be Philly's chief elected prosecutor, I promised to try to reverse the damage done by traditional prosecution. I wasn't supported by the usual centrist powerbrokers, but I wasn't alone. I and other progressive prosecutors who were elected before and after me ran to be technicians for a growing national people's movement for criminal justice reform, arguably the most important civil rights issue of our time.

That movement rejects that the United States should be the most incarcerated country in the world. It intends to decarcerate. That movement embraces prevention, rehabilitation, and public health over punishment. For people who are suffering from addiction and mental illness, it prefers to treat rather than jail. That movement would reduce what we spend on jails and excessive policing to reinvest in public education, economic development, antiviolence efforts, treatment, and everything else that actually prevents crime. That movement embraces racial justice. That movement recognizes that traditional prosecution's grievous missteps don't just fail to prevent crime—they actually cause it by stealing resources from crime prevention programs that restore communities. Traditional prosecution breaks the people it should protect, which breaks their communities, their cities, and their towns. Ultimately, mass incarceration destroys so much of what we care about that it will eventually destroy itself.

But how does an extremely punitive criminal justice jurisdiction built on traditional prosecution destroy itself? Philadelphia has built two pricey, brand-new courthouses in recent years to handle its boom in criminal cases while simultaneously closing and selling public schools. What is the impact of defunding Philly students' public education and failing to graduate young people—robbing them of resources in exactly the years when young men are most prone to commit crime? Philly suburbs' public school funding remains much higher; its crime is much lower.

And what does a rapacious criminal justice system do to a city's economy? Is it a surprise that a city that has convicted and incarcerated and oversupervised so many of its youth, especially its men, also made them unemployable? Is it surprising that such a criminalized workforce is unattractive to businesses considering whether to locate in the city? Pernicious criminal justice turns those young people into poor taxpayers and poor providers for the rest of their lives. And all this incarceration and supervision is expensive. Not only does it lead to the economic disenfranchisement of the youth caught in its net, but it also helps explain how Philadelphia's economic decline and its chronically burdensome taxation incentivize even more flight from the city and a downward spiral in the tax base.

What alchemist drew water from the well of ignorance to come up with this poison brew of expensive criminal justice, lost businesses, lost tax revenues, lost employment, underfunded education, and despair? The legacy of Philadelphia's traditional prosecutors and institutional partners includes their impoverishment of the city. And poverty and despair catalyze more crime. Philadelphia is a glaring example of the need for criminal justice reform—but it is no outlier: Its problems are the problems of cities around the country. When I chose to run for office, I knew the bad news: Our decades-long radical adventure in an authoritarian, punitive, and broken criminal justice system had not merely failed to prevent crime: It had caused crime in ways a working system would prevent.

The good news is that profound change is possible in cities, their institutions, and their politics, just as it is in people. At its core, the movement for criminal justice reform recognizes that people change; it rejects a comic-book version of people as unchanging saints or monsters. That binary, fictional narrative is the cracked foundation of a system that tilts toward retribution and punishment rather than rehabilitation and prevention. The criminal justice reform movement recognizes that, just as people can profoundly change, so can institutions and so can the politics and the media that prop up those institutions, even after decades of failure. The real question is how?

This book is about facing the reality that traditional prosecutors and their institutional friends need to go, which will never happen until the rest of us take over their power. For most of my life before becoming Philadelphia's chief prosecutor, and even during that campaign, I have wrestled with the same questions: How and why is our criminal justice system so broken? How do we fix it and move forward? Where are the nuts and bolts to turn, and what tools will work to turn them in order to repair criminal justice? How do we fix the injustice of the past? How do we prevent injustice in the future? In our democracy, can we take power back when leadership has failed? If so, then how? Why are we afraid to seek power?

The miracle is that, after a long life of watching and wondering from the outside, I have a job now as a mechanic on the inside of a broken system, in support of this unrelenting grassroots movement to address the key civil rights issue of our time: criminal justice reform. But the story of our time in office in Philadelphia is not this book. Our wins and losses in office to date are a matter of public record, an open source and imperfect repair manual that incorporates the wisdom and battle scars of my fellow American criminal justice mechanics—the progressive prosecutors who, like me, are nothing more and nothing less than technicians for a national movement for criminal justice reform.

# CHAPTER 1

# Chasing Power

## *Campaign Announcement*

*Don't you know*
*They're talkin' 'bout a revolution*
*It sounds like a whisper*
　　　—TRACY CHAPMAN, "Talkin' 'bout a Revolution"

For thirty years of my career, I did the kind of work that makes you unelectable, or so the political insiders say. Voters said something else.

I was in the dark, holed up in the control booth of a television studio in Philly's public access television station, getting ready to announce my candidacy for district attorney. At fifty-six, I'd spent my career in court as a criminal defense and civil rights trial lawyer. I had tried and won a lot of cases. I got some justice for a lot of individuals, but that justice was never quite ideal. It was unbalanced, incomplete, and unsatisfactory. Even the wins showed me that the system needed to change. But as I tried case after case and the decades passed, the system didn't change. It was only getting worse. Our city was one of the most jail-happy cities in the most incarcerated country in the world. Too many serious crimes went unsolved, especially when the victims were powerless. In one area of concentrated poverty in Philly, the solve rate for shootings was only 15 percent. And, rather than being cared for and supported, too many victims were used for political purposes. Day after day, driving around Philadelphia, I saw for-sale signs on too many of our public school buildings. For years, while visiting clients in custody and their families in their homes I kept wondering why jails and prisons and new courthouses just kept growing like an unchecked tumor, while the things we all needed fell apart. The problem behind it all was the criminal justice system. We were coming together that day, to change it.

It was February 8, 2017, only ninety-eight days before the primary election, the only election that mattered in a one-party town like Philadelphia. The incumbent district attorney, Seth Williams, was in trouble: He was under federal investigation for improperly accepting gifts he didn't declare, possibly in exchange for special treatment in his handling of cases as DA. His potential indictment had drawn into the race five other candidates willing to challenge him. I knew most of them well—and, as always in Philly district attorney races, the challengers were like the incumbent—predictable, conventional, connected. None of them was a real reformer, regardless of what they claimed. I was frustrated by the lack of change in the system—by the never-ending squandering of lives and resources. So, despite my dislike for politics, I decided I had to run for DA, at least as my own kind of protest. Yes, my team and I wanted to win. But more than that, we had to speak the truth as we saw it. At least our platform might move the conversation.

I hadn't found the light switch yet in a room full of switches and controls. Sitting in darkness, I looked through the glass that separated the control room from the brightly lit, black box studio. The studio was starting to fill up with my people, many of them activists I had defended for free over the years.

"My people" looked powerless to others. They were anything but powerless. They had fought AIDS, fought for disability rights, were disabled themselves, gave out clean needles under elevated train tracks, did pirate radio, were advocates for homeless people or were homeless themselves, said their Black lives mattered, worked to end global warming, were queer, camped out with Occupy, fought pollution, opposed casinos, wanted peace, were sex workers fighting to be safe, were addicted to drugs and seeking treatment, were clergy who shut down dirty gun shops with hymns. Or they weren't activists at all, but they cared deeply and found ways to support the ones risking arrest. I admired them all for having already changed the world with their selfless pursuit of justice and for aspiring to do more.

At some point, I had begun to refer to the activists and organizers I usually represented for free, or to people in their worlds I respected who provided support for their work, as "my people." I used the phrase to mean they were doing God's work, fighting the good fight, willing to sacrifice so that others would be okay. "My people" and I weren't the same. I didn't control or possess them any more than they possessed me when I did their legal work for free. But we were a team of people who wanted the same things: We wanted fairness, equality, freedom, the protection we deserved from our government rather than its contempt, justice for marginalized people. We liked to knock down bullies and to speak about it as the Constitution mandated we had the freedom to do.

Sometimes when I referred to "my people," they were under my umbrella; other times I was under theirs. The phrase was meant to be humorous. It was meant to be ironic, to highlight that we were starkly different but somehow together. "My people" was the only tribal claim I liked—a descriptor for a group of people whose basic belief in equality made them skeptical of division and tribalism. My people were a tribe that could include everyone; call them an anti-tribe. As I looked around the studio, I saw my people, but there wasn't a politician in sight. That was fine by me.

My people were outsiders, but they were the opposite of powerless. Activists are more than people yelling in the street and blocking traffic. They are often visionaries who see the future we need before the rest of us see it. At their best, they are a fascinating bunch of theorists and communicators who catalyze change. They'd taught me that being outside the narrow halls of traditional power doesn't mean you're powerless—that power doesn't just take one form. Power can wear a badge or a black robe, but it can also be nothing more than a courageous voice. Power can be any of us.

A few days prior, I had sent out a couple hundred deliberately vague text messages to my people, inviting them to "an announcement." A mild buzz of speculation had followed among the invitees and the few press members who showed up, but most of them had no idea what I would announce.

I concentrated on the typewritten outline of my speech while I paced, whispering my way through several minutes of a solo rehearsal. Each time I rehearsed, it sounded okay until it didn't. Then I stopped and drew arrows to change the sequence of phrases or add one or change a word. A couple of times I scratched out my new edits. The original sounded better. Then it didn't.

Lisa, my life partner of more than thirty years, wasn't there, even though she was the one who'd taught me what I knew about electoral politics. Almost twenty years earlier she had gotten herself elected judge as an insurgent candidate, against all odds. But now, as a sitting judge, she was required to stay away from politics, including my announcement. It would have been nice to see her eyes through that glass, on the inside of the studio. I checked my watch and noticed a couple of my fingernails were slightly chewed, which usually happened when I was mid–jury trial on a heavy case. The seeming impossibility of my risky choice to run for district attorney weighed on me.

For a minute, I was a broke thirteen-year-old again, wearing secondhand clothes and riding in the back seat of a squeaking, rusty car with my much older parents. For a minute, I felt slight and ridiculous again, was afraid of being laughed at and dismissed, was in that back seat dreaming of something bigger with no basis for believing it would ever come. My speech needed to turn everything I knew from a thirty-year criminal justice career into a ten-or-so-minute platform that was short enough for social media but long enough to explain our plan for reforming criminal justice in Philadelphia. A few other major cities had already elected some amazing progressive prosecutors, enough to create a nascent national movement. Now it was Philly's turn to try to join that movement. Win or lose, there would be consequences for my family and for me.

When I decided to run for district attorney, I knew that when incumbent chief prosecutors run for reelection, they run unopposed over 80 percent of the time. Almost no one dares to run against them, and for good reason. Qualified candidates come from two camps: current prosecutors who work for the chief prosecutor they would run against, and criminal defense attorneys who work in courtrooms where losing means they could be badly hurt by the office of the chief prosecutor they would run against.

Life was not going to be easy if I lost. I knew the drubbing I could expect as payback for my campaign against the incumbent DA if he won: pettiness, dirtier tactics, worse plea offers for my clients for the rest of my career. If another candidate beat the incumbent and beat me, it still wouldn't be easy. But I had to put fear out of my mind for this announcement and for the campaign, or I'd start acting like a politician. People hate most politicians for being self-absorbed weather vanes, chameleons—frightened, hedging, poll driven, unprincipled putty ready to conform to any shape to get approval. They are proud of their ability to answer yes and no simultaneously, and equally proud of their ability to "pivot"—and respond to anyone's question by answering a question they weren't asked. Just ask them and their operatives, who brag about it. We call it ducking, evasion; to them it's artful. Most politicians struck me as less truthful than many of my criminal defense clients, whose motivations weren't always great, either, but who sometimes told the truth even when that meant admitting to a crime. I viewed most incumbent elected officials as politicians to whom people had given all the resources and all the power to make things better for them, but who wouldn't make things better for reasons that were almost always selfish.

In 2017, the activists and organizers I knew or had studied inspired me much more than most politicians. I was born in 1961 and grew up with civil rights movements on television, especially the Black civil rights movement. I was fortunate that this was my first, formative lesson in activism. These black-and-white forms on television were men and women who faced down violence to fight a genuine evil; they weren't just brave and disruptive but also strategic and persuasive. They didn't just fight. They won. Or at least they won more often than they should have. But those wins changed the country—and the world. As a small child, I watched them wage their campaigns, and ever since I had lived in the better world they dreamed into existence. There were other great movements besides the one for Black equality that played out on our television screen—movements against war and pollution, for labor, for women's rights and Latinx and immigrants' rights.

The sacrifice of the women and men who fought for others felt brave and real. At worst, activists merely failed to improve things. At best—embodied by people like Martin Luther King, Jr., and Cesar Chavez and Rosa Parks—their righteous work lured in and crushed their opposition, without money or violence. They were strategic and smart, but fully committed. They risked it all as the movements they served gained ground.

I went to law school inspired by the legacy of America's civil rights era, of its activists and organizers. Even before I graduated from law school in 1987, I was too driven by goals and deadlines and financial needs—and fear of how an arrest might wreck my unrealized future as the first lawyer in my family—to become an activist myself. I didn't put myself on the barricades, but I found my own way to fight as a young lawyer: I could defend activists who got arrested in a courtroom. Defending them meant I had to study the history and theory of protest to explain the motivations and intent behind their actions, which are central to any criminal case. I did, and was particularly inspired by civil disobedience strategy: the how-to of righteous, non-violent action that provokes the oppressor to reveal its claws. Once those claws are exposed, the public sees the oppressor's true nature and everything changes. During the civil rights movement, authorities used dogs and fire hoses on well-dressed idealists while they prayed. The world watched. We know the result: The haters lost. Illegitimate, violent governmental power lost those crucial battles, even though the war has not yet ended.

My people were the same. They had engaged in non-violent direct action to achieve positive social change in Philadelphia, so police arrested them, and prosecutors went for their throats. Philly prosecutors charged them with crimes, demanded jail time, and nearly always lost, as haters do, failing to convict them of anything. Far from intimidating or dissuading my people, the Philly prosecutors and police radicalized them. We won cases at trial time after time. The unfairness and injustice the protesters endured in the process only built their capacity and resolve. Their movements had already changed the city against the force of institutionalized power. They had wins: countless lives saved from HIV, AIDS, and hepatitis; better public schools than the government was prepared to provide; the closing of a dirty gun shop; advances toward equality for poor people, labor, Black and brown people, and LGBTQ people; reductions in pollution; increased mobility for disabled people via curb cuts now enjoyed by every tourist in Philadelphia hauling a rolling bag; greater access to addiction treatment; casinos pushed away from the city's center toward its outskirts; and even the very existence of the public access television studio where we were all gathering. My people knew their unrecognized power. And they disdained the subset of police and prosecutors who had chosen to treat them, and everyone else inaccurately seen as powerless and marginalized, so unfairly.

For a certain stripe of Philly prosecutors and police, the antipathy was mutual. Rather than simply keep the peace when demonstrators gathered to advocate by peacefully protesting within their rights for these causes, these government agents were so affronted that the protesters had gathered at all that they attacked with bogus arrests and overblown charges. They hated the protesters precisely because they were different, effective, dramatic, and loud as they called out powerful interests, including the governmental authority that paid and employed police and prosecutors. When protesters chanted "Whose streets? Our streets!," they were right. But much of the Philly criminal justice system went all out to prove them wrong. At times, the Philadelphia District Attorney's Office assigned homicide prosecutors—their elite trial lawyers, who should have been handling the most pressing criminal cases—to go after non-violent protesters who had committed no crimes. In Philly, the place where our constitutional rights to peacefully protest were written, government through its police and prosecutors tried to destroy the protesters' futures with more zeal than in any other American big city at the time. For ordinary, seemingly powerless, outsider defendants, it was terrifying. It radicalized them; they persisted. Some attended the announcement.

The public access television station was a welcoming, no-frills venue to announce the campaign. It was a populist and egalitarian place, one that existed only because of activist friends and ex-clients who had fought for years to make the cable TV industry in Philadelphia reluctantly do what the law required from the beginning: give up a sliver of nonprofit bandwidth to the public in exchange for the massive windfall generated by their much larger, for-profit bandwidth. The public access station was also my choice.

I'd chosen it partly because I believed in its mission and what announcing there said about our campaign, but also because I wanted a studio event where I could control and record the message and deliver it for free on social media repeatedly, at any moment of our campaign's choosing. I had learned about media from defending activists in the AIDS Coalition to Unleash Power (ACT UP), a grassroots group founded to end the global AIDS epidemic whose tactics were epic. Nobody understood media strategy better than they did. They taught me that to own your message, you need to be concise, to tell it your way, and to do it all at once. And then repeat it with discipline. Media will have no choice but to take your message.

I wasn't well-known enough for mainstream journalists to dignify my upcoming and mysterious announcement with a story, or for them to take our unlikely campaign seriously unless they saw it getting traction. So if word of the campaign's announcement leaked early, it would probably mean scoffing coverage in the mainstream press that might obscure our message and our difference from the other candidates. To avoid that, I decided to announce my campaign and my platform all at once, as I had learned from ACT UP, as briefly as would cover all that territory. My hope was that the platform itself, its goals, and the movement would become the story, and would overshadow the usual horse race coverage of the obvious improbability of my being elected.

The typical horse race coverage is all about who will win rather than who should win; more about polling and conflict between candidates and sensationalism than about serious ideas and actual experience. Horse race journalism betrays democracy for the sake of ratings and advertising revenues. In a horse race story, we were losers. But our platform was full of ideas that were far more winning than we seemed to be. I hoped that by making the platform and the campaign announcement the same message, it would resonate with people's lives and experience.

When I was a trial lawyer, scripted closing arguments had never worked for me. Looking down at notes to read them made me look away from the faces and reactions of the people I needed to reach. Memorization of a scripted closing didn't work, either. I wasn't an actor who could make a memorized script sound fresh. And I couldn't write my own word-for-word script without turning on an endless cycle of editing and overthinking that inevitably wrecked whatever was direct, genuine, and emotive in the first draft. So when I prepared a lengthy closing argument after days of obsessively thinking about it, I scribbled down short notes on a page or two of a yellow legal pad, a checklist to pick up late in the closing, a way to jump-start my memory if I forgot a point. When I was on, my closing arguments flowed from those days of thinking. I used notes only toward the end to ensure I hadn't skipped anything that needed to be said.

The morning of the campaign announcement, I huddled in the lobby of my law office with Brandon Evans, the main strategist in my new campaign, and Jody Dodd, my office manager for a decade and an experienced activist. Brandon was in his mid-thirties, Black, broad-shouldered, strategic, focused, no-nonsense. That day, he was hyper-focused, all business. Brandon was raised by a single mother who held down two jobs during most of his youth. She worked for decades in high-level administrative spots for a criminal defense lawyer and then for a federal judge in Florida. His childhood around lawyers and courts helped build his real insight into criminal justice. Brandon went to college, then worked as an organizer and political consultant for labor, including in the South, where Stacey Abrams mentored him, and then for the Working Families Party (WFP), developing his political chops.

Before I decided to run for district attorney, I met Brandon in

WFP's West Philly office, where his title was Pennsylvania state director. He and a national WFP director vetted me, as they had a few other potential Philly DA candidates. We met at a small table in WFP's storefront office located in the commercial corridor of a mostly Black, working-class, and moderately poor neighborhood—one skinny, gray-haired white man in a suit and tie facing two younger Black men in casual clothes. It looked like an unlikely but intense poker game during which the other players, chips, and cards had been raptured.

Brandon repeatedly knocked me sideways with polite questions that invited no platitudes. He was testing whether I was serious about change, whether I could connect to marginalized people, whether I could manage my end of a campaign, whether I could raise money, and whether I had the stomach for an election that would be an ugly fight and the uglier fight that would come later if I won. I could tell from his questions that Brandon had already studied my career and asked around. As a career trial lawyer, I loved the stealthy questions. He knew his craft and had no tell. I was comfortable on the criminal justice questions. I was off balance on some political questions, but I stuck to what I knew and thought. I was too old to overpromise. I wasn't sure how my vetting had gone by the time I left, but I knew that if I ran Brandon needed to be on my team.

After I left the office, a few men were standing around admiring my parked red Tesla, an unusual sight that year in Philly. They asked about the mechanics. We spoke for a couple of minutes about the electric car's mechanics before I got in and drove away. Brandon later told me he and his D.C. colleague were watching through the plate glass to see how I interacted with the men standing near my car in a neighborhood where the candidate they selected would soon have to be comfortable going and getting votes.

Once the campaign was under way, Brandon's office would consist of a cellphone, a backpack, and a laptop so he could keep moving. He made a point of keeping everybody in the campaign in their lane partly by keeping them out of his, including me, by disregarding my novice candidate questions. Most of the time he came off as stern, a progressive pragmatist and theorist focused on winning elections for the select politicians he believed would actually walk their talk. In a lighter mood most people didn't see, he was a hilarious, deeply expressive storyteller with a slightly southern flair and a nerdy Civil War historian whose satire of campaign dysfunction and holier-than-thou infighting among liberals and progressives was priceless. As the campaign wore on, I was increasingly aware of how lucky I was to have his experience in organizing and political campaigns.

Jody was slightly older than me, a white career activist and hell-raiser from West Texas, the part I like to call Willie Nelson Texas. I first met her in 2000 when she came to Philly to protest at the Republican convention, liked the city, and stayed. By 2017, Jody was the den mother of all Philly's activists and organizers, a wise and trusted rock whose twenty righteous arrests for free speech activity layered experience on her deep knowledge of non-violent protest, direct action tactics, and movements. In the world of street protest, notoriously against hierarchy and its trappings, she was still revered—an OG. She also enjoyed treating me like a pesky, slightly younger brother despite the fact that she supposedly worked for me.

My Center City law office, where Brandon and I met on the morning of the announcement, was in two joined antique row houses in the middle of a narrow, historic street in the area old-time residents still call the gayborhood because of its history as a center of queer life and activism. Gentrifying real estate developers preferred to call the area Midtown Village, much to the chagrin of the longtime locals. I'd had my law offices there since 2000, before the real estate developers caught on, when some other lawyers and I bought the vacant building—holes in the roof, water in the walls—with an SBA loan, and began fixing it up.

Brandon and I were sitting in the office lobby on squeaky, tufted leather sofas and chairs by the giant fish tank. I was staring through its glass at the oblivious fish, which looked like a bunch of moving flowers bathed in light, amused by the irony of their aquatic incarceration as we worked on the campaign announcement. I was riffing, rolling through the platform topics with Brandon. Jody and other people from the campaign or from my law office were in and out of my conversation with Brandon. Intermittently, Jody fielded calls and kept the law-firm ship on course. Over several days we had debated whether to announce all the platform's planks this early, but by the day of the announcement we agreed that we should. Ours was not a personality or experience campaign: It was a campaign of specific ideas that were unfamiliar and even hostile to the status quo. Our voters needed to know that from the jump. With only ninety-eight days to go, there was no time for a slow roll or ambiguity.

The platform summarized the lessons I had lived and learned and heard by listening closely in my time in the justice system. It was what I knew to be true and what needed to happen if we were to move toward a truly just justice system.

We are all equal and deserving of our government's protection, provided with transparency, respect, and restraint. In such a system, equal treatment is justice. And that kind of justice restores society—restores the relationship between people and government, and makes us safer. Safety and justice are symbiotic and complementary, not trade-offs between opposing forces, as the status quo would have us believe.

Our current criminal justice system is broken; it is unjust and unsafe. Its unfairness and its mad love of retribution have given us a network of mostly hidden gulags that, upon even light inspection, reveal the profound racism of the system that stretches back, largely unchanged, to slavery. This broken system causes crime; it makes us unsafe.

And what is the answer? Where are the nuts and bolts to fix

this old, broken car—to change out the parts too dysfunctional to go on so we can keep the rest of the machine moving toward a better place and modernize it yet again?

We need to get people out of jail. Our jails and prisons fail to rehabilitate; often they are so jammed they don't even try. This means turning away from everything that has caused mass incarceration, including the unnecessary charging of cases, the overcharging of cases, the use of cash bail, policing and prosecution that are lawless and lacking in integrity, and the failure to divert cases away from conviction toward other forms of accountability and rehabilitation. We need to eliminate mandatory sentencing schemes and sentencing guidelines that are too high and that tie the hands of judges, stopping them from doing their job—judging. A death penalty that is unjust, burns money, and never results in executions serves no purpose.

Our broken system also needs prosecutors to stand up for victims, rather than manipulate and use them for political and career-building purposes, only to discard them once there is a conviction and the case file is closed. This requires closely considering and counting the many kinds of victims, their needs, and their trauma. It requires hearing what they say and seeing them as they are, rather than imagining them as traditional and inaccurate stereotypes. Vulnerable victims include sex workers, people suffering from the disease of addiction, innocent people sentenced for others' crimes, survivors and victims whose crimes are never solved, and immigrants afraid to protect themselves within the system for fear that Immigration and Customs Enforcement (ICE) will deport them. And it requires doing everything in our power to prevent more victimization in the future, by investing broadly as a society in what will prevent serious crime.

By fixing this broken system, we can allow police and prosecutors to focus on the most serious crimes rather than using the ever-widening net they have now for poor people and Black and brown people. That wide net only makes it harder to apprehend and appropriately sentence the much smaller group of people whose crimes tear the fabric of society.

By fixing this broken system, we can save the massive resources spent on unnecessary incarceration and reinvest them in the things that we know for certain actually do prevent crime: education, treatment, job training, and anti-poverty measures, carried out by social workers, public school teachers, and police officers committed to community policing, the annual cost of which is about the same as the unnecessary and destructive incarceration of another human being. This is how and this is why justice makes us safer.

It was what we believed. There were no pollsters to tell political operatives to tell us what we should think, thank God. Even if we had money for them, no thanks. We didn't want recycled truisms from centrist has-beens, mainstream journalists, the prosecutors who gave us mass incarceration, or anyone else whose criminal justice knowledge was not learned in their bones, on their block, in their community, or at a criminal justice job that became their life's work and where the fight they fought was good. We just wanted to say what we wanted to say.

There were some wonderful, smart, and strategic people who knew of our plans to launch a campaign with our full, progressive platform and reached out to preach caution. "Do you really need to mention the death penalty? I mean . . . are we really trying to win?" We listened to these well-wishers, thought it through, and decided, ultimately, this was no time for caution. Our shot at winning was to tell the truth—the most powerful and exciting weapon in our arsenal, maybe the only one—and see if we could get Philly to join a growing national movement.

Time was getting close. I looked up from my notes again and through the glass that separated the control room from the studio. Brandon and Jody and the rest of the team were out there somewhere in that growing crowd of people, I guessed. It occurred to me it was midafternoon; the day so far had been a blur. I shrugged and rubbed my face, noting the light afternoon stubble. I ducked into the bathroom, checked the already snug knot in my tie, and used water from the sink to plaster down a few unruly gray hairs. I cracked my neck.

It was time. Everything slowed down as I walked the few steps to the brightly lit black box studio. I was crossing a line from lawyer to politician, from sideline commentator to activist campaigner. I headed for the fake wooden podium the studio had wheeled in and was, even now, wiring for sound.

Walking into the studio, I was glad to be surrounded. I felt old for this adventure, but also ready, and my people were with me. If the announcement went well, it would lay out our platform in full, stir up social media, and energize a Philly piece of the movement. If it didn't go well—if my nerves overwhelmed my trial experience or if our platform fell flat—it would be an embarrassing failure, a defining landmark of my later career, and criminal justice in Philadelphia would go on as usual, unjustly penalizing the poor, the politically engaged, and the powerless. But everyone in that studio had taken wins and losses, so it would be okay. I waited a second for my words to show up.

"Thank you for coming," I said.

I stopped, took a deep breath, and started talking. Flop or not, here I was. In the next ten or so minutes, I announced my candidacy for district attorney of Philadelphia, and explained our entire platform. I paused occasionally to look around the studio to see if people were leaving or laughing. Everyone was right there. They were looking back, some nodding. When I talked about decarceration, about getting people out of jail, a few shouted encouragement as if we were all together in a lively house of worship. Others joined them briefly. There was some applause; anticipation was giving way to enthusiasm.

I kept an eye on the clock, as I did during closing arguments, trying hard to keep the announcement to about ten minutes. I spoke slowly, paused occasionally, and breathed deeply to ward off my scrambled emotions. These were useful tactics I had learned from watching other lawyers whose jobs required their standing before juries that would decide whether or not to execute their clients—or whether their clients were even guilty. There was an economy of words, an unhurried pace. I managed my emotions and nerves well until about nine minutes and thirty seconds in, when I was wrapping up my speech thanking the many lawyers, activists, and organizers in attendance who had for so many years fought "the good fight."

And then, suddenly and for a moment, when I heard myself say those words I choked up. What I saw moved me: A circle of people facing one another who had chosen throughout their lives to take the hard way, to make trouble, to bear the abuse heaped on them by the insiders and their institutions that would later reap the benefits of reform at no real cost to themselves. I had watched these people do battle in "the good fight" for others who couldn't easily fight for themselves. Having these fighters surrounding me in a circle—these activists and advocates and angelic warriors—so attentively staring back at that moment humbled me, and started to make me wonder if we would win. I concluded by asking everyone in and outside of that room to "join us." I checked my watch: ten minutes on the nose.

I called up my campaign chair, the activist lawyer Mike Lee, whose buoyant, youthful optimism and humor were reflected in his bright floral bow tie and especially bright smile. Mike ended the event with a quick list of next steps and a call to action. I knew that Mike and his partner were expecting their first child, whose gestation and birth would overlap and coincide with the campaign. Then came a circle of powerful applause, including mine, for everyone else there.

The announcement video spread quickly on Facebook in Philadelphia, including my choke at the end of the speech. Within a few days, the announcement video's views far outnumbered those of the slick commercial that Dick Rubio, supposedly a leading candidate, had been circulating for months. His ad was a high-resolution scare tactic, a shadowy three-minute piece that showed him all over the city looking and sounding like Batman making Philly Gotham safe for little boys wearing football uniforms (a detail to remind us that Dick had briefly played pro football, as if that mattered). Dick's professional commercial, which included no real platform, got a couple thousand hits in three months. Our low-tech video was a stationary shot from a single camera in a black box studio of a fake wood podium and a talking head—mine. Within one week, more than twenty thousand people had viewed our video. We could feel the ground moving under us because we said something, and because activists do what they do.

One day after the announcement, the news hinted that Seth Williams, the incumbent DA who was seeking reelection, was about to be indicted in federal court on corruption charges for improperly accepting gifts he did not disclose as the law required. The timing was surprising, earlier than expected, although everyone knew that Williams was under investigation. Most people expected that he would face whatever might be coming after he was reelected. Only three days after my campaign announcement, Williams ended his campaign for a third term. Within months he was charged with crimes Ultimately, he was sentenced to five years in federal prison. But on that day, the day he withdrew from the race, every current and wannabe candidate knew the election was wide open. I was the sixth candidate to declare; soon enough there would be a seventh.

I was an older, unlikely novice candidate running as an outsider against insiders. My team and I were doing things our way, regardless of the consequences—and we started late. It was time to go looking for our voters, with only ninety-eight days to go.

# CHAPTER 2

# Early Outsider

*You get mistaken for strangers by your own friends*
*When you pass them at night*
*Under the silvery, silvery Citibank lights*
*Arm in arm in arm and eyes and eyes, glazing under*
—The National, "Mistaken for Strangers"

I've introduced you to some outsiders at our campaign announcement. Now let's talk about what made me run. Law and politics are dominated by insiders: people who work in rooms and go home to neighborhoods that most of the rest of us will never know. Even the most well-meaning politicians often live far away from the life experiences of the people they serve. But there's no law that says politicians have to be rich, or to come from political dynasties, or to be connected to power players and in service to them. There's nothing about wealth that says anything about the wealthy besides that they were lucky, maybe from birth or before—they are not necessarily smarter, harder working, more humane, more resourceful, or more resilient than anyone else. We all know this intuitively, but the play of luck and misfortune in our own lives is our strongest lesson in this truth. The trick is making sure we don't forget it.

When I was about eight, I was watching cartoons in our living room one afternoon when my dad opened the front door of our recently bought, basic Philly-area two-story home. It was after school, but he was home from the office early. He wore a dark gray suit that matched his silver hair, big black "gunboat" shoes, as he called them, a white shirt, and a skinny dark tie. My dad was a funny man who liked to fake being a curmudgeon, and I waited for him to say something amusing, or just something, as he usually did when he walked in. But he limped across the living room, not even looking in my direction, and disappeared quietly into a first-floor bedroom, where my mother was waiting for him. They closed the door.

I went back to watching cartoons, a little distracted. I could hear my parents speaking but couldn't tell what they were saying. When my dad came out, his face was flushed. My mom walked out after him, and I heard her saying as she followed, "God will provide." My mother was a woman of deep Christian faith—a former tent evangelist and seminary student—and this was the kind of hopeful thing she would have said to a firing squad from the crosshairs. I forgot the cartoons. I knew there was trouble and, even more alarming, that my parents were trying to shield me from it. It felt like someone had yanked a blanket off and suddenly everything was a little colder and less certain.

After that day, my dad mostly worked from home. Even at eight, I knew that jobs worked in an office funded by someone else, the kind you dressed up for in a suit and polished shoes, were the ones with steady pay. In 1970, my dad's daily working from home in casual clothes was another signal to me that we might need some help.

My parents were older than anyone else's parents I knew. Dad was forty-five when I was born; Mom was forty. They had weathered the Great Depression, early jobs and careers, World War II, higher education, and next careers before they found each other. By the time I was born, Dad was increasingly bothered by arthritis, especially in his hips, and jungle rot in his toenails from serving in the Pacific during the war.

We had moved to Philadelphia when Dad was hired away from an editing job at Washington University in St. Louis—where he and my mother both had roots—to become a full-time staff writer in Philly for a Big Pharma company. My parents bought an affordable house in a Philly suburb where there were good public schools and hoped to build a more comfortable, secure life. And then he and a dozen other professional writers who were hired with him were all laid off, without explanation. Once my father lost the job that anchored it all, and far from any family who could help out, my parents were struggling. My father's unexpected layoff was the first time I really grasped that power does what it wants to outsiders, and not necessarily with malice. Sometimes power is just indifferent, self-absorbed, blindered and clueless, or guided by a star that points far away from where the rest of us need to go.

After getting laid off, my dad became a full-time freelance writer. He co-wrote a book on European treatments for drug addiction called *Drug Trip Abroad* for some professors at the University of Pennsylvania. He wrote government reports for the National Institutes of Health and corporate propaganda, did some journalism, and wrote scripts for one-minute-long commentaries read by a local TV news anchor. The freelance writing was a hustle of short-term deadlines and short-term payments up against a long-term mortgage and other steady bills. All the while he continued writing novels, all but one under his name. Before and after he had a family to support, he wrote novels with good publishers and good reviews, but that didn't turn into much money in his lifetime. Meanwhile, my mother was busy with kids and part-time work, including at our public school library for a while.

Probably my parents' wisest decision after moving from Missouri was to buy a cheap house and live in a neighborhood that provided good public schools. We lived in a mostly white, moderately affluent, politically conservative, Christian (at least in the performative sense) suburb that was proudly unburdened by big government in 1970. Most of the houses had cesspools rather than sewers. There were no public swimming pools. Even the local YMCA pool was unaffordable, possibly by design. Sidewalks were scarce. Some of the richer areas near us had big lawns that went all the way to the curb, and kids got yelled at by homeowners for walking on the grass next to the curb. Cars were permitted in that part of town; human feet, not really. The lesson was clear: You got exactly what you could afford and nothing more—not even a sidewalk.

In high school, I worked hard. My mind was set on going to a really good and prestigious college, as I was sure that would lead to unlimited opportunity. I thought that a strong work ethic and a good education would be my armor against the trouble my parents had in their lives, even though I knew that my parents' education and work ethic had failed to protect them.

At school and in the neighborhood, I usually kept to myself or hung out with a hardy band of outsider kids. I had reasons to feel like one: My parents were older and didn't socialize with a lot of the other parents. My dad's limp was increasing and obvious even before arthritis disabled him—other kids used to ask me if he was my grandfather. My dad was Jewish, unlike nearly all of our neighbors, in a place where young boys played a rough game of tackle football they called "Screw the Jew." My mother was a devout Christian married to a secular Jewish man, which worked for them but was even more unusual. We were a little different in any gathering of Christians or Jews, no matter how welcoming. Our politics didn't match the neighborhood. Also, everybody could tell we were broke: The car was beat if it was even running; the clothes were secondhand thrift-store items, hand-me-downs, or from Kmart if they were new. And our gradually

becoming supported by government programs was embarrassing for my parents and, by extension, for me. My dad had no
control over his physical illness, had volunteered and served in a
war, and was a good man his whole life. My mom was a bright
idealist who graduated from high school at sixteen before completing college and attending divinity school. She came from a
family of Missouri dirt farmers and raised a family. My parents
were decent people who had tried hard. Their troubles felt embarrassing and unfair.

I learned to embrace the outsider identity and its broke principles: Get by with less because you must; fix things yourself;
spot pitfalls and avoid them because you have no resources to
climb out of the pit; know that all jobs are worthy and so are the
people who do them; no one "deserves" anything. My competi-
tive spirit showed up. I enjoyed figuring out how to get things
done with less, learning to fix or replace the part that was broken
rather than replace the whole machine, avoiding waste, being
self-reliant, thinking critically, getting ready to overcome whatever came next. I was a kind of survivalist, a fan of people who
were self-reliant enough to make or fix or figure out anything. I
felt like a saner version of the guy with the backyard bunker full
of canned food.

I learned valuable lessons from trash picking and then fixing
broken furniture, clocks, and lamps; from building bicycles with
cannibalized dumpster-dived parts; repairing our roof; replacing
the clothes dryer belt and motor assembly; replacing the frozen,
cracked toilet tank and its mechanism; and eventually fixing and
tuning up cars. Working on cars taught me to reject the idea that
everything is a trade-off in a system—that improving one thing
always makes something else worse. It turns out that a well-
tuned car is faster, more powerful, quieter, smoother, more fuel
efficient, and pollutes less all at the same time—no trade-offs
needed.

Fixing cars and machines taught me that in any repair there

are always a couple of details that delay or derail the whole project, like a couple of stripped bolts or rusted nuts that take more
time to remove and replace than the other twenty-five combined.
Working laboring jobs—as a janitor, landscaper, painter, and
carpenter's flunky—taught me how skilled and how interesting
these jobs and the people who do them can be. And all of it taught
me that things other people are eager to discard in their entirety
can be fixed, repaired, repurposed, and rehabilitated enough to
move us further down the road. There's almost nothing that
can't be made better immediately and last awhile until something
completely new and much improved comes along.

Even as I learned broke skills, I had no grasp of affluent skills
necessary for a life I wasn't living. I wasn't good at feeling comfortable in airports and airplanes, understanding the basics of
banking and finance, buying nice clothing, acting right in nice
restaurants and vacation spots, being socially capable around affluent people, or accepting gifts gracefully.

As a teenager, I wanted to outdo the comfortable kids, especially the mean ones who rode around in their parents' nice cars
and wore pricey clothes. I would leave class and jump straight
into my parents' squeaky old Rambler with my vinyl "bobo"
sneaks and drive away. Outside of school, the comfortable kids
and I were seldom in the same spaces; we didn't see each other's
lives. I simultaneously idealized their lives and rejected them.

My parents' challenges and losses made it easier for me to feel
my wins. I was already overcoming challenges in high school and
at home. They were proud of me for my achievements, even the
humble ones. And, though it made me uneasy, I already knew
that in a polite, racist society, I might have the disadvantage of
being broke with an increasingly disabled dad, but I had the for-
midable advantage of being white.

Classes in my Philly-area suburban public school were a lot
different from those in my diverse St. Louis city public elemen-

tary school, where I attended kindergarten through third grade. Race wasn't talked about in my high school, except awkwardly in history class. But the effects of institutional racism were everywhere. Like many suburban public high schools at the time, my school was officially integrated but actually segregated, one classroom at a time. Our high school was separated into three tracks. Track 3 was predominantly Black and brown kids with a few broke white kids. Track 2 was mostly working-class and broke white kids, or affluent kids who were acting out. Track 1 was primarily affluent white kids. There was a smattering of Black and brown kids in Tracks 1 and 2, but the pattern was clear. I saw the separation, but said nothing and did nothing. I stayed busy scheming on good grades, the troubles at home, and what great things might come next if I just worked hard and got into a good college.

Toward the end of my high school career, my dad's health crashed. For a couple of days, he had been upstairs gobbling aspirin, hoping that his hip joints would loosen up one more time and worrying about how to pay medical bills if he went to the hospital with no private health insurance. Then, one night, I watched two burly EMTs struggle and sweat carrying him on a gurney down the narrow stairs in our house before loading him into an ambulance. Strapped in on the tilting gurney, he was trying hard not to call out in pain from the unavoidably rough handling on his frozen, crunching hips. I could see it in his grimace and how tightly he grabbed the gurney's sides.

My dad would spend most of a year in Bryn Mawr Hospital for bilateral hip replacement surgeries and lengthy rehabilitations. Hip surgery is moderately intrusive and highly effective now. But in 1978 in his case it meant incisions from mid-thigh to his lower ribs on both sides, lots of old-school bone carpentry, and lengthy rehab. There were separate operations for each hip. My mother kept us together. We visited him a lot, transported mostly by me in the older-model Plymouth Fury my aunt had handed down to us, which I tuned up and maintained. My previously strong grades suffered, but I kept visiting anyway.

The summer before the year I graduated from high school, I would often visit him in the hospital after my workday, wearing painter's pants covered in drywall dust. I would roll him up and down the hallways, standing with one foot on the back of the wheelchair like a skateboarder, while pushing with the other foot or dragging it like a rudder on the shiny floor tile to steer around corners at speed. As we skated by, my dad would greet and wave to the other long-term patients. He was a predictably popular raconteur with the hospital staff.

He was mobile for a few years and happy about it, until the artificial joints failed. Even worse, he had developed osteomyelitis, an incurable bone infection that meds kept under control for the last twenty-five years of his life. The artificial hips had to be removed but were never replaced. Spongy tissue filled the gaps where bone had been. He was mostly confined to a wheelchair until he died in his mid-eighties. Fortunately, Social Security disability payments stabilized his moderate income. To the end, he never really complained—fake curmudgeon though he was. But I didn't know all of that was coming when I visited him in the hospital during high school, hoping and expecting a more favorable result.

My dad was from a big immigrant family of Russian Jews and talked to everyone. He had always talked to everyone, whether as a kid helping his dad sell fruit and paint houses, as a St. Louis public high school grad working as a hospital orderly, or as a U.S. Postal Service letter carrier for six years after high school before Pearl Harbor. He enlisted right after Pearl Harbor, and served as a weatherman stationed on a U.S. Air Force base on the Pacific island of Kwajalein, where military planes from all over would constantly fly in and out. In freer moments, the troops stationed there and those laying over would gather on the beach to cook fish, drink beer, and talk. But that was over thirty-five years before his hospitalization.

With the Bryn Mawr Hospital workers, he told stories and joked around. They responded with hospital gossip and their own stories; he'd tell us the best ones he heard when we visited. I remember watching an indulgent smile form on the face of a Black nurse while she drew his blood as my dad ran through a small catalog of Shakespearean quotes about blood: "Blood will have blood" and so on. His performance looked like an encore. The nurse drew his blood all the time, but she didn't seem to mind passing the time with an old storyteller. The kitchen workers, med-techs, maintenance engineers, janitorial workers, orderlies, and nurses were a multiracial and multi-ethnic group, far friendlier than the doctors. They usually smiled at my dad when I wheeled him around. The doctors were all white, more occasional in their comings and goings at the hospital, mostly aloof and talking among themselves about their work, their cars, and golf.

Even my dad's ordinary interracial engagement at the hospital was a revelation to me, a nostalgic, nearly forgotten echo from my youngest school years at Pershing Elementary in St. Louis. In my high school, there was almost no contact between Black and white students, thanks partly to the different tracks. Black students were mostly behind the walls of other classrooms and out of my sight during the school day. There were virtually no Black teachers or staff who regularly dealt with students. In the hallways, even different racial and economic groups within each track hung together.

I still remember making my way to class and noticing a new student, a tall pale white kid with a shock of black hair who had arrived from England and was a phenom on the soccer field, immediately popular with the girls, unlike me. I'd seen enough British comedy on television to figure his cockney accent and casual clothing meant he was working-class. He was talking and laughing with a Black kid who was a star on two other sports teams when they began to raise their voices and square off. A few other Black kids were also talking, standing nearby. None of them were in my classes. They suddenly got quiet. The English kid hollered, dramatically bobbing his head up and down: "I'll beat you black and blue!"

The Black kid was already grinning before he finished: "You got that half right!"

At that, the two of them and all the Black students nearby dissolved in laughter. My immediate sense that this was a real fight turned to surprise when they all began laughing, giving dap, and shaking hands. I didn't know engagement like that was possible in my high school. Obviously, in my Track 1 classes and on my block, I was missing something that was happening elsewhere— a familiarity, an affection that was capable of crossing racial and cultural barriers and exploding them, even in public. I longed for that kind of exchange. It felt like something I'd touched when I was much younger, in St. Louis, had slipped away in this Philly suburb as I grew up. I had seen it in the hospital. But, owing to the bitter logic of racial segregation in America, I wouldn't see it again until I was in law school, working for homeless people one semester in New York.

It was the winter of 1986 and around 20 degrees outside the gigantic, magnificent doors of St. Patrick's Cathedral in New York, and next to Rockefeller Center—two icons of institutional power in America's most powerful city. I was twenty-four years old. It was midnight.

I was standing in the shadows of the cathedral with six or seven white, Black, and brown homeless men. Our beds for that evening were a row of thick cardboard garment boxes that each of us had dragged to the site earlier that day. Each box was shorter than a coffin, but roomier. We lined them up against the gothic stone retaining wall that separated the cathedral's grounds from the wide adjoining sidewalk where tourists lingered in day-light. The men I was with were talking.

"You think he's coming tonight?"

"Who?"

"The veteran."

"Oh. He's around? I heard he wasn't around."

"He went off over at the other place a couple nights ago, I heard."

"I just stay in my box. I just stay in my box if it happens."

I listened closely, but didn't want to show my confusion. I was a different kind of tourist, merely observing homelessness for the night with a friendly homeless client, Frank, who had volunteered to be my tour guide. I was the only one who wasn't really homeless; Frank was keeping my secret and I didn't want to blow it.

Lisa was my girlfriend at the time. She and I were spending the first semester of our last year of law school as unpaid interns for different nonprofits in New York. We were also living together for the first time after being a couple less than two years. She was interning at CARE helping feed the world, a passion of hers and an homage to her pre–law school Peace Corps years and her childhood as an Air Force "brat" who lived overseas. I was interning at New York's Coalition for the Homeless helping homeless people get housing, or something like it, in the biggest city in the richest nation in the world. The Coalition had gained a national spotlight after it persuaded New York State's highest court that the New York State Constitution contains a human right to housing, a right the U.S. Constitution lacks. I wanted to be in that fight. Lisa and I were contemplating careers as public interest lawyers, drawn to the drama and mission of the work.

The men's breath rose as glowing gold vapor in the cold, illuminated by yellow streetlights. I gave up on figuring out what their conversation meant and focused on imitating their movements so they wouldn't know I was a fake. I got distracted, wondering if I could actually sleep in a garment box in 20 degrees, even with my multiple layers of cloth coats, gloves, and hats.

The day had started normally enough. I'd spent a few hours in the Coalition's modest offices in my worn, button-down oxford shirt, dealing with individual homeless people's issues. Some had lost crucial belongings in the shelter system. Others had civil citations to answer from police who'd been "moving them along." In the afternoon, I rode the subway to recount the number of working toilets at one of the city's shelters. My task was to inspect to see if the city shelter was in compliance with a consent decree that required an adequate ratio of toilets and sinks per shelter occupant. The city had been faking compliance by showing inspectors toilets, urinals, and sinks to count that were being used only by staff or that weren't even functioning. The shelter itself was poorly lit, with an open grid of beds laid out on the hardwood floor of a forgotten Victorian basketball court. A cast iron balcony above served as a skinny running track. There was heat and shelter, but it was also a good place to get your stuff stolen or get hurt or get no sleep or get lice before the staff followed strict policy and pushed you and your belongings out early in the morning, allowing you and your belongings to return only after dark. Understandably, many homeless people preferred to sleep on the streets. After counting the plumbing fixtures, I returned to the office.

Late that afternoon, as planned, I left the office to meet up with Frank, an older man I knew as a client, at the Coalition's offices. Frank had agreed to show me how he spent his evenings and nights on the street in New York. Frank was a white man in his early sixties, nearly blind. We walked the city for a few hours. Frank showed me how he collected aluminum cans, which could be redeemed for a nickel each at the time. Other can collectors, he told me, overlooked the ones that were dark and flattened from tires or foot traffic. Somehow Frank spotted even the faintest glint of metal in sunlight or streetlight, despite his near blindness. He found more intact cans in city trash cans or on the street, and if they weren't already crushed he stomped them flat before bagging them to manage the load; he traded in trash bags full of cans for cash once or twice a day. He told me stories about the family life and career he'd had in early IT before things fell apart. I knew he also had a story to tell about his spiral into homelessness, but he didn't offer it. I didn't ask. What he told me confirmed the lessons of my childhood—that most of us are walking a ledge and should call ourselves lucky rather than deserving if we don't slip off.

Shortly after sundown, Frank and I headed for Grand Central station, one of a few nearby places to obtain a free meal. As we lined up behind a hundred other people with their paper plates, I recognized two of the servers as my co-workers from the Coalition. They were my peers—well-educated people my age who had been working with me almost daily for two months. They had no idea I was playing homeless with Frank. Not wanting to be detected or freeze, I had dressed like many of our clients. I was wearing old, worn clothing in dark colors. Everything was thick cloth, in multiple layers. I pulled my hat a little lower and kept quiet as my co-workers put food on my plate. Even as they served me a full plate of spaghetti and watery meat sauce, they didn't see me. No matter how deeply they cared about homeless people and their issues, the people they served were blurring. I was just another hunched silhouette in a long line of people who had slipped off the ledge and couldn't pay the rent anymore, who had become unemployed, who were suffering from mental illness or addiction, or who were chronically leashed to poverty. I walked away amazed that my open-hearted, friendly co-workers at the Coalition had mistaken me for a stranger.

Frank and I got our boxes for the night in a garment district alley, taking care to select ones that weren't wet and didn't stink of food trash. We took them to St. Patrick's. After bidding Frank good night and watching how it was done, I climbed into my garment box and lightly folded the cardboard flaps inward to block out the wind and light from the street, keeping the flaps loose enough to make sure I could exit in a hurry. For a couple of hours I lay in the box, listening to street noises like a tent camper listening for bears, then fell asleep fitfully wearing everything I had brought, arms folded and knees pulled up to preserve warmth.

Around four A.M. I woke suddenly to the sound of shouting. Disoriented, I kicked open the box flaps and jumped out to see a man running down the long row of boxes butted up to the stone wall of the massive cathedral. He was kicking every box as he ran, cursing and threatening to kill or fight or maim or do something I couldn't make out to everyone in every box. People were coming out of their boxes. When one yelled to the man that this wasn't Vietnam, I realized this must be the veteran. Two of the men were now cursing and agitated, going after him to fight. A couple of others tried to calm him down. Twice the veteran appeared to be walking away, but quickly turned around and came back to renew the commotion. Boxes were displaced, some punctured and torn. After a few more minutes, he stomped off toward where I first saw him and kept going, still shouting until he was too far away for us to hear his words clearly. Once the veteran crossed the street two traffic lights away, the people standing next to me said with authority that he wouldn't U-turn again and he was done for the night. It got quiet again in the still, frigid air. We all crawled back into our boxes until dawn.

At sunup, we dragged the boxes away. This was the informal deal these homeless men had worked out with St. Patrick's to allow them to sleep on the wide pedestrian sidewalk next to the church's walled yard during the frigid night: They had to clear out and clean up at sunrise. They could get close to the iconic power—but not too close, and not in the light of day, and not so people could tell they had sheltered there the night before. Forcible removal of homeless people from that location would have been too public a contradiction of the values that these icons represented: a welcoming, inclusive, and prosperous city of opportunity; a welcoming, inclusive, prosperous, and charitable church. After all, these were a mass of tired, poor, and huddled men. These men were the least of these.

The monolithic and mostly monoracial institutions had disappointed that night; they had given up their stinking secrets. Thanks to the Coalition's groundbreaking legal work, the law required city government to provide adequate shelter. But the government's institutional response was to cheat on something as mundane as counting toilets. Charity from whatever source is a virtue, but that night it looked like a soggy paper plate of food for men who were making the reasonable choice in freezing weather to sleep in boxes outside rather than to sleep less protected in shelters. Even my do-gooder peers at the Coalition for the Homeless, who worked so hard for homeless people every day, had disappointed. That night, they were less capable of seeing the individuals they fed than was my guide Frank, who was nearly blind. And religion's admirable directives to sacrifice and to love your neighbor felt more like slogans—the ephemeral words of a homily delivered behind the giant doors of a shining, gilded space—than what I was seeing on the street, outside those giant doors. That night, my expectations were exceeded only by this mutually supportive, loose affiliation of Black, brown, and white homeless men in worn clothing. Under the streetlights, only the energy of their rising breaths was golden. They were true outsiders. But together they had succeeded in making the institutions let them sleep where they wanted, albeit in a space that was frozen, as hard as rock, and outside the institutions' walls. The institutions weren't beyond fixing, but some of their parts were badly broken. The people making them a little better were on the outside.

Exhausted, but feeling infinitely lucky to have a home, I headed back to what I knew would be the warmth of our temporary sublet in Chelsea, where Lisa was surely still in bed. When I got there, I climbed the stairs and opened the door. A wave of heat emanating from the cast iron radiators pushed past me as I went inside. Rubbing her eyes, Lisa hugged me and told me she'd been worried about me, sleeping out in twenty degrees, as I took off layer after layer of clothing. Then she threw me out of bed because she said I smelled bad.

# CHAPTER 3

# Death Penalty

## *First Interview at the DAO*

*Here is a fruit for the crows to pluck . . .*
*Here is a strange and bitter crop.*
—Billie Holiday, "Strange Fruit"

As a young man, and before law school, I was given an education in the death penalty that determined my career. The death penalty changed my life. Since its beginnings, America has structurally guaranteed its own failure when it comes to criminal justice issues in our democracy, including matters of life and death. Across the country, and across parts of three centuries, we have taken the vote from Black and brown people, from poor people of all types. We take the vote from convicted people, often permanently, but at least while they are in jail or for years after. We suppress the votes of those most likely to be victims of violent crime and most likely to be charged with crimes. Without a vote, vast groups of Americans have no say with elected officials. We get an American criminal justice system designed by and for everyone but the people most personally affected by it. A lot is at stake, sometimes including our very lives.

It was 1984, the year I turned twenty-three, after I finished college. It was the year I was trying to figure out what career to pursue—what to do with the rest of my life.

I was working as a carpenter's flunky when the defense and prosecution selected me to serve on a death penalty jury. I knew my selection meant both sides thought I could be fair answering the daunting question of whether another human being who was guilty of a terrible crime should live or die. I wanted to get picked. While some other potential jurors were worriedly trying to get out of jury service or indifferent, I was quietly excited and hoping for a seat on the jury.

Crime and solving crime had repulsed and fascinated me since early childhood, especially terrible crimes like serial murder that were covered so often on the nightly news. They were my Grimm's fairy tales, but more disturbing. Most of the killers were caught and tried. Serial murder—or at least its detection— was prolific from the end of the 1960s through the end of the 1970s, which were my late childhood and teen years. The Manson family killed seven people over two nights when I was eight years old; I was nine when Charles Manson's trial began. When I was nine or ten, I watched the ongoing coverage of the Zodiac Killer, who murdered five known victims over time. He taunted the press with coded hints and claimed, probably falsely, to have killed thirty-seven. The Zodiac Killer was never caught. David Berkowitz, the "Son of Sam," killed six victims over the summer of 1976 before he was caught in the summer of 1977. I remember hearing about Ted Bundy when I was about sixteen. Bundy was a charismatic law student whose vaguely handsome, generic looks seemed to change before your eyes, making him hard to identify. He escaped custody twice, including once mid-trial in Colorado, before being caught, tried, and eventually sentenced to death for dozens of murders and rapes of young white women who had straight hair, parted in the middle. My senior year of high school, the so-called Hillside Stranglers—Angelo Buono and his cousin, Kenneth Bianchi—were caught for kidnapping, raping, and killing girls and women. Ten of their victims were found in California, and two more in Washington State.

But the one I remember the most was John Wayne Gacy, whose victims were most like me. He was caught when I was about seventeen, although he'd started his murders when I was only eleven. I still remember watching the TV screen as the details of his crimes and capture played out over several days on the nightly news, the count of recovered bones and skeletons rising every night. Gacy posed as a contractor looking for help, a friendly clown for children, or a phony lawman with badges, handcuffs, and a black Oldsmobile equipped with spotlights that suggested it was a police car. His known victims were thirty-three young men and boys who were raped and tortured over those six years before his capture, all of whose bodies he had buried beneath his home until he ran out of space and threw the last five in the river. When he was caught, nearly all the bones pulled from beneath his Chicago home came from victims killed when they were in my age range over that six-year span.

At twenty-three, I had been picked to sit on a jury for a crime that was also truly terrible: An elderly woman had been raped and murdered. Her house was lit on fire in an effort to burn it down around her, likely to destroy evidence of the crime, including her body. The defendant had worked for the woman doing maintenance. Her son was an FBI agent, and the bureau flooded the jurisdiction with agents. Within twenty-four hours, they caught the man who would be charged in the case. He was renting a room in a motel near the house. In the motel parking lot they found the woman's car. On the car's rearview mirror they found the man's fingerprint captured in her dried blood.

An autopsy indicated the woman had been raped and her ribs fractured, either during the rape or by stomping, before or after death. The case was sensational not only because of its lurid details and vulnerable victim but also because it came just after the end of the U.S. Supreme Court's moratorium on the death penalty, the period of several years when even our highest court said that the death penalty was too cruel and arbitrary to be practiced . . . before it changed its mind.

For an ambitious chief prosecutor in 1984 almost anywhere in America, the case was also a career builder: The victim was white, the defendant black, the death penalty was in play. And we were in Chester County, Pennsylvania—a suburban/rural and, more so at that time, somewhat racist area just outside of Philadelphia. No Democrat had been elected in the county for more than one hundred years. Because the stakes and the publicity were high, the chief prosecutor persuaded the judge to proceed with a legal rarity, the sequestered jury—in our case, a jury that stayed in a hotel together and would return home only after delivering its verdict—in order to ensure there would be no jury tampering, intimidation, or undue influence from media or family.

I was living in my parents' house and working construction for a kitchen remodeling company, trying to decide what was next. I was drawn to three main options but open to others: language professor, divinity school, law school. I was in the process of applying to law school, among other things, but no one asked me a question that would have uncovered that detail during jury selection. The prosecutor saw a young white male novice carpenter who had attended and graduated from local public schools before college, and picked him. The defense and the judge said I was okay.

The trial started. After several days of observing testimony and other evidence at trial all day while staying in a hotel at night, the other jurors and I heard closing arguments on whether or not the defendant was guilty of the charges. We understood that finding the defendant guilty of first-degree murder would bring on a second phase—a second trial, really—to determine whether he deserved execution or a life sentence. In my mind, as jury deliberations started, the evidence seemed strong that the defendant was guilty of first-degree murder and rape. But my job was to listen to everyone before judging guilt or innocence.

Shortly after we left the jury box to begin to deliberate privately in a conference room that adjoined the courtroom, one of our quieter members stood up and pulled a small Bible from his back pocket, which he held up, opened, and eyed. The Bible was upside down. He mumbled a version of "Thou shalt not judge." We were silent for a moment. A woman on the jury gently asked him a few questions to suss out what the quiet juror was doing and why. His affect was distant. He answered obliquely, but slowly made it clear that he could not try to render any verdict in the case, which was our purpose. We listened to him, looked around, and huddled while he sat apart. I told the other jurors he had been reading the menu upside down when we ate lunch together earlier, which I had noticed as he sat next to me and corrected. I incorrectly assumed at the time that he had vision issues or must have been tired after several days of trial. We decided to tell the judge. I quickly drafted a short letter to the judge with wording approved by other jurors explaining what had happened and asking the judge to tell us what to do.

The quiet man was removed from the jury without our being told any specifics at first. We later found out that he had major mental health issues that were not disclosed or discovered during jury selection. When asked, he had indicated he had no health issue that would interfere with jury service. He had also specifically answered no to the question of whether he required medication, which was untrue. The quiet man took prescribed psychotropic medication daily. While sequestered in the hotel, he'd had no access to necessary meds at home. After several days without them, he decompensated shortly before deliberations began, and there we were. Perhaps he was too embarrassed to reveal his condition, surprised to be sequestered, and then too afraid to reveal he had lied during jury selection. The judge instructed us to try to render an eleven-person verdict anyway, and without his participation or presence in the deliberation room.

We went back to deliberating. But the trouble didn't end there. To the consternation of the judge, a couple of jurors sneaked booze into the hotel and led a rowdy party of sequestered jurors that I somehow managed to avoid. More troubling, one of our members, who lived in Pennsylvania but dressed like his idea of a Texan (complete with cowboy boots, big decorative belt buckle, and hat), told everyone early on in trial deliberations, "We know what we're here for—we need to get that boy." Another juror, a German immigrant woman in her late sixties who spoke with a thick accent, said something about "these pretty Jews" in a dismissive tone, apparently referring to another juror. When she was only half-heard and was challenged to repeat it, she went silent. The juror sitting next to her apparently heard her comment, but refused to repeat what she had said. Later, an agreeable middle-aged male juror selected to be foreperson delivered a tearful plea for us to hurry up and come to a verdict quickly because his son would soon be home from college and he wanted to get home to see him.

Despite our jury's failings, there was also brilliance in how it operated. If we were all strangers and maybe a little strange, when we joined together to deliberate we were also a super brain made up of twelve (or, in our case, eleven) people's special talents in recalling and analyzing the evidence at trial. Some jurors had perfect memory for details other jurors forgot, and offered thoughtful comments on timing or physical evidence. Others locked on to police procedures and documents or could recite testimony almost word for word and expound on witness credibility and reasonable inferences from the evidence with logical, sharply reasoned arguments. When our different and unique talents and experience led the way, we were an effective team. But when human frailty led, we weren't much better than a mob whose ability to decide another's fate was built on emotion and bias. The super brain could also be a super-bad brain.

We came back into the courtroom after a couple of days' deliberations and rendered our eleven-person guilty verdict on murder in the first degree and rape. We were expecting to hear more evidence before deliberating a second time on a different issue— whether a person deserved to live or die for his heinous crimes. As our foreperson read the first-degree-murder guilty verdict, I looked around the jury box. Some jurors were at ease. Others were ashen, sitting in twisted-up positions, perhaps dreading the decision that we would have to make next. We stood, raised our right hands, and confirmed our guilty verdict, one by one, eleven times.

But there was no second phase after all. We faced no such thing because the county, having spent a small fortune to try the case and to house and feed the sequestered jury, had cut a deal. Or maybe because the DA thought it was better politics than starting the trial over again after a mistrial. In order to proceed with an otherwise illegal verdict of eleven, the county and the defense agreed that the state would not seek the death penalty. For its convenience and to save some money, or maybe for politics or some other reason I'll never know, the prosecution bargained away the death penalty.

Being a young juror made me choose law school, and a career as a trial attorney in criminal justice. I entered Stanford Law School, still riveted by my jury experience: the clear evidence; the able, swift, and careful investigation by law enforcement; the heinous crime; the variable quality of the lawyering; the madness, wisdom, unfiltered bigotry, and decency of the jury. I saw on display the justice system's volatile mix of excellence and mediocrity. But one particular observation from the experience stuck with me: I was not persuaded that juries that decide momentous things, such as whose liberty should be taken or who should live or die, are perfect. Or that the process that decides the death penalty—which in this case hinged on one juror's hidden mental illness and the dominoes it knocked down—was flawless.

The death penalty, informed by my jury service, followed me to law school. Not only was it discussed and taught in coursework, but it was our law school class's unique topic for moot court. Nearly all law students in American law schools participate in class-wide moot court competition at least once before graduation. It's shadowboxing for future lawyers, or maybe pilot training in a flight simulator. You make all the moves, but it's not for real. Performing well is a résumé builder, and also an exciting opportunity for students drawn to brief writing and the theatrical aspects of law.

The topic professors selected that year for our moot court was as dramatic as it gets: Is it constitutional to execute people who commit murder when they are children? As we prepared our moot court briefs and arguments, juveniles had received death sentences in different states; some juveniles had already been executed.

The social justice lawyer Bryan Stevenson would resolve that question in arguments before the U.S. Supreme Court decades later: NO, it is not constitutional to execute people for murders they commit as juveniles. The Supreme Court reasoned that juveniles who commit murder should not be executed due to their mental immaturity, which reduces culpability but also increases their potential for rehabilitation.

But that seminal U.S. Supreme Court ruling would have to wait until decades after our law school years. This was appellate moot court, which meant we would research and write legal briefs arguing both sides of an issue different courts had already decided in opposite ways. We would also argue and answer questions on the fly asked by professors or lawyers playing judges (or real judges who volunteered) in a courtroom.

The competition required teams of two. I cajoled Lisa into being my partner, which was probably a better deal for me than for her. She was less enthused than I was about taking the class, and she made me promise to find a different partner if I could. I didn't try very hard. She was a gifted debater in college and a stellar legal writer in law school. I was more drawn to storytelling and the drama of courtroom than to the formality of writing briefs.

My research turned into a transfixed tour of the rich history of the death penalty in U.S. Supreme Court opinions and thought. The opinions detailed arguments for and against the death penalty, explained in wonky terminology such as "deterrence," "general deterrence," "specific deterrence," "incapacitation," and so on. I worked my way through the sociological studies relied upon in those opinions. Grasping so much detail burned a lot of time, but prepared me well to answer the judges' extemporaneous questions we would face during the various rounds of moot court competition.

In that research, I heard the steady drumbeat of Justice William Brennan's opinions. His dissents are revered for their eloquent persistence, as if he were speaking to a future America that would be more open to his arguments after his death. Brennan, a former state court judge whose legal experience prior to the Supreme Court was closer to the reality of criminal justice than the experience of nearly all his Supreme Court colleagues—with the notable exception of Thurgood Marshall—went to his grave opposing the death penalty.

We were only a few miles from Silicon Valley in 1986, but we couldn't afford computers. So we stayed up all night in the basement of the law school using the law review's computers. We finished in time, but we missed our deadline by about ten minutes due to unforeseen printer problems. Our score on the brief got docked severely for that lateness, a deficit that would follow us through every round of the competition. But at least the brief was good. Lisa's writing was brilliant, as always. Mine was decent.

The courtroom rounds started. We hadn't rehearsed, so we were nervous at first, but we did well in early rounds and started having a great time. After Lisa and I had a particularly strong round in the moot court competition, I still remember one of the judges, who turned out to be a criminal defense attorney in private practice in San Francisco, finding me in the hallway outside and offering me a permanent job. I had already decided I was headed for public service work as a public defender or prosecutor, the two sides I had watched from the jury box before law school. I declined too quickly.

The death penalty followed my national job search as well, in my final year of law school, as I interviewed with chief prosecutors' and public defenders' offices in big cities around the country. I had a lot of interviews, and got offers from both sides. Interviews generally went well, with a couple of tumultuous exceptions. In Oakland, during my second interview, a senior prosecutor was so disgusted I liked the ACLU that he angrily ended the interview and chewed out the less senior prosecutors who had recruited me. One especially ideological public defender's office was cold to my interest in both defense and prosecution; it disqualified me in their eyes. But no interview was harsher than the one at the Philadelphia District Attorney's Office (DAO) around December 1986. Having received offers from prosecutors' offices elsewhere, I guessed my hometown prosecutor's office would look favorably on my law school summers spent in public service, my strong academic background, and especially my deep roots in the area. I assumed this interview, like most of the others, would go well. It didn't.

My Philly DAO interviewers were a team of two. One, a man whom I got to know and like well enough later when I was working as an assistant public defender, was cordial. The other, a woman only a few years older than me, was cryptic and gave no eye contact when I first greeted her and sat down. She asked me early in the interview what I thought of the death penalty, which was unexpected. No new prosecutor in Philly was going to be involved in a death penalty case anytime soon in their career. I assumed it was a litmus test, a bad sign for my chances since my answer was somewhat nuanced. We began discussing my death penalty jury service and the case law and sociological research I remembered from moot court. At one point I blandly referenced the uncontroversial notion that there is a lack of scientific consensus on claims that the death penalty deters crime. She was not favorably impressed and angrily snapped back that executions deter the person executed. I wasn't impressed by what she knew or how she reacted. I politely corrected her misunderstanding of what "deterrence" means, knowing it might inflame her. Polite wasn't good enough. She jumped up and exploded anyway, making very clear that the interview was over, and at step one. As I endured her outburst, both disappointed and amused, I got up and looked toward the other interviewer. He was quietly looking back at me as if to say he was more interested and somewhat embarrassed but had no real say. I gathered my things and left.

A cartoon of the event would have had me flying out the DAO's front doors, feet over head as if the building had spit me out, my papers fluttering in the air and falling around me as I hit the sidewalk. That cartoon wouldn't be far from the truth. No complaints, though. Looking back, I have to admit it was for the best: I was telling an uninformed, traditional prosecutor she didn't know what she was talking about, which is not how you ask for a job you actually want. She was angrily telling me that I didn't make the cut for the Philly DAO circa 1986 and what that team stood for at that time. We were both right.

My legal career began on a different team, at a different government office in Philly where I did belong in 1987, the office of the public defender. Although I tried and won a lot of serious cases in the first several years of my career, I didn't try my first homicide until I was in private practice, hired by the family of a defendant facing the possibility of a death sentence. The defendant was found not guilty of all charges on a shaky identification. A death phase was avoided.

After trying more homicides over several years, I eventually found myself in a second death penalty case. My client, the defendant, testified well during hours of questioning at trial. He had shot and killed another man with several shots to the back and side and was caught close to the scene by police who happened to be in the area. The number and location of the shots, as well as there being no weapon found on the victim's body, were strong evidence of first-degree murder that would enable a death phase if the jury convicted on that charge. But the defendant testified for hours about the victim's intimidation of him and his family, which he attributed to the victim's trying to silence him for knowing the victim had killed the defendant's friend. The defendant's testimony was somewhat supported by the victim's own Facebook postings, which tended to show the victim's prior involvement in killing the defendant's friend. My client was found not guilty of the higher murder charges, but he was convicted of a lower-level homicide charge, voluntary manslaughter, sometimes referred to as "imperfect self-defense," which carries a maximum sentence of ten to twenty years in custody plus other charges. He got a total of twenty years. A second death phase was avoided.

Just before I decided to run for district attorney, in 2016, I tried my third death penalty case. It was the most wrenching case of my career as a criminal defense attorney and involved nearly five years of preparation before the trial began. The defendant and his codefendant were accused of killing three adults in a botched bodega robbery. The victims were the bodega owners—mother, father, and aunt to two traumatized teenage girls who witnessed the murders. At trial, the defendants were convicted of all three murders in the first degree, and faced the very real possibility of a death sentence on each case. A death phase went forward, but the jury narrowly rejected death, in my opinion based on evidence that the defendant was raped as a child. That evidence was absolutely crucial to our chances of persuading a jury not to sentence the defendant to death. His first manifestations of schizophrenia appeared after the rape. That evidence also arrived very, very late. It would be a stretch to say prosecutors provided it.

The prosecutors had the evidence of my client having been raped, but kept it to themselves before and during trial, including when experts (whose opinions should have been informed by this fact) took the stand. Instead, the prosecutors waited until the experts had finished testifying before giving me a fat, oddly shaped pile of half-legible records the night before the death phase started. They didn't tell me what it contained, possibly hoping I wouldn't look closely.

Even then, they handed the documents over only after I noticed them sitting on the prosecutors' counsel table and started asking what they were. Late that night, I read the records for hours. Around two A.M. I found the documentation of my client having been raped as a child, buried at the back of more than one hundred pages. The defendant, who was in his thirties, had never reported to me, my co-counsel, or anyone else who would admit it, including his troubled mother, that he had been the victim of childhood rape in an alley by a stranger. He was what the courts call a "poor reporter" in the sterile language of death penalty litigation—someone so mentally impaired that fully communicating or even remembering everything in their past is impossible. Yet here it was, obscure social services paperwork from his childhood that our death penalty investigator had been unable to find after diligent work, indicating the defendant's immediate report of extreme and damaging trauma when he was a child. There was no clear indication of any treatment having been provided to address the rape. This was crucial information, especially layered on what was already known of my client's blasted childhood and the long, documented history of hallucinations and paranoid delusions we already understood. My experience as a lawyer did not convince me that the process by which some prosecutors and defense attorneys try to persuade jurors who should live or die is perfect.

For decades, prior administrations in the DAO relentlessly pursued the death penalty in Philadelphia. Lynne Abraham was known for her DAO's office obtaining death sentences over one hundred times in nineteen years and for her self-described "passion" for the death penalty. Sadly, her office was less passionate about integrity in the process of pursuing executions. The prosecutorial threat to seek death was cynically used to coerce guilty pleas for sentences of life in jail with no chance of parole, even when the circumstances of a case and the defendant's history did not support a death sentence. Everyone in the system knew that a jury picked for a death penalty case, all of whose members have confirmed they could impose a death sentence, was more likely to convict during the guilt phase than a jury that includes people who are opposed to the death penalty. So some prosecutors' pursuit of the death penalty was really about fixing the trial on guilt by getting a jury biased toward guilt during the guilt phase. And there were other ways to fix a trial. In many cases, the prosecution did not disclose essential and constitutionally required information to the defense. Outlandishly illegal closing arguments by Roger King and others in death penalty cases caused retrials. But prosecutors were not the only ones to blame for a crooked system.

The game was also fixed by the system as a whole to disadvantage the defense by paying court-appointed defense lawyers next to nothing. People charged with homicides are overwhelmingly broke, unable to pay for counsel, and locked up through trial. Homicide defenses in general and death penalty defenses in particular have been routinely conducted in Philly and elsewhere by a small cadre of underfunded, court-appointed defense counsel whose underperformance was almost unavoidable and became the norm. They often did not obtain or present the legally necessary records, experts, and witnesses a death penalty jury must hear in order to consider life or death. The court system, including the judges who repeatedly appointed these same defense lawyers (two of whom I used to call "Team Hemlock"), did far too little to even up this one-sided mess. The system was okay with the outcomes.

Philly's chief prosecutors didn't interfere. In my opinion, they were okay with such a flawed system because it fed the sensationalist journalism and politics of fear that built their political careers. And so the lack of integrity in failing to disclose required information to the defense in those death penalty proceedings was almost universally covered up post-trial by prior administrations. That cover-up violated fundamental notions of justice as well as the chief prosecutors' sworn oath—to seek justice without regard for politics.

How flawed were these Philadelphia death penalty proceedings? Before I became district attorney, nearly three out of four Philadelphia death sentences rendered since the end of the U.S. Supreme Court's moratorium on the death penalty—a nearly forty-year period—had been overturned. The other death penalty cases remained in litigation; even more were likely to be overturned in the future.

And how many years passed from the time of the death sentence until it was overturned? Lawyers who did nothing but death penalty post-trial work for a living said it usually took more than fifteen years between the time the death sentence was given and the time it was overturned. Over fifteen years of litigation that was costly to taxpayers but even more costly to survivors of homicide and others touched by it—the victim's family and friends, as well as the defendant's—who endure all those years of an adversarial ping-pong game invading their daily existence; more than fifteen years of wounding notifications and dreadful anticipation prior to attending damaging hearings. There is no closure.

How bad is a reversal rate of nearly three out of four death sentences? Understand that appeals judges very seldom overturn verdicts in other contexts. Defendants ordinarily win only a small portion of all post-trial legal challenges in criminal matters. I would estimate the defense succeeds in overturning trial outcomes on appeal about 5 percent or less of the time; prosecutors win the other 95 percent. But the government's obtaining authority to execute a prisoner under its control, which must be based on proceedings with factual and legal integrity, has overwhelmingly failed to meet that standard.

And why were these death sentences overturned so frequently? My sense was that about two out of three of the overturned sentences came from the defendant's counsel failing to do their job. In court it's called "ineffective assistance of counsel"; think of it as professional malpractice. Experts who could have established a defendant's early trauma or psychological damage from educational and other records or events were never hired. The records those experts needed were never obtained. Neighbors, teachers, employers, and family who witnessed the defendant's life and could have provided insight on the defendant's history were not interviewed, or subpoenaed, or presented to testify in any meaningful way.

As a result, the court records of some of the death phases span a skinny couple dozen pages of brief testimony and improvised argument. Juries carrying the yoke of deciding between life and death heard next to nothing about the defendant's life.

Well-prepared defense attorneys will explain every mitigating fact about their client during the death phase. It's a careful process of sifting through educational and social service records, and interviewing witnesses—schoolteachers, neighbors, relatives—to determine victimization and trauma in their childhood, neglect, physical and sexual abuse, mental deficits, and mental health problems among other things. Experts and testing are often required. But that's hard work. It takes time and money.

A hack lawyer who represents the defendant during the death phase skips getting the records, doing the testing, interviewing witnesses, getting the experts. A hack job looks a lot like putting on the stand whoever happened to be in the hallway on the defendant's side right after the guilty verdict comes in. Maybe Mom testified and said, "Don't kill my baby." Or maybe the defendant testified and said he's sorry right after his lawyer spent weeks saying he's innocent. Or maybe no one testified in the death phase, and the same lawyer who argued that he was innocent of a heinous killing at trial then argues, "Okay, he's guilty, but don't kill him anyway."

And what comes next when a sentence of death is reversed, so many years later? The reversal of a death sentence, like the reversal of a trial conviction upon appeal, ordinarily means prosecutors can try again. But, curiously, that doesn't happen; the prosecutorial fire to pursue a death sentence a second time goes out. Usually, in Philadelphia, prosecutors did not seek another death sentence the second time around, abruptly giving up on the ultimate sentence, a sentence they adamantly claimed at trial was necessary and the only one that fit the crime. It's inconsistent and hypocritical to routinely decide that the ultimate penalty—the execution you sought—is no longer necessary after the passage of time. We are talking about human lives here. So why does it happen?

There is more than one anecdotal theory of why prosecutorial zeal for death sentences wanes when a death sentence is overturned and a second death phase is allowed. The first theory is about politics and its symbiotic relationship with the press. The entire trial on innocence or guilt is not redone on a death penalty redo. So the evidence of the killing, in all its gory drama, is toned down in a second death penalty phase hearing. Journalism about the death phase is a grimmer story, especially in recent years as voters have become less inclined to support the death penalty. There's less drama and less favorable press coverage to fluff up a prosecutor's career.

The second theory is that capable trial lawyers simply know better. Prosecutors sometimes know that a fair fight on a properly redone death phase is something they will lose. When all the information about the defendant's traumatic background and sometimes severe mental health issues are fully presented at a new death phase, they may lose. In addition, after years on appeal there is evidence that most death row defendants have few disciplinary infractions or additional crimes. Where that is true, any jury is less likely to choose death. No prosecutor likes to lose, so why try?

The third anecdotal theory is that in some cases, the victim's family and survivors have already experienced the prior death verdict being overturned and are simply tired of the lack of closure. They have no appetite for a second death phase and more decades of legal challenges. In other families, the leading voices are new or have changed their views. They have come to a different stage of grief or are guided by a new faith or philosophy that rejects executing the person who killed their loved one.

Systemically crappy, inconsistent representation on both sides is unacceptable in a fender bender lawsuit or any other civil matter. But it happens in the most serious criminal matters, where life hangs in the balance, for one reason: There's money to be made in civil cases and almost none to be made in a death penalty criminal matter where the defendant is represented by court-appointed counsel. These defendants may be presumed innocent by the law, but they are presumed guilty in a criminal justice system that is driven by politics and power. The crimes are heinous, and so the defendants are presumptively despicably guilty, rather than presumed innocent, as the law requires. The most powerful players in the system traditionally prefer the politics of a guilty verdict and a death sentence, so power sets the rules and gets what it wants.

What has happened in Philly is nothing new. In 1989, when Bryan Stevenson established the Equal Justice Initiative in Alabama to represent people in death cases, the total compensation for a court-appointed attorney representing a defendant through all phases of the case, including appeal, was $1,000. Prosecutors have no equivalent challenge; they are salaried and generally do fine with their funding compared with other governmental entities. The matchup of resources is so lopsided and the likely outcome so predetermined that Stevenson felt compelled to establish an independent and (eventually) better-funded alternative in order to make Alabama fulfill its constitutional obligations—and to obtain more accurate results. Once the defense could operate with similar resources, the outcomes began to change. Stevenson was right.

In Philly, the system by necessity mostly picked among the few attorneys so desperate for clients that they would work for crumbs. They are mostly a motley crew of lawyers who have no better source of revenues and no overhead. Many of them have few private clients, and seldom have full-time staff or decent offices or a stable of happy vendors that includes investigators and experts ready to take their calls for underpaid court-appointed work. So when the system chooses what to pay these lawyers, it's not just about money; the low pay guarantees poor representation.

Before I became DA in Philadelphia, dismally low flat fees encouraged underpreparation—for example, a homicide case preparation fee of less than $2,000 no matter how much work was done. The low fees don't just attract a pool of desperate lawyers, but the incentives built into the fees led the worst of those lawyers to hurt their clients. For instance, lawyers made more money trying death penalty cases than they made by trying to achieve a non-death plea ($400 for every day of trial; $0 after a plea), which incentivizes some of the worst of them to unwisely try cases even when doing so puts their clients' lives in jeopardy.

In general, public defenders do a much better job with death penalty defense in Philly due in part to their idealism, extensive experience, and moderate but steady salaries. Given how inadequately compensated public defenders are for the important work they do, we should be alarmed that public defender money looks like a ceiling compared to the floor of court-appointed pay in matters of life and death. And there are idealistic private defense lawyers who take some court-appointed work, rightly viewing it as charity since their office overhead alone far exceeds the compensation they will eventually receive. I was one. In 2011, at fifty years of age, I decided to take several court-appointed homicides and handle them as well as I could. It was public service; I thought it was giving back, God's work, the good fight. It was also a nightmare of bureaucratic catch-22's and passive-aggressive pushback when I tried to do something more than the normal, do-nothing approach. In one case, the judge became amnesiac about commitments he had made to ensure payment of my vendors—experts and investigators—after the work was done. His forgetfulness led to the vendors blaming me. My staff's payroll was due every two weeks, but compensation for my services was ordinarily due only after sentencing—which meant upon completion of what ultimately became five years of work. Unless a lawyer is independently wealthy, this economic pressure is real and its effect is real as well—which brings us right back to that crazy high reversal rate for death sentences.

In 2015, shortly after he began his first term, the new Pennsylvania governor imposed a moratorium on executions in the state that he kept in force during his second term, and for his own good reasons. Most Pennsylvania experts will tell you that the death penalty in Pennsylvania's sixty-seven counties is either beyond fixing or can be fixed only at tremendous cost with benefit that is at best debatable. Further, there is no consensus among criminologists that the death penalty deters murder or any other crime.

The irony is that in Pennsylvania and many other states, death sentences are just words; they are not carried out. In 1962, a Pennsylvania killer was executed against his will. Despite former Philly district attorneys' mad love for executions, no one has been executed against their will since then. There were two or three people executed in the late nineties who purposefully abandoned all post-trial appeals and challenges in order to expedite their executions. They included Marty Graham and Gary Heidnik, two serial killers who arguably added their own bodies to their piles of victims with the help of the government when they stopped fighting their executions. Objectively speaking, former DA Abraham's passion for executions has been unrequited. I suspect her real romance with death had more to do with political ambitions.

Thirty-three years after I sat on that death penalty jury, I was campaigning to become district attorney. I was being considered by the voters to make decisions about life and death again. I was hoping to sit in a different chair, in a chief prosecutor's office, where I would hold discretion to seek the execution of people for having committed truly terrible crimes. I campaigned promising to give the defense all documents and information that the law and fairness require, and to consider all aspects of each case meticulously before exercising individual discretion. I campaigned promising to use very well-informed common sense. We need common sense in each case we review when we decide whether or not to seek a penalty that is irrevocable and final. Common sense includes what I know from having been a death penalty juror, seated at a different table, so many years ago—what was said and what was muttered and what it all meant. Common sense reminds me to question what I have witnessed prosecutors do in seeking executions I opposed as defense counsel, and what their conduct in those cases means about how prosecutors handled other cases in the past and what needs to change in that office's culture. Common sense tells me to question whether people involved in death penalty cases are perfect or imperfect, strong or frail—jurors, judges, the defense and the prosecutors, the survivors and the accused, even the ones who only hear about it all on the news. And my common sense has answered that question for me. Yes, we are all frail and strong, but none of us are perfect who are given power to determine whether another person should live or die.

# CHAPTER 4

# Frank's Long Shadow

*I did it my way.*

—Frank Sinatra, "My Way"

Cities, especially old and storied ones like Philadelphia, can feel fixed in time, like their culture doesn't change. But seen from the perspective of history, a city's culture is far more fluid and changeable than it appears to the living. The moments of change are sometimes visible, though, captured in stone or bronze—in the city's statuary. Philly's dead, including two men whose statues have characterized the city's ideals at different times, made admirable and despicable choices that changed the city, pointing it in opposite directions. Their statues were our daily reminder that choices we made long ago can be unmade, too. No monument is permanent. One of those statues had to go. In our campaign, it was bedrock that the living get to choose the future.

I met the legendary and reviled Frank Rizzo just off Ninth and Christian streets, outside the mostly open-air Italian Market on a sunny weekend in July 1991. The former mayor of Philly was nearly seventy-one; I was barely thirty, nervously anticipating the birth of our first son, Nate. Eight days after I met him and four days before our son was born, Frank died of a heart attack.

I was four years into my legal career, still a public defender but now dreaming of starting my own civil rights and private criminal defense practice. Thanks to a Federal Housing Authority loan that required almost no deposit, Lisa and I had just bought and moved into our "starter" home, where we would remain the next twenty-six years. Frank was well past his political prime but still politicking in his old South Philly neighborhood stronghold, running for a second set of terms as mayor. He had never wanted to leave office in the first place. He had been mayor from 1972 to 1980 but had to step down after his effort to eliminate term limits failed. Now, more than a decade later, he was trying to get back into City Hall for a new pair of four-year terms. His main opponent was Ed Rendell, who became Philadelphia district attorney in 1978 at age thirty-three, completed two terms, and then ran for governor in 1986. Rendell lost for governor, but five years later, he was trying to become mayor, running as a centrist to the left of Rizzo. Times had changed from Frank's heyday of old Democratic machine politics, but he still had a real shot when I met him.

I was waiting at the Italian Market with Ed Rau, my father-in-law. Ed was an ex-career-military pilot who had flown in Korea and Vietnam and endured the deaths in battle of most of his flight crew. Later he served two years as a pilot for the American ambassador to Afghanistan. Ed hunted in the hills with the locals, and carried his Leica camera to shoot "scenery" as the United States kept an eye on the USSR twenty years before the ill-fated Russian invasion of Afghanistan. He continued ascending the officer ranks, becoming a lieutenant colonel, before hitting a ceiling after putting a MCGOVERN FOR PRESIDENT poster in the front window of his home in a neighborhood full of military families at his last stop, Strategic Air Command HQ outside of Omaha, Nebraska. Ed was a man who kept secrets and had been in the fight. When he said things, you watched his eyes. Though I'd been married to his daughter for two years, Ed still intimidated me. Lisa was still his baby girl.

For a hunter and traveling foodie like Ed, the Italian Market on a sunny day was irresistible. The neon signage of Italian bakeries and butcher shops faced brightly colored piles of fruit and vegetables on sidewalks full of vendors hawking in the open. In the winter, vendors kept warm by burning crates in fifty-five-gallon drums. Ed and his second wife, Gretchen, were visiting from retirement in Colorado—retirement from the military and from his post-military law practice in aviation law and employment discrimination on the side of aging airline workers. As Ed and I wandered through the market, I spotted Frank, who was surrounded mostly by well-wishers on the hot, sun-drenched sidewalk across from the St. Paul Church on Christian Street.

I knew all about Frank. Frank was not my people. To me, Frank was still the racist mayor my dad had railed against. He was still that black-and-white menace on our nightly local news when I was a kid, the one who famously showed up at a black-tie event with a nightstick stuck in his cummerbund. To hear my dad's view, when Frank was on TV the rabbit ears antenna on top of the screen might as well have been Frank's horns. My dad used to grin when he called Frank "Mussolini." Having volunteered and served in World War II, I guess he was entitled to call out a fascist.

Frank exchanged mutually suspicious looks with Ed and me— over the years he must have honed his senses to detect the presence of enemies, especially liberal lawyers. Insincere pleasantries and the obligatory shaking of hands followed. I remember the thin lapels of his immaculate Rat Pack suit, retro even then. I remember the flash of a threatening demeanor that smacked of suppressed rage, the easy power of his charisma wrapped in a

Sinatra tan. Ed Rau's steely gaze belied his diplomatic words. Ed could also spot an enemy. I could tell Frank was not his people, either.

Frank Rizzo started as a beat cop in the 1950s and rose to become the police commissioner of Philadelphia. Whether he was a cop or a commissioner or the mayor of the city, Rizzo's record for racism and brutality was widely known—and widely embraced in some parts of Philly. He opposed school desegregation. One-way streets were redirected to isolate Black neighborhoods. While Frank was police commissioner and then mayor, scores of unarmed young Black men were shot in the back by police only to have their killings excused with copycat stories made up later. The usual tale was that the police had spotted some object, often the ubiquitous Afro picks of the era, that supposedly looked like a gun for an instant in the hand of the unarmed man they shot. The absurd story that the victims brandished Afro picks at armed officers—and the picks somehow reflected the light as if they were guns—was good enough for Philly prosecutors and police at the time, no matter how many times it was repeated.

Frank directed the police to strip-search young Black men in the middle of their streets to make sure the residents all saw and understood that their neighborhoods were occupied and by whom. Rizzo's rhetoric was so memorably brutal, bigoted, and foolish that the Southeastern Pennsylvania chapter of Americans for Democratic Action circulated a widely read compilation of his quotes titled "The Sayings of Chairman Frank." It included such gems as "The way to treat criminals is *spacco il capo* [break the head]. If you [the Rome police] need some help, we'll transport some guys over here and they'll straighten them out right away." Or: "I'll make you a rich man. I'll give you five dollars for every liberal who jumps off the Walnut Street Bridge when I'm elected." Or, on the Black Panthers: "They should be strung up. I mean with the law. This is actual warfare." Frank's brother became fire commissioner during his reign. On Frank's mayoral watch, the city's economic future was sunk by the permanent entitlements he gave to his beloved clan of police and firefighters, who were treated better than other city employees. In Frank's era, high school graduates who became police at eighteen retired by forty-three with fat pensions for life. His affection for other unions outside his tribe was more limited, transactional at best.

Frank's politics were insider, patronage politics in a patronage town. The metropolis-destroying cost for these entitlements would sink the city long after his terms in office ended. He was wildly popular with his white ethnic, working-class base, and generally unpopular with the marginalized people he could look down on from the high second-floor windows of Philly's monolithic City Hall, a shrine to democracy and governmental power that is open to all its people, a place where a man like him made little sense.

Frank Rizzo's isn't the only legacy to shape Philadelphia. City Hall is planted right at the center of the city, where Broad Street and Market Street cross. The magnificent and antique building was once the largest masonry structure in the United States, a full city block of pillars and archways supporting lounging statues of human figures. Its stature would make more sense in Washington, D.C., or ancient Greece, but somehow it ended up in this mostly working-class town. The structure's highest point—the equivalent to about twenty stories in a modern building—is a single domed tower topped by a statue of William Penn, the founder of Pennsylvania, who fled England after being arrested and prosecuted for his egalitarian Quaker religious beliefs.

It is unusual to top a government building with a gigantic statue of a man who was arrested and prosecuted for crimes, much less to mandate that no structure in the city can be taller than the top of his bronze hat (a rule that remained in effect in Philadelphia until the 1980s), but there stands William Penn even now, who went to trial as a criminal defendant. Penn's supposed crime was protest in England, a place where religion and speech were not free. When England clamped down on a Quaker religious service by locking the Quakers' meetinghouse, Penn went ahead with the meeting in public anyway. He was arrested and charged. At one point during Penn's trial, the jurors, who were disinclined to convict him, were jailed without food by the judge to force them to find Penn guilty. The jury resisted anyway, and Penn was acquitted before the young aristocrat left the country altogether, probably to the great relief of the English establishment and his father.

Penn's experience of being prosecuted unfairly in England likely helped shape his wish list of rights in the New World. He wrote *The Frame of Government in Pennsylvania*, a mini-constitution for the Pennsylvania colony that protected against the repression he experienced in England and was intended to attract freedom-loving new residents to Pennsylvania. *The Frame of Government* evolved into Pennsylvania's constitution and its famous declaration of rights:

> That all power being originally inherent in, and consequently derived from, the people; therefore all officers of the government, whether legislative or executive, are their trustees and servants, and at all times accountable to them.

Pennsylvania's constitution eventually informed the U.S. Constitution on matters close to Penn's heart and neck: religious freedom, separation of church and state, the right to a jury trial, and jury independence.

Although the record is mixed, Penn's and the Quakers' egalitarian philosophy was mostly reflected in efforts to abolish slavery. As early as 1688, German Quakers protested slavery, and many Quakers engaged in other anti-slavery work for two centuries. The Quakers' egalitarian impulse would be reflected in

Philadelphia's architectural simplicity; affordable row houses helped Philadelphia to have the highest rate of home ownership among the ten largest cities for many years, despite Philadelphia's becoming the poorest city among them. The city's economic decline has helped preserve the unadorned and functional early American Bauhaus style.

Arguably this history of abolitionism, egalitarianism, and respect for human dignity and human rights was the foundation for the diversity Philadelphia now enjoys. The demographics today are roughly 42 percent Black, 41 percent white, and 17 percent other people of color who are mostly of Latinx and Asian heritage. The Philadelphia area is also home to the densest grouping of Quakers in America, about half of the American Quaker population. In modern times their members include those who also call themselves Buddhists, Jews, or Christians, and plenty of agnostics and atheists. For many years the affluent Chestnut Hill section of the city's quarterly Quaker meeting was populated by aging European Jews who had survived the Holocaust and were welcomed in by the Quakers in the area. Their gratitude attracted many of these survivors to the Quaker tradition and its Sunday meetings, which some of them attended for the rest of their lives.

Philadelphians like to think that Penn's struggle and the best part of the Quaker tradition birthed a city with egalitarianism and justice in its DNA. I like to think that. But for many years, if you really wanted to understand criminal justice and governance in Philadelphia, or maybe just understand Philadelphia, after you looked up at William Penn at City Hall you could go across the street and do what I did in 1991 on that sunny day in the Italian Market—meet Frank.

You used to just have to cross the multilane car circle that surrounds City Hall to face him. There you would see an imposing, larger-than-life bronze statue of Frank Rizzo: unsmiling with an immaculate suit, his right arm raised, elbow slightly bent, presenting one right palm in what the sculptor may have intended as a wave to the multitudes but always looked to me like a fascist salute. Or maybe the artist was slyly sculpting something his patrons didn't see. That statue is gone now.

The Frank Rizzo statue was Philly's version of a bronze Confederate general on a horse. Many considered it shameful that Frank's statue was so proximate to Philadelphia's home of governmental power, especially with no other mayor's statue around. Over the past few years, and before Frank was removed, the Rizzo statue was frequently enclosed by police barriers and sometimes protected by a police guard during large gatherings or protests. It was splashed with paint repeatedly.

The statue was not the only Rizzo image to attract negative attention. Philadelphia is rightly famous for its murals. For the past twenty-five years, the city's Mural Arts program, run by Jane Golden, has covered the city in almost four thousand gorgeous murals created by professional artists assisted by street artists, at-risk youth, people returning from jails and prisons, and inmates who painted on sail cloth that was later attached to buildings beyond their prison walls. Nearly all of the murals stay spotless, devoid of graffiti tags or other marks, because they are created in collaboration with the communities they reflect—the result of a careful process of research, interviews of neighbors, and group meetings in the murals' surroundings to determine their content. The murals are everywhere and intended for everyone. The most vandalized mural for over a decade was the one of Frank Rizzo, a head-and-shoulders shot of Frank looming on a three-story-high wall adjacent to the Italian Market.

Rocky Balboa ran through this market in the same era that this neighborhood was Frank Rizzo's base. The market remains a gem but is no longer all Italian, and the neighborhood around the mural has changed. Gone are the shops with signs saying NO PERSONAL CHECKS, a policy enforced only against Black customers. Gone is the white butcher I saw and heard ask a Black customer if he hadn't been in the shop for a while because he'd been "making license plates at Graterford" prison. In recent decades, waves of Vietnamese, Cambodian, Mexican, and South American sellers joined the Italian food purveyors on Ninth Street. The neighborhood is not Frank Rizzo's base anymore. Soon after Frank's statue was taken down, the giant mural of him was painted over. Unlike Frank's mural, the solid-colored wall that replaced it is no longer smeared in paint ball splatters, Philly's commentary on the fifty-year legacy of Rizzo's hateful approach to racial and criminal justice—an approach that lives on in the powerful police union's throwback leadership.

Philadelphia is a city of 1.6 million people; the sixth largest city in the United States, it has the fourth largest police department. That department is represented by a single police union. Like it or not, and many active Philadelphia police officers do not, every Philadelphia police officer is required to pay dues to and be a member of "the Mighty Lodge 5" of the Fraternal Order of Police (FOP). Even retired officers remain members and pay big dues, producing the bizarre result that most of the voting members are retired. The union panders to its retired members, and reflects the voices from the past. They sound more like Frank than they should. The retirees are far more male, white, and conservative than the active officers. Lodge 5 is only one source of the Philadelphia police union's historic power, which is only now beginning to ebb.

Perhaps more than in any other major American city, police have ruled Philadelphia's politics for decades. This is in part because they formed the stronghold of Frank Rizzo's power but also because Philadelphia, like most big cities in this country—from Los Angeles to Houston to New York City—is a predominantly progressive city in an otherwise rural, conservative state with, at least in the case of Pennsylvania, an alarming history of hate groups. The well-worn saying is "There's Pittsburgh and Philly and Alabama in between."

Why was this relevant to Philly or to my campaign? Because

for over a century in Philadelphia—and big cities throughout the country—the chief prosecutor's office has been a launching pad for ambitious prosecutors to run for statewide elected office, and eventually national office. And the era of ambitious politicians becoming elected chief prosecutors in order to become elected to even higher office coincides with the rise of mass incarceration in the United States for a reason.

For those politicians who want to win statewide office in Pennsylvania, pleasing the leadership of Philadelphia's FOP has been a key to unlocking votes in rural counties, the places where people know little about urban life or crime and where jail industries profit from harsh urban policies. Philly candidates for statewide office who please Philadelphia's FOP are assured of FOP support statewide, even in places where rural bias against a Philadelphia candidate is a potential hurdle. No other public office works as directly with the Philadelphia Police Department as the Philadelphia District Attorney's Office. All an ambitious district attorney in Philadelphia thinking of running for statewide office has to do to get statewide FOP support is pander to the leadership of the Philadelphia FOP, actively favoring police or looking away when politically advisable, which really means sometimes stepping on the necks of everyone not wearing blue.

Philadelphia DAs in the past few decades have included political juggernauts like Arlen Specter, who was voted in at thirty-five before he became a career U.S. senator and the most powerful gatekeeper to the federal bench; and Ed Rendell, who took the post at thirty-three, before he was elected mayor and then governor, and then became the chair of the Democratic National Committee. Rendell was buddies with Bill Clinton, and remains an enduring and powerful centrist voice within the Democratic Party.

Other DAs in Philadelphia of recent memory failed to win other offices, but were no less politically ambitious, including Lynne Abraham (best known nationally for being dubbed "the deadliest DA" by *The New York Times*), who liked to speak of her "passion" for the death penalty and crowed about the more than one hundred death sentences her office wrestled from Philadelphia juries during her nineteen-year tenure. I used to call her "the Queen of Death." After Lynne Abraham came Seth Williams, Philadelphia's first elected African American DA, who styled himself as a reformer while campaigning for DA, only to disappoint, reversing direction once he entered office. Perhaps he imagined running for statewide or even higher office later. He hinted at some dubious similarity to Barack Obama until an indictment ended his second term early and landed him in federal prison.

How did these ambitious prosecutors pander to the police? My thirty years in criminal justice before becoming DA taught me the rules. They are easy: Don't hold the small number of criminal cops accountable when their conduct is violent or corrupt. Don't push back against constitutional violations of individual rights committed by police, or against selective, discriminatory law enforcement. Do issue unnecessary subpoenas to police so they will receive overtime pay for appearing to testify in court. (It's an invisible political bribe that adds up to tens of millions of dollars, sometimes providing more than the individual officers' base salaries. Taxpayers be damned.) Cover up the integrity issues of a few bad officers, and cover up evidence that might lead to an acquittal of a defendant when that information reflects poorly on police. Violate the constitutional requirement (known by the name of the U.S. Supreme Court opinion that established it, *Brady*) that police and prosecutors turn over to the defense information that shows innocence or otherwise helps the defense. Deliver unequal treatment that favors bad police over good ones, inevitably pushing the bums toward supervisory positions. Favor police over civilians. Above all else, if you, a Philly chief prosecutor, want to rise to higher office statewide, you must climb a staircase made from the bodies of powerless people—the politically disconnected, the poor, and Black and brown people—in order to make yourself more palatable to the powerful, including the Philly FOP.

In early 2017, it was the decades-long stench of this pandering by ambitious politicians and Philly DAs—so habitual it was its own institution—that we were running against. Rizzo's legacy of over-punishment and a racist politics of fear, corruption, insider-ism, tribalism, officially sanctioned violence, and destruction of the city's budget and resources overshadowed Penn's legacy and the entire city. Throwing paint at Rizzo's statue hadn't fixed it. It was time to take away his shadow's power, even before his statue went away. We had to go inside government and turn on the lights.

I still remember my surprise in 1991 when Frank died suddenly of a heart attack a few days after I met him. A couple of days later I was walking by the Cathedral Basilica of Saints Peter and Paul, the gorgeous red-brown stone cathedral that sits midway between City Hall and the art museum. It's where Philadelphia's Catholic elite are baptized and married. I didn't know before I walked by that Frank Rizzo was lying in state. The hours-long line was out the giant doors and went on for blocks. Police cars, barricades, and uniformed cops were everywhere, gathered like a tribe at the death of its chief. I saw a well-dressed, dark-haired woman in heels walking with uniformed officers through the police barriers that excluded everybody else. She was in her thirties, maybe just forty. The fashion looked like money, slightly retro. She was escorted past the long line and immediately entered through the cathedral doors without delay or explanation. I asked someone who she was. No one answered or even looked my way. They heard me. A few minutes later, I overheard one of the officers tell the other that she was Frank's girlfriend. Frank had been married forever.

Some things in Philadelphia are for insiders to know. The woman's significance or her reason for jumping the line wasn't supposed to be for an outsider like me. But what I did know is that, in Philly, outsiders can wait in line or they can find another way. I stayed behind the police barrier with the others for a few more minutes before heading home, a walk that took me past City Hall and the stairs where Frank's statue would be erected, with private funds, seven years later, in 1998.

Frank came down in 2020, removed by the city twenty-two years after he was installed. People were sleeping when it happened. There was no prior notice after years of controversy and delay in its removal. Frank was disappeared, extraordinarily renditioned—tactics he might have liked to use on the living in his day. But Frank's day was over. His bronze image was plucked by a crane, covered in a tarp, and driven away on a flatbed truck to an undisclosed location during days of protests around the death of George Floyd that were led by Black Lives Matter. Philly can't find Frank, or his shadow, at the moment. Some Philadelphians would break it if they could; a few others would try to put it up somewhere else, surrounded by the throwback culture and support that Frank in bronze represents. But Frank's renditioned statue is in a secret place for now, which William Penn's statue is not. Frank's statue came and went beneath the watchful eyes of William Penn on top of City Hall, where he was first installed more than a century ago. Penn remains like a restless guardian angel swathed in lights and fog, dusted and oxidized by the weather and the years, as he keeps watch. Even with Frank gone, Penn still has much to guard against.

# CHAPTER 5

# Decarceration

*No man born with a living soul*
*Can be working for the clampdown*

— THE CLASH, "Clampdown"

Racism, police brutality, corruption, and the myths that justified all three not only persisted in Frank's long shadow but also morphed into mass incarceration, disproportionately of Black and brown people. Mass incarceration has catalyzed the dismantling of crime prevention, including a social safety net partly to pay for more jails and prisons, and partly because a safety net was at odds with the myths held dear by a country full of prisons.

In 2017, there were a lot of Franks holding power all over America in policing, prosecution, and politics—which explains a lot about how we got to be so catastrophically over-incarcerated. We see some of mass incarceration's many drivers in the operation of our cash bail system, mandatory sentencing laws, sentencing guidelines schemes, excessive supervision of people on bail and parole, and knee-jerk violations of parole and probation that too often lead to more incarceration. But behind the mechanics and tactics of any oppressive system, there are always myths—sometimes in the form of unquestioned assumptions. These myths become so familiar and universal that we barely see them.

The omnipresent jails built by Frank and his ilk rest on the cracked foundation that is the myth that people don't change. People are either very good or very bad—saints or monsters, you see.

The Franks of the world have their reasons for liking this self-serving narrative of people not changing and its corollary myths—of criminality being constant and distinct from victimhood, of victimhood being constant and distinct from criminality. I say "self-serving" because the narrative implies that even our elected leaders are where they are for a reason. It means their identity as insiders and leaders and their incumbency and ongoing power are based upon their being very good, now and forever, which means their incumbency and power should remain unassailable. The myth never concedes that chance, fortune, and help play a role. People always get what they deserve.

The rest of us don't need this myth. But Frank's kind of insiders do. They need it to make people who might challenge them skeptical of change, even to the point of disbelieving in their own experience, their own joyous evolution. The insiders need the myth to keep outsiders from trying to come inside, so that they can stay in power longer. Frank's fans need it because they are mediocre—at best—and don't want the rest of us to know.

If the world is divided between monsters and saints, that means we need to identify who belongs in which camp. The Franks of the world make it easy for you: They say you can tell the difference between monsters and saints by race, ethnicity, neighborhood, poverty, gender, sexual orientation, politics, criminal record, or some other easy marker.

Having established who's who, they then build walls between the camps by pushing the myth's corollary notions. Push the notion that victims are never perpetrators. Push the notion that perpetrators are never victims. It's not true, but push it. Push the notion that police and accusers and witnesses are always accurate and always truthful—that only the guilty are charged and convicted. Push the notion that anyone who disagrees with the police or witnesses called by the prosecution is lying even though it's not true—no group has a monopoly on the truth. Push the notion that the supposedly unchanging nature of criminality calls for an unchanging response that is simple, punitive, and retributive—because people who commit crimes are criminals for life, right? One crime tells us all we need to know about its perpetrator. None of this is true, but they push these fictions to stay on top.

My saying that people change is not aspirational. It's fact. Decades after my law school moot court argument, the U.S. Supreme Court decided it's not okay to execute people who committed murders as juveniles. And then it took another step: The Supreme Court decided it's not okay to keep them in jail forever, under a mandatory sentence of life without the possibility of parole. Both decisions were based upon psychological research establishing that juveniles' and young adults' brains are immature, making them less culpable for their actions but possessed of greater potential for rehabilitation and change due to that mental immaturity. As a result of these two momentous decisions, we are seeing what happens after children who took part in murders are re-sentenced and exit jail. Overwhelmingly, they have changed for the better. People find new selves, or maybe their new selves find them.

Years before I ran for office, these decisions set into motion an experiment no academic institution would allow: First, human children who have in varying ways been involved in murders are deemed monsters. Very young, they are brought into courtrooms and told by authorities wearing black robes and sitting higher than anyone else that, by execution or by incarceration until their natural deaths, they will die in a prison. They are locked in cages for years or decades, sometimes enduring the blight of sensory deprivation for extended periods in solitary confinement. Then, fairly suddenly and unexpectedly, their fates are revised: All of these people are re-sentenced and many are released due to the U.S. Supreme Court's opinions. They exit prison at many different ages, from their thirties to their seventies or even eighties. They have completed wildly varying but always lengthy periods of time in custody—nearly all the human subjects of this experiment have served between fifteen and fifty years. And now, suddenly, they are free.

A separate, unacceptable experiment was set in motion and is going on in parallel. Simultaneously, siblings and lovers and parents and friends of the victims of these crimes are suffering and trying to heal and to bear what is beyond remedy: the death of their child, brother, sister, cousin, parent, colleague, schoolmate, employee, co-worker, friend, spouse, lover. First, these human subjects are told by authority figures, in real courtrooms, that the sentence of life without parole or the sentence of death for this juvenile perpetrator is just and that it is justice—the only type of justice being offered. A decade or many decades later, the survivors who can be found are told there will be a re-sentencing and possibly a release from custody of the convicted perpetrators. More specifically, these survivors are told the U.S. Supreme Court has determined that the life or death sentence they were told was justice was in fact unjust—a violation of the U.S. Constitution. For some survivors, scars are torn open and the bleeding begins again. For others, who have been able to heal more, this news will lead to the questions and conversations and support these survivors need. For some, the idea of their loved one's killer dying in jail is already inconsistent with their faith, their philosophy, or their progress in healing. They embrace forgiveness and rehabilitation. For every one of these human subjects, these survivors, it's hard.

At the end of the experiment we find out what happened to these children, now adults, who were released. We find out whether the people we called monsters have changed. Can people change? We no longer have to guess. There are facts, and those facts are kryptonite for the myth of monsters and saints.

Nowhere in the world has this experiment been more important than in Philadelphia. Philadelphia is the world's epicenter for juvenile lifers. Philadelphia has put in jail for life more juveniles convicted of taking part in murders than any other city in America; other countries don't give juveniles life sentences. As a result, in 2017 Philly remained the most extreme and the largest experiment in the world on what happens when many of them are re-sentenced and leave custody.

By 2017, I knew that most juvenile lifers had evolved profoundly in jail, shaking off their impulsive and violent tendencies during their first years of incarceration and as they matured. Many had worked thousands of hours in prison jobs that paid pennies per hour. Many had obtained college degrees and credits. Some "old head" juvenile lifers had become the most stabilizing influences in their prisons, mentoring and calming the younger, more recently incarcerated inmates. And mostly these juvenile lifers did these positive things before the Supreme Court changed their fate, with no real hope of freedom, of ever living or dying outside prison walls. Even with nothing to gain and negligible resources to aid in their rehabilitation, they improved.

In 2017, among those juvenile lifers who had been released, recidivism was so low that it fell below the rate of a random sample of the general population. We will continue to see their progress over time. They don't need to be *safer* than everyone else for us to know the vast majority of them have profoundly changed—but the truth is, when I set out to run for office, they were. The truth is, the crimes juvenile lifers committed in childhood were monstrous, but they themselves were not monsters.

Their being sentenced to death or incarceration for their entire lives on the theory that only death in prison would stop them from killing again or committing other serious crimes was wrong, but only partly because it was factually incorrect. It was also morally wrong: When they committed these acts, they were children. Those death and life sentences reinforced the message that served the people in charge, the myth that people don't change. Those sentences assumed that killing was in these children's *nature*, that their criminality was constant and inherent rather than what it really was for so many of them: temporary and situational. Even so, and in the most damaging of places, the juvenile lifers affirmed that the core of human dignity, our capacity to improve, lives in all of us. They evolved.

The parallel experiment—the survivors' experience—will be harder to evaluate. Simple metrics, like recidivism, are not available for this group and their process of healing. But for many survivors, their experience will be affected by the outcomes of the main experiment itself—the juvenile lifers who are released. For many survivors, it will matter that the people released overwhelmingly do not kill or commit serious crimes again, especially violent crimes. It will matter that others will not be harmed the way their loved ones were. And for those survivors more wedded to retribution and punishment than they are to the prevention of victimization in the future, it will be hard. Trauma goes deep; profound healing is not universal. Like anyone who is suffering, they will be vocal in ways we can only hope are also helpful to them. Bryan Stevenson was right when he said you're not the worst thing you ever did. We should add that you're not the worst thing ever done to you. All victims and survivors deserve their second chance as well, our resources, and our support to try to heal. The fundamental causes of America's mass incarceration crisis—racism and slavery, profit, politics, a false view of people as unchanging that drives us toward retribution rather than rehabilitation and prevention—are obvious. But the mechanics of mass incarceration are more obscure, especially for those whose professional and lived experiences have not been in America's criminal justice courthouses.

I remember sitting onstage one block from City Hall during the campaign, looking out at a thousand people in the pews of the Arch Street Methodist Church during an important and well-attended public forum. The church's pastor, Robin Hynicka, happened to be an ex-client of mine who was arrested during anti-casino protests in Philly. His progressive church was known for supporting protest against racial injustice, poverty, and anti-immigrant laws. The church hadn't backed down from a fight with the city over its practice of allowing homeless people to sleep in its basement on freezing nights.

A few of the most conservative candidates had skipped the forum, sensing that the diverse and casually dressed audience wouldn't receive their message well. From the stage, I saw a good presence of mainstream and volunteer journalists, who broadcast the event well beyond the pews and gothic stone walls. Community members were lined up at two floor microphones situated in different walkways between rows of pews, alternately asking questions of the candidates.

Someone asked us to explain in two minutes or less specifically how to combat mass incarceration, which was not much time to answer such a big question. A couple of other candidates answered generally, with one or two ideas. I had been butting up against mass incarceration daily in court, for my entire law career. It was time to talk about it. I quickly scribbled notes on the back of a couple of my campaign business cards, listing ten ways while even more came to mind as my turn came. The mechanics of mass incarceration are like parts of a giant machine that interconnect: a handful of main drivers, each with subparts, that affect and counteract each other. No one person designed this mess. Depending upon how they are adjusted, those drivers can either further incarcerate or decarcerate massive numbers of people relatively quickly. I stood to address the crowd and said I had ten ways to attack mass incarceration, and dropped them one by one with quick explanations of a few seconds each, mindful of the time. Some members of the audience counted them down out loud, correcting me when I lost count. With more time, I could have listed more. Or I could have focused on a smaller group of key drivers of mass incarceration.

Four in particular stood out and became frequent talking points both that night and as we campaigned, part of our mantra: cash bail, sentencing guidelines and mandatory sentencing laws, mass supervision, and violations of supervision on probation and parole.

Cash bail, otherwise known as money bail, is what defendants pay to stay out of custody before trial, after they are charged with crimes. Philly, and every other county in Pennsylvania, is a cash bail jurisdiction. Nearly all American jurisdictions are cash bail jurisdictions, with a few notable exceptions such as D.C., Kentucky, and New Jersey.

Two of the biggest problems with cash bail are these: (1) Poor people who pose no real danger to the community get stuck in jail pre-trial for non-serious offenses. (2) Rich people who pose a real danger to society get out of jail pre-trial for truly serious offenses.

Cash bail's rationale has never made much sense. The ostensible premise is that people who have paid cash bail won't skip court and won't commit new crimes, while people who don't pay cash for their release will skip court and become one-person crime waves while their other case is pending. This theory imagines a world where people charged with crimes are wholly rational decisionmakers primarily motivated by money over everything else, including their freedom. That's nonsense.

But cash bail's real function, whether conscious or unconscious, seems to be something else: to create revenue, both for the government and for private companies, while taking freedom from the poor. After the killing of Michael Brown in 2014, a federal investigation revealed that Ferguson, Missouri, relied on dunning its relatively poor and Black residents with tickets and fines to raise a big chunk of its municipal funding, a regressive fundraising tool that punished the poor in the name of criminal justice. Cash bail practices reek of the same kind of kleptocracy.

Even though, after a criminal case is over, bail money is supposed to be returned to defendants who show up in court, counties come to view the bail funds they are holding as a resource. For nearly all of my career as a criminal defense attorney, Philadelphia took a big bite out of bail money and kept it even when a defendant was found not guilty and never missed court. Other counties view bail money held by the county as a piggy bank for whatever fines, fees, and costs a judge imposes on a defendant at sentencing. The system incentivizes judges to assess fines, fees, and costs more heavily when defendants have more money tied up in bail. And legislators have steadily increased the amount of money government takes from defendants, often making fees and costs mandatory so that judges who believe this dunning is unjust in a particular case are required to impose them, which further incentivizes state and local authorities to support and expand a cash bail system. Those fees and costs generally go to fund the state budget, and in most jurisdictions they keep going up.

State and local government legislators in many jurisdictions have been corrupted by the steady pressure of private bail industry lobbyists, whose gifts and friends' campaign donations some legislators enjoy. Prosecutors and judges within the courts can become corrupted by viewing unjust cash bails as leverage to force an eventual guilty plea rather than do the time-consuming work of trying a case. Even the seemingly mundane issue of moving defendants who are in custody between jails and courthouses becomes problematic when too many people are stuck in jail for lack of a few dollars to pay bail on non-serious cases. Having too many people in custody slows the disposition of their cases, and that delay alone forces some guilty pleas when the number of inmates needed in court exceeds the system's capacity to bring them.

Cash bail results in the incarceration of the poor for minor crimes while liberating the rich for serious crimes; it is a system that in practice restricts the presumption of innocence to the wealthy. Its effects are devastating on the people most directly involved in the system. For the poor people charged with non-serious offenses, even a temporary inability to pay cash bail can mean stranded and suffering children, suffering or dead pets, and loss of employment and healthcare. And that job loss may mean one fewer taxpayer. For all the other taxpayers, the jailing of the person unable to pay cash bail means a crushing tax bill to pay for that incarceration; the cost sometimes exceeds the cash bail after a single day. For the rich or resourced defendant charged with serious offenses, immediate liberty by cash can enable swift intimidation or retaliation against victims and witnesses who trusted law enforcement and the courts enough to engage them, which degrades and undermines the prosecution of serious criminal cases. These well-resourced defendants can return to their criminal enterprises without interruption to endanger people, often including themselves. Consider the following opposite examples of how cash bail systems fail us.

A young single mother who cleans houses is stopped and arrested for having a couple of ounces of weed in her car. She uses the weed herself, but only buys in ounce amounts to reduce the risk of getting caught. Police and prosecutors incorrectly assume she is a dealer. A moderate amount of cash bail is ordered on the dealing charge that is too much for her to pay. Immediately, she is up against the following: caring for her children, who are with a sitter when she works; caring for her dog at home; informing her next day's employer that she won't make it and probably being asked when she can; paying all the bills that are coming in while she is in custody; and facing the trauma of incarceration for the first time—she has no prior record. Within days, she will be up against losing all the cleaning jobs she has with homeowners who employ her and possibly losing custody, at least temporarily, of her children. Who will take her dog and care for it? What will happen when she can't pay her rent? Later, when she goes to court with a few weeks or a month of separation from her children under her belt, she will want to do anything—including pleading to drug dealing, a crime she did not commit—to get out. And, if she does so, that conviction will forever limit her ability to support herself and provide for her children, improve her education, and obtain housing, among other things. For a broke person who poses no danger, a little bit of bail can be a big injustice.

A major heroin and cocaine dealer whose drugs are sourced overseas from a cartel is arrested for drug dealing when a shipment involving several kilos is intercepted based on information obtained from an informant. Social media indicates the dealer has access to firearms, although none are found during the drug interception or arrest of the dealer. The prosecutor seeks and a judge imposes what is high bail for any normally resourced person. But the drug dealer and his allies have access to money far in excess of the bail and promptly pay it, gaining his release. From the street, the dealer pursues his suspicions about the identity of the informant and pays an associate to kill the informant, thereby eliminating a potentially crucial witness whose death weakens and may undermine the case. The dealer's drug operation and the violence surrounding it continue, albeit more cautiously in light of the arrest and in ways that are even harder for law enforcement to detect. For a rich person who poses great danger, even a lot of bail can be too little to do justice: Detention in custody with no ability to pay to get out is what works.

And what is the alternative to a cash bail system? It's pretty simple: Abolish it. Divorce the payment of money from deciding whom to hold in jail and whom to release. In a no-cash-bail system, judges hold people charged with crimes in custody or release them from custody based primarily on the danger their release presents to the community. In the District of Columbia, there has been a statute for thirty years that forbids judges from using any amount of money in setting bail. In D.C., about 12 percent of all criminal defendants are held in custody until trial because they are viewed as presenting too much risk on the streets pre-trial. On truly serious cases, where the defendant poses a danger to the community, billionaire defendants sit in jail just like anybody else pre-trial. No amount of money can buy their way out. And, in D.C., about 88 percent of all criminal defendants are released without having to pay any money, although they may be required to report for some type of services or monitoring. For example, a homeless defendant won't pay money but may have to report to a homeless services center once a week— call it sweat bail.

One of the greatest virtues of a modern, no-cash-bail system like D.C.'s is that immediately after arrest it allows the system to address underlying issues for which the criminal charges are just one symptom. For example, a person suffering from addiction or mental illness can be released and required to seek treatment services right away as a condition of their freedom before trial. In a traditional cash bail system, it's all about the money, with no or minimal services available before trial—any mental health or addiction services show up only after conviction and sentencing, as a condition of parole or probation. The early treatment and support available to people who are released in a modern no-cash-bail system have another great outcome in fighting mass incarceration and improving justice.

In a no-cash-bail system, unnecessary convictions for non-serious offenses are easier to avoid. Defendants who comply with their conditions of pre-trial release by going to drug or mental health treatment before trial, for example, are proving they will be compliant with post-trial rehabilitation, which makes them good candidates for diversion rather than conviction and other forms of accountability that do not require convictions and prison sentences. Prosecutors who are deciding whether or not to offer diversion rather than go to trial have reliable information on who may do well with diversion. Root causes that may have led to the arrest are addressed earlier. Individual justice is served by its elimination, but cash bail is only one of the drivers of mass incarceration.

Sentencing guidelines and their slightly more evil cousin, mandatory minimum sentencing, are another cause of mass incarceration. Sentencing guidelines and mandatory minimums boil every individual situation down to numbers. Sentencing guidelines are a range of numbers judges choose from in sentencing defendants, such as 24–30 (meaning twenty-four to thirty months of custody) for a certain class of cases. Mandatory sentencing differs in that it is an absolute floor below which a judge has no power to go—for example, life without possibility of parole is a mandatory sentence in Pennsylvania that gives judges no choice in certain cases, regardless of the facts and equities.

With sentencing guidelines, the sentencing range usually depends on two factors: the supposed seriousness of the offense (reflected in a point system) and the defendant's prior record (reflected in another point system). The two point systems become the axes of a table that presumes to reduce the intense complexity of all types of criminal conduct and life history to reductivist simplicity. In the worst jurisdictions, judges have no choice but to rigidly follow sentencing guidelines. In slightly better jurisdictions, judges have some discretion if they overcome a variety of challenges and are able to show that the case or the defendant is special and somehow different from what the guidelines cover. And in some jurisdictions that are less benighted, the sentencing guidelines actually adhere to the definition of the word "guidelines": They are ranges to be considered by judges, but they do not prevent the judge's exercise of discretion in deciding what sentence to give in a particular case.

For example, someone convicted in Pennsylvania with an assault for a bar fight who had a minor prior criminal record may face a sentencing guidelines range that suggests a sentence of anything from probation to several months in county custody if the victim's injuries are not too bad. But if the same punch by the defendant causes slightly more serious injury, the sentencing guidelines may suggest a much longer and more life-altering sentence, between two and four years in state custody—the kind of sentence that can wreck family bonds and steady employment permanently, two factors known to prevent future crime and encourage rehabilitation.

In most jurisdictions, the chart of sentencing guidelines can fit on a single page. Simplicity is supposed to be part of the point. After all, the criminal system is built on the myth that people are all good or bad and don't really change. But the definitions and point systems laid out in the manuals that come with the chart are not simple and consume tremendous time at sentencing, and afterward on appeal. Most sentencing guidelines manuals betray their control-freak authors' fevered, predictive dream of all the characteristics of every crime, every prosecution, and every defendant in the future. The deceptive impression created by these hefty books full of definitions and complex number systems is that they reflect something of substance, something written after years of criminological research and based on data, tested and scientific. They don't.

They represent someone's or some group of legislators' gut feeling or political scheming on what sentences should be for certain crimes and certain defendants. Far too often, those legislators have no experience in criminal justice and their positions reflect whatever they think will get them reelected, which historically has been a draconian approach to sentencing. Even when the sentencing guidelines are written by people with experience in criminal justice, they nearly always reflect the philosophy of criminal justice's old-guard power players: traditional prosecutors.

Pennsylvania's sentencing guidelines scheme, for example, dates from the 1980s, a time when there were zero progressive chief prosecutors in Pennsylvania. At first, Pennsylvania's sentencing guidelines were nothing more than an averaging of what sentences were already being given for similar crimes and defendants across Pennsylvania's sixty-seven wildly different counties. In theory, the purpose was consistency across different jurisdictions and among different judges that limited judicial discretion. But consistency alone is not justice, and consistency codified in excessively lengthy guidelines is terribly unjust when it forces judges to impose consistently excessive sentences. Individual justice is justice's goal, even when it appears or occasionally results in outcomes that are somewhat inconsistent. And consistency can be dangerous when less populated rural, suburban, and exurban counties set the sentencing guidelines for what densely populated urban counties' judges should do with crimes seldom faced outside of cities. It's a real culture clash, an invasion of cities' authority to handle their own criminal matters and higher levels of crime in the ways city judges believe will work. Some states' sentencing guidelines updates have added complexity and some nuance, but remain orchestrated by politicians and their traditional prosecutor cronies who view too much sentencing as not being enough.

Mandatory sentencing schemes don't require a fat book of rules because they are even simpler than sentencing guidelines schemes, which is the only good thing I can say about them. And they are even more problematic for justice, completely stripping judges of their ability to give a sentence below a certain floor when the specifics of the case call for it, even when the result is unjust. A defense lawyer's logical arguments and silver tongue don't matter anymore, either. That stolen judicial power finds a new home in the toolboxes of traditional prosecutors, who are the only ones empowered to undo a mandatory sentence where that is even possible. With mandatory minimum sentencing laws, prosecutors hold nearly all the power. And prosecutors are able to use that power to get defendants, through their beleaguered counsel, to do exactly what they require. Often that means prosecutors are able to coerce defendants into pleading guilty rather than trying their case and accepting whatever negotiated sentence the prosecutor feels like offering. Any mutiny by the judge or defense counsel against the prosecutor's use of the mandatory sentencing law is futile. The prosecutor can always revive the mandatory minimum sentence. Judges frequently impose mandatory minimum sentences while commenting that they disagree with them or view the mandatory minimum as an example of the legislature "going haywire," but have no choice but to impose it.

Every now and then, even prosecutors are offended by mandatory sentences and have to find creative ways around them, as I experienced once representing a man named Juan Ramirez on drug charges in federal court. He was facing life without the possibility of parole due to a combination of the weight of drugs involved and his two prior drug convictions. He had no real record for violence or guns and was one of a few dozen defendants in a large drug conspiracy where he was a mid- or low-level participant. Had this been his first offense, the mandatory minimum he would have faced was ten years.

Juan Ramirez grew up impoverished in Puerto Rico. He told me he remembered sitting on a bar stool as a young child next to his mother, who would periodically disappear into the back with male customers for money. His parents would binge on drugs and stopped feeding him and his younger sisters for days at a time. By age ten, Juan was washing cars in a cemetery for money and dealing dime bags of drugs to users so he could feed himself and his younger sisters. When he came home with money for food, especially after his parents' benefits checks were exhausted later in the month, his mother would assault him to steal the money so she could buy drugs, sometimes biting him in the process. When he switched to buying food before he got home, she would beat him or try to sell the food for drug money. He always persisted, supporting his sisters even after both parents died of AIDS while he was a teen.

I got his case a few months after he was arrested and indicted, unusually late in the process. Juan spoke little English and his prior attorney spoke no Spanish. The lawyer was a bum who apparently made no real effort to help him before being replaced by me. Helping Ramirez, in a federal case where the evidence was overwhelming and the likely sentence life, meant helping him to snitch—to provide truthful information to the feds that would aid them in prosecuting other people. If his information was truthful and successful, he could obtain a sentencing reduction to something far below a life sentence.

But it was too late for Ramirez to effectively snitch by the time I got the case. The feds already had all the evidence they needed. A couple dozen other defendants, many of them far more involved in the drug conspiracy than he, had already talked. Ramirez was truthful and he was willing to tell everything, but had nothing new to give. We tried snitching at a proffer, a meeting where Juan did what he was asked and truthfully told the prosecutor and federal agents everything he knew. I made sure Juan also told them everything about his background; the federal prosecutor got quiet but said he was unable to help. Juan had nothing new. The prosecutor said his supervisors had no choice but to disapprove a sentencing reduction. A life sentence was inevitable. We were all up against a bad system.

But the prosecutor, who had been in street law enforcement before law school, found a way to help out. The information Ramirez gave wasn't new or necessary, but it was all true. But for the crap lawyer who ignored him for months due to a language barrier, Juan would have qualified for a sentencing reduction. So the prosecutor took bits and pieces of the information Juan provided in his proffer as additional, albeit cumulative, support for search warrants and arrest warrants he was already writing based on other defendants' information, without any information from Ramirez. The prosecutor didn't need Juan's information to get the warrants, but he threw it in anyway. When the warrants were executed and produced evidence, the prosecutor told his supervisors that Juan's information had been used. He was stretching to give Juan credit, and it worked. At sentencing, the prosecutor got Juan a ten-year sentence that the judge and I had absolutely no power to give. On his way out of the courtroom, the prosecutor gave me a toothy grin. We both knew the feds had come up with a system so ugly that even an ex–law enforcement officer turned federal prosecutor couldn't stand it and stuck his neck out to get some justice.

Here is where the big view helps more than the details: How can sentencing guidelines and mandatory sentencing schemes be sound when their only fruit has been steady increases in mass incarceration in Pennsylvania, and in the United States? They can't, which raises the question of why America continues to use them. Who benefits?

The answer is politicians, elected officials, and the prison industry they made. More specifically, mandatory sentencing schemes and excessive sentencing guidelines are the legal framework of a profitable and political trade in human beings. In Pennsylvania—but also all around the country—public state prisons have been a major industry outside cities, especially in many rural counties. State prisons dot the state map, but none exist in Philadelphia. Of the roughly 50,000 Pennsylvania state prisoners in 2017, about 27 percent (over 13,000) were Philadelphia residents before being exported to other counties' prisons, where they would be included in that county's population for purposes of the census. Where these Philadelphians went and were counted in the census, tax funding followed that fed the local economies at approximately $50,000 or more per inmate per year. That's a lot of money, especially in a broke county. The rough math on 13,000 Philadelphians locked up at fifty grand a year is $650 million spent all over Pennsylvania except in Philadelphia, the urban center where the vast majority of these men and women were born and nearly all resided prior to their incarceration. And with these other counties' counting Philadelphians in their census, increased highway funding and gerrymandered political power have gone to the same counties by counting people who live locked up in prison cells, unable to drive or vote. No wonder, then, that with so many other Pennsylvania counties' inflated payrolls and tax bases and fluffed-up political power dependent on locking up Philadelphians, the elected officials of an otherwise economically moribund county economy vigorously push mandatory minimum sentencing and sentencing guidelines laws that fill their prisons with Philadelphians who are disproportionately poor, Black, and brown.

Even after being released from custody, people who have been convicted of crimes face supervision on parole and probation that is no less troubling or massive. Mass supervision refers to mass incarceration's counterpart, the even larger number of people who are living under the supervision of parole or probation officers. In the short run, supervision on probation or parole can be constructive. The science around it is clear: Three years or less of supervision on parole or probation is usually beneficial. More than three years of supervision generally just makes things worse. Not only does excessive supervision fail to improve things, but it actually causes people who have been convicted of a crime to fail. They often end up re-sentenced and back in custody when a judge decides the probationer or parolee has violated the terms and conditions of supervision. Those violations can be as insignificant as a probationer missing a monthly payment to fund his own supervision or missing a single appointment with a probation or parole officer.

Imagine the position of a landscaper on parole, holding a growling chain saw in both hands on a worksite. His decent boss hired him despite a criminal record. He has been a good worker for five years. He reunited with family, is a provider again, pays taxes, and has had no further involvement with crime since his conviction. He has made all of his biweekly probation appointments until the day his boss tells him he just can't spare him this time—other workers out, a looming deadline, bad weather coming, and payroll due, including the paycheck of the parolee holding the chain saw. If the landscaper leaves work to go to his parole appointment that day, he'll be fired. Keeping employed and paying monthly fees and costs are requirements of his supervision. Without a job, the parolee faces a supervision violation. If the landscaper skips his parole appointment, he faces a supervision violation for merely skipping the appointment. None of this would be happening if the landscaper's supervision had ended at three years, but it didn't. After five years of successful rehabilitation, two decent people—the parolee and his boss—are up against a bad system.

Whatever choice he makes, the landscaper is likely to end up in front of the judge who sentenced him in the first place and his chain saw won't be the only thing growling. He may face a weirdly parental dynamic, with the judge playing the angry parent role and a parole violation, a re-sentencing, and a return to incarceration coming next that will likely do far more harm than good for the future of a man who has profoundly changed. And if the landscaper is sent upstate, money and power will go with him. Someone or something's interests will be served, but it won't be justice and it won't be ours. There is no binary world divided between saints and monsters. Stereotypes always fail us; each person is unique; truth is individual; each case is individual; justice is individual. Simplistic one-size-fits-all approaches do not remedy crime; they cause it. Rehabilitation works because it helps people change. One-size-fits-all approaches to criminal justice—in the form of extremist sentencing, mandatory minimum sentencing, "three strikes" laws, sentences of life without possibility of parole, death sentences, mass incarceration, mass supervision on probation and parole, the use of cash bail, and more and similar dumb ideas—do nothing to heal society or to make us safe. Stereotypes and their codification in criminal law are just shortcuts for people inclined toward simple answers rather than the hard, careful, and sometimes uncertain work that pursuing justice, case after case after case, requires.

# CHAPTER 6

# Do Less Harm

*Oh brother are you gonna leave me wasting away*
*On the streets of Philadelphia.*
—Bruce Springsteen, "Streets of Philadelphia"

A perverse, unjust system harms the bodies of the people in it. Our society has a history of addressing the overall health of our privileged classes, even in an epidemic, by pursuing or at least allowing the selective harming of our outsiders—Black, brown, indigenous, gay, and poor people, and people suffering from mental health issues and addiction—rather than protecting them. The nature of contagious disease, of any epidemic, is that it spreads. Our system comfortably disregards the deaths of marginalized people to its peril. It's not just immoral, it's suicidal in the end. Our history of facing HIV and COVID-19 proves that even as epidemics kill the outsiders first, in the end they are not as selective as people in power might prefer. Epidemics harm everyone. Even a perverse government bent on self-interest should have learned by now that protecting anyone's body, no matter how marginalized and stigmatized that body is, protects everyone, including the people who hold power.

The Kensington neighborhood in Philadelphia has been the city's epicenter of heroin use since at least the late 1960s due in part to the relative purity and low price of heroin available there, a by-product of the neighborhood's proximity to the ports, highways, airports, and train tracks where drugs—and the guns that come with them—move up and down the East Coast. There are other reasons beyond its geography. Industry died here in the 1950s and '60s, at first slowly, so that it degraded wages and drove out its population of white ethnic workers. Then industry died here completely, but only after a substantial population of Puerto Ricans moved here to work in industrial plants for low wages. They were effectively stranded. The next industry to arrive was the illegal sale of drugs, offering what became the only real economic opportunity in a neighborhood that remains desperately poor, even by Philadelphia's standards. Notably, Philadelphia's primary answer in Kensington has been to wage a failing war on addicted people through arrest and incarceration rather than to address their disease through public health approaches, which work far better. The story is not completely one-sided, as public health approaches have made moderate inroads and reaped benefits, benefits that I witnessed long before 2017 but that informed our platform as we campaigned.

I got to know Kensington in the late 1980s through my work as a public defender and later as a lawyer representing Prevention Point, Philadelphia's needle exchange program that activists built in part to stop the spread of HIV/AIDS among intravenous drug users during the AIDS crisis. Drug users shared needles frequently, spreading the virus rapidly, as they shot up three or more times a day. The needle exchange collected dirty needles and syringes and exchanged them for sanitary ones. The fact that HIV/AIDS was spreading through intravenous drug use, blood transfusions, and sexual contact meant we needed to simultaneously slow its spread and do the research that could offer a medical solution down the road. I saw no reason why criminal laws meant to protect us should place us in danger.

My attachment to Prevention Point's work to fight the spread of AIDS via intravenous drug use—and the related work of ACT UP, the AIDS Coalition to Unleash Power, to fight the spread of AIDS via sexual contact and to fund research to find a cure— was partly personal. Having gone to law school in the Bay Area from 1984 to 1987, Lisa and I watched the catastrophe of AIDS and HIV unfold in San Francisco, in particular, and quickly spread elsewhere, including Philadelphia. We were seeing a world ravaged by a growing plague my generation had so far failed to address. And it was getting worse. AIDS was already devastating certain marginalized groups—gay men, Haitians, hemophiliacs, at first—and was daily finding more groups to slaughter. My generation's ongoing failure to cure it or to slow its spread meant that every human was or would soon be at risk. Intravenous drug use and insecure medical blood supplies were killing people. And so was mere sexual activity.

Lisa's first job as a lawyer was representing workers who were discriminated against by employers. Many of those workers were people who had disabilities, including life-threatening illnesses. One of her fellow lawyers, a hemophiliac, contracted AIDS from a tainted blood supply and died. Other clients and organizations she represented connected her, and then me, to members of ACT UP and its remarkable non-violent work for social change. In the late 1980s, two American presidents—Reagan and the elder Bush—declined to fund medical research that might find a cure or at least flatten the curve of the spread of HIV. Televangelists intoned that AIDS was God's plague on homosexuals.

When Bush visited Philadelphia he was greeted by activated and angry members of ACT UP, who with characteristic theatricality imagined for the impact of the photograph they could create and place above the newspaper's fold. Protesting pallbearers carrying a symbolic coffin filled with symbolic ashes of the dead, to confront the president's indifference to the growing epidemic. When jostling at the police barricade surrounding a prominent Philadelphia hotel caused the mock ashes to spill from the mock coffin, some panicky police wrongly assumed they were real ashes from the bodies of AIDS victims that could somehow infect them. A police riot ensued, with officers who had nothing to fear from the ashes violently swinging police batons that broke one protester's skull and drew blood from others who might actually have been HIV-positive. A scandal ensued. The outgoing mayor appointed a blue ribbon panel to investigate the event, find facts, and make recommendations about how such a fiasco might be avoided in the future. The mayor allowed ACT UP to pick a panel member. The organization picked me, a baby public defender whose instincts they trusted and whose knowledge of police procedures, albeit limited, was an upgrade from their own. Other panelists included prominent members of law enforcement, academia, LGBTQ activism, and so on.

We worked for months, producing a bombshell report of about eighty pages that documented a lack of police training and policies around HIV and AIDS to reduce panic and prevent riots. We recommended the establishment of a civilian board to make policing more accountable. The whole process made me want to go beyond criminal justice, to do civil rights law for people whose skulls were cracked or who were otherwise stepped on by government for simply trying to protect lives. Serving on the panel changed the course of my career.

After five years as a county public defender and then a federal public defender in Philly, where I exclusively represented poor people charged with federal crimes, I set up my own private practice—the practice where I would continue solo, and with a few partners over time, for twenty-five years. Only a few years into my private practice, in the early 1990s, I was hired by Prevention Point, which had grown out of the work of ACT UP.

Back then, Lisa and I had just had our two sons. One was walking. Their births reminded me that the generation of children now arriving on this old planet were watching a worldwide epidemic expand, with no cure in sight. If we did nothing for all of our babies, as teens or adults many of them would unknowingly infect and eventually kill themselves and tens of millions of others. As usual, our government was not acting to prevent harm that did not yet greatly impact its beloved, powerful insiders. I wanted a piece of that historic, good fight and was excited to represent Prevention Point for the pittance they could pay.

Under Pennsylvania law, there is a simplistic legal argument that providing clean syringes to drug users violates the law against disseminating drug paraphernalia. But there is a better legal argument that providing clean syringes to drug users follows the law of justification, which includes the law of self-defense. Justification allows us to commit a smaller offense to prevent a greater harm, mostly when we are trying to protect ourselves or other people from suffering injury or death. In my view, protection of others—everyone, really—was the mission of Prevention Point and its needle exchange. Contracting or spreading HIV and suffering or dying from AIDS were great harms to be prevented by the smaller offense of giving clean needles to intravenous drug users. So, in my view, Prevention Point's work was morally required and legally justified. Not everyone agreed with this analysis.

In the early 1990s, Pennsylvania's statewide prosecutor, the elected attorney general, railed against needle exchange programs like Prevention Point and suggested he would arrest and prosecute the activists who worked for them. His comments were friendly to upstate conservative voters uncomfortable with everything that HIV/AIDS and drugs and needles represented in the event he tried for higher office statewide, as so many other state attorneys general have done. I believed he meant business, and so did Prevention Point. We prepared for arrests and prosecution. But concern about the attorney general's cynical enforcement subsided when he resigned his office after taking secret campaign contributions from video poker machine operators that were omitted from the finance reports he signed. Shortly before beginning his fourteen-month custodial sentence, the former law enforcement chief prosecutor reportedly told the press: "I can do federal prison standing on my head."

Although the threat of Prevention Point being prosecuted by the Pennsylvania attorney general had been removed, Philadelphia police were initially unsupportive in a culture that still gave room to the laughable notion that providing clean needles increases drug use. It made no more sense than the fiction that access to condoms causes teenage sex. Science backs neither theory.

But Philadelphia police still rousted users who showed up for clean needles at the card tables Prevention Point set up in Kensington under the elevated train tracks. Rather than getting clean works, the users got arrested for possession of drugs, or witnessed their clean needles and syringes being stomped and broken by police boots.

But as time passed and public health information spread, the wisdom of stopping the spread of the disease by providing clean needles gained momentum with a new mayor, Ed Rendell, and policing in Philly changed. The cops left the exchange's card tables alone. Over time, Prevention Point was accepted by government insiders because it reduced harm in the middle of an epidemic. The people of Prevention Point did a lot to reduce the spread of HIV, AIDS, and hepatitis C in Kensington and therefore helped to flatten the curve of their spread to everyone everywhere. In 2017, it was still being debated whether Prevention Point also reduced harm in Kensington by eliminating countless dirty needles from parks and sidewalks where everybody uninvolved in drugs walked around every day. Some neighbors blamed Prevention Point for the used needles' presence in their community because Prevention Point supplied those needles and did not always require people to return dirty ones in exchange for new ones, as the phrase "needle exchange" suggests. Prevention Point's better resourced and city-funded work was ongoing when I ran for district attorney. By then, it was efficiently distributing a few million needles annually, under punches from some neighborhood residents who blamed it and the absence of an idealized second war on drugs for their painful, daily struggles with the addiction and misery that surrounded their homes and affected them and their families daily. Prevention Point had saved a lot of lives. But it didn't end Kensington's problems.

Heroin use was worse than ever in Kensington during my campaign, thanks to the massive and reckless distribution by doctors of opioid pills manufactured by big pharmaceutical companies that corrupted healthcare with false marketing, lobbying, and cash that bought the U.S. government's complicity. The U.S. government allowed the quadrupling of the U.S. opioid pill market over more than a decade while other, healthier countries reined in Big Pharma's capacity to flood their national markets. American doctors were actively misled into becoming drug dealers who stuffed their patients' hands with opioid pills that eventually enabled heroin and fentanyl addiction.

The United States was consuming approximately three-fourths of the world's supply of opioid pills while other countries with long-standing heroin problems had turned widespread medical distribution of those pills away and were no worse off than before. For years, doctors and dentists had routinely written opioid prescriptions for a broken wrist, removed wisdom teeth, bariatric surgery. According to the U.S. Centers for Disease Control and Prevention, 20 percent of patients who take a ten-day prescription of opioids become addicted. For some people, the addiction starts the second day of taking the pills. Once the prescriptions expire and doctors refuse to write more, some people who are suffering addiction resort to street heroin. But, since at least 2015, Philly's street heroin increasingly had been laced with fentanyl, a highly volatile and unpredictable anesthetic of such intense potency that tiny amounts are fatal, especially when they are roughly mixed with heroin or cocaine and crack by drug dealers rather than chemists. Fentanyl allows drug dealers to increase their profits while placing their customers in even more danger. By 2017, it was involved in more than 70 percent of fatal overdoses in Philadelphia.

Philadelphia was chronically among the worst jurisdictions in the United States for its rate of fatal drug overdoses. By comparison, New York, which is five or six times larger than Philadelphia, has about the same number of fatal overdoses per year as Philly. In 2017, more than one thousand people died from fatal drug overdoses in Philadelphia, more than died of AIDS per year at the height of the AIDS crisis there. That's about three souls a day. One dies before I have breakfast; one dies by lunch; one more by dinner.

Opioids of all types kill primarily by suppressing breathing. Users nod off, sometimes when their necks are in a position that restricts air. For this reason, experienced opioid users take drugs with others nearby as lifeguards. Sadly, the other users are often impaired and may be simultaneously injecting the identical, potentially fatal mix. Opioid users who fatally overdose overwhelmingly die alone, behind dumpsters, in their bleak homes, or in the bathrooms of fast-food restaurants or libraries where no one sees them.

For many, addiction is self-medication for mental illness or severe trauma in its many forms—rape, abuse, or the weighty accumulation of terrible experiences in childhood that correspond directly to criminal conduct later, especially when they go untreated. I knew from my years as a criminal defense lawyer that many addicted people were healthy and vigorous before opioids got them. Several were injured athletes or construction workers who trusted their doctors' prescriptions. The *DSM-5* says substance addiction is a mental disorder: Substance Use Disorder. But unlike other medical problems we suffer that invoke compassion, our culture considers people suffering from addiction worthy of blame.

There is plenty of blame to ascribe to both our legally protected and our illegal opioid dealers—profiteering medical companies, medical providers, street drug dealers and their networks, and corrupted government. We have a punitive criminal justice system so wrongheaded that its failed war on drugs and program of mass incarceration have resulted in more street drugs at lower prices and more addiction than ever before. Go to jail and you will be massively delayed in getting treatment if any is available at all. There's more access to treatment out of custody, woefully inadequate though it is. We should be outraged at this outcome, especially when we consider how other countries have avoided a similar crisis simply by limiting widespread medical distribution of opioid pills and providing low barriers to treatment, including national health programs. Instead, much of our outrage is directed at the person suffering the addiction, whose daily experience is fear mixed with stigma that erodes any feeling in them that their lives have value. So they hide from our government, its police and prosecutors, and with great frequency die alone. Stigma kills them, and we are all the source of that stigma.

Repeatedly, during my campaign in 2017, I was asked whether or not I supported Philadelphia copying what had already been done in places like Vancouver, Berlin, and Portugal. The answer wasn't hard for me and has been the same since early in my career. Other candidates adamantly disagreed, or were tongue-tied, or just pivoted as always. Some people call them safe injection sites. Others, wary of the notion that injection of hard drugs should ever be called safe, call them supervised injection sites. I call them harm reduction sites, because to me that's what they are. The thing about these sites, whatever you call them, is that no one dies there. No one. Not since 2003, at least. No one dies in them in Canada or Germany or elsewhere, where they are legal. No one dies in them when they are run by idealistic doctors and med students. And there are no reports of deaths in the ones started by activists in the United States, where they are underground and illegal.

Most people who first hear of harm reduction sites conjure up images of medical doctors or maybe other drug users providing drugs and helping people inject in some post-apocalyptic urban ruin. Not so. There's a roof. There is heating and cooling. Bathrooms are available. Opportunities for treatment are always available and encouraged in ways that are not intrusive. Some have detox facilities upstairs or offer help in other forms (copy machines, coffee, food, washing machines, advice on obtaining benefits) for people who are often homeless and whose daily grind is to avoid the physical and mental agony of coming off a drug that was fun only once, the first time they used.

Yes, these sites reduce harm to drug users. And they do more. By saving drug users' lives, they reduce harm to their families and communities. The vast majority of syringes are either disposed of safely as medical waste inside red plastic sharps containers at the sites or collected on the streets, rather than remaining on sidewalks and in parks. Users inject indoors and in private rather than in public for children to witness on their way to school. The spread of HIV and hepatitis C and hepatitis A is reduced throughout the entire population, including among people who never inject drugs because these diseases also spread in other ways. And the sites build a relationship of trust with users that is a catalyst for drug treatment the only time it will work— when the user is ready.

In Vancouver, where harm reduction sites had been legal and

prevalent for roughly fourteen years when I ran, some supervised injection sites looked like a hair salon. Each site had numbered open booths, with cleanable surfaces and chairs. There were two-way mirrors at each booth, making what happened there more visible. Drug users entered the site with their own drugs. At the safest sites, they could put their own drugs into a drug spectrometer that provided information on the drug's ingredients—information that might have steered them away from an overdose, or a poison dose. Then, at the time of their appointment, they were provided clean needles and syringes. They discarded their old ones safely. They injected themselves under the watchful eye of trained people, many of them medical professionals. The lines of sight and the mirrors at each booth allowed workers to keep an eye on a couple of dozen users at the same time at a distance of twenty feet or so.

At a harm reduction site, resuscitation was not complex. If a user nodded off, a worker saw it. The worker would nudge or bump the user, rub their shoulders, rub their sternum, or provide oxygen through a mask from a tank to wake them up. As in any medical facility, oxygen saturation in the blood of a nodding user could be monitored via plastic clips that fit onto the user's fingertips if the user was slow in waking. In the rare instances when easy resuscitation methods did not work, naloxone was used to reverse the overdose, or an ambulance was called, or both.

In more than a decade of legal harm reduction sites in Vancouver, people suffering from addiction had injected themselves over three million times. A few hundred had overdosed. None had died. And everyone who went there to inject saw people and felt compassion that gave them at least one more chance to feel their own value, to remember their own decency and find their own salvation from drug addiction—or at least their own peaceful way to abide a little longer with a shred of dignity despite suffering from a disease they might never shake. The supervised injection sites stopped people from dying, and I told people on the campaign trail I was okay with that. I was okay with that whether those people eventually succeeded in making a complete recovery or not. I was okay with giving them a shot at their own redemption. You have to survive to recover.

Historically, Americans have reacted emotionally in rejecting harm reduction efforts, especially supervised consumption and needle exchanges, as if harm reduction were untested and new. The next time you're having a drink in a bar, ask the other patrons their opinions on harm reduction or supervised consumption. They should know something about it. In a bar, information on the potency of each dose is provided and available—percent alcohol by volume (ABV) for beer, percent alcohol for wine, proof for liquor. The widespread availability and common use of alcohol in its milder versions (lite beer, beer, wine) rather than hard liquor is the result of ending Prohibition in the United States, when hard liquor of unpredictable quality and potency ruled because its higher potency was better suited to transport and commerce in a black market.

Alcohol is America's most ubiquitous and fatal drug. It kills ten times as many people a year as all other drugs combined. It shortens American lives by millions of future years annually. But because it is legal and regulated, purity and lack of adulteration are assured. A bartender is trained to watch the patrons and monitor their well-being, providing water or coffee or refusing to serve more if intoxication is out of bounds. And the bartender and waitstaff are trained to provide or call for medical assistance if intoxication becomes medically emergent, just as you would expect in a supervised injection site. But bartenders do more than workers at a supervised injection site do. Bartenders provide the drug. The bar owners and bartenders profit from it. And despite the fact that alcohol abuse is the third worst cause of preventable death in the United States, Americans are okay with it being legal for adults to consume it under supervision in bars and restaurants, because legalizing alcohol and reducing its harm work far better than Prohibition ever did, back when the illegal trade in alcohol drove official corruption, gun violence, and murder.

Or check out Lisbon and Portugal's highly successful public health approach to using civil court to address drug addiction by addicted people's voluntary participation, which works infinitely better than our punitive criminal justice approach, thanks in part to Portugal's decision more than twenty years ago to treat addiction as a public health problem rather than to criminalize it.

A neighborhood built into a few steep miles of hillside in Lisbon used to be a hellacious death zone for heroin use in the 1980s and '90s. These badlands were the primary home to about five thousand addicts who bought, sold, used, lingered, lived, unwittingly spread HIV and hepatitis C, and often died there. The rest of the city loathed this district, and its blighted existence made drug dealing and public drug use crucial political issues. This was the genesis of Portugal's decriminalization approach, created by a medical doctor.

Things had gotten much better by the time of my campaign. Lisbon's badlands had become a residential area that, in discrete pockets, was still home to a sparse group of mostly aging drug users. Approximately one thousand remained—an 80 percent reduction. The fact that they were an aging population whose young members were a rarity was encouraging evidence that Lisbon's methods were working. Users in Lisbon were usually in their forties or older and were often undergoing a relapse from their youth after many years of being clean. There were very few new or young users of heroin or crack anymore in Lisbon.

In 2017, Portugal prosecuted drug dealers in criminal court and always had. But it treated drug users differently. Rather than arrest them and prosecute them in criminal court, Portuguese police wrote civil tickets (much like parking tickets) to drug users that required them to attend a meeting with a "dissuasion committee." The committee generally consisted of a few people with psychology and social work backgrounds who interviewed the user to determine whether the user was addicted or was engaging in recreational use. Users in both categories were recommended services of different types. Other factors that underlay or exacerbated the drug use were explored—trauma, homelessness, mental health issues, and extreme poverty, among others. Users were encouraged but not required to voluntarily pursue the services. The ones who were ready accepted the services. The ones who were not ready might accept the services later, after multiple contacts with the dissuasion committee and multiple citations. But the users were not arrested, held in custody, or sentenced to incarceration for using or for failing to stop. They were offered support and treatment, just like sick people are offered in hospitals for any other disease. And this public health approach worked, unlike the prohibitionist and punitive system we had in the United States—the failed one that other candidates stood for to greater and lesser degrees when we ran for district attorney.

Arguably no area of criminal justice policy has been more flawed than America's punitive, prohibitionist approach to the use of drugs. Just as Prohibition failed with alcohol, the war on drugs has utterly failed to stop drug use or mitigate the health effects. There are more drugs available now, often of increasing potency at a lower price, and more people using them than ever before. Treatment for addiction and its underlying causes has been replaced with absurd levels of punishment and starkly racist incarceration.

There is a link between justice and public health. It is the height of abusive government to stand with disease and fight for it against the bodies of its own people—any of its own people. For the people harmed, there is little difference between government attacking them and government standing by while disease attacks. Whether the disease is HIV, COVID-19, or addiction, we and our government's legitimacy depend on doing less harm and feeling the justice inherent in harm reduction's contribution to public health.

# CHAPTER 7

# Police Integrity

*We ain't never gonna change*
*We ain't doin' nothing wrong*
*We ain't never gonna change*
*So shut your mouth and play along*
—Drive-By Truckers, "Never Gonna Change"

There was a question I heard frequently during the campaign from police officers and their staunch supporters who were uncomfortable with my campaign's emphasis on police accountability and equal treatment for all. They asked, in a tone more accusatory than curious, "Do you have our backs?" as if it were obvious that any candidate's answer should simply be yes. Mine wasn't. My more complicated answer was "Yes, I have the backs of police when they follow the law, just like I have every civilian's back when they do the same. But no, I don't have their or anyone else's backs when they commit crimes." Should I? It's basic: Don't commit crimes, regardless of your job or your group. Accountability has to be equal in a just system.

The subtler assumption of the question "Do you have our backs?" is a blurred line between police and prosecutors, the false implication that police and prosecutors are a single team. That implication would negate the prosecutor's job to be a check on illegal police behavior and to hold their criminal conduct accountable, as required by the prosecutor's oath and basic fairness. Too often within police ranks, the unquestioned notion is that police, whose job it is to hold others accountable, shouldn't really be held accountable themselves. Underlying the police culture that expects a free pass is the inflated notion that police officers' jobs are the most dangerous of all (factually untrue), or perhaps more important than any other (I can think of a lot of really important jobs). No such free pass can exist for any tribe, including any tribe defined by their job or profession.

But police culture expecting a free pass is what happens when you let a small number of rogue cops run the show and establish the culture. But it's also the result of bad incentives and procedures. When a system has rogue elements for long enough, the rogue elements start to feel like the system itself. What do you do when certain behaviors are so widely accepted that they seem institutional? And how do the rogue cops get to run the show? In most major American cities, police know it's because the city "has their backs." For reasons that are primarily political, city governments have acquiesced to removing control from police chiefs on discipline and firings, instead giving it to police unions, to the great detriment of the best cops and civilians. Even the small number of police personnel who are terminated, demoted, or disciplined by their police commissioner or chief usually succeed in reducing or reversing that accountability due to a rigged system that gives insider arbitrators more power than the commissioner. Rogue cops are enabled by rogue arbitrators. And the whole fix is enabled by state and local politicians who look the other way, more interested in pleasing the police union to advance themselves than they are in achieving police accountability, police integrity, or stopping crime.

As I campaigned, I knew there were rotten cops just like I knew there were rotten lawyers. The incumbent DA had withdrawn his effort at reelection and was facing federal charges that called for jail time. In the absence of any real police accountability coming from the Philly DAO, during my career I had played private prosecutor with few tools, spending more than my share of time in criminal and civil court pushing back against police officers who thought the badge meant they could do whatever they wanted: lie, steal, brutalize and abuse, and leverage their police power in personal disputes. And those officers knew their business. Prosecutors and the police department had looked the other way for decades. As a busy criminal defense attorney and civil rights attorney in 2017, I had seen an indefensible culture of abusive power of the type that can grow only in a vacuum of accountability.

Around 2010, a woman named Maria sat in my office and told me that her police officer husband, Peter, was cheating again. She said she had caught him for the second time and this time it would mean divorce. There would be important, ordinary issues to be resolved in ordinary ways: They had a daughter and owned a home together. But, as a Philadelphia police officer, Peter Acevedo had the means to do things that were far from ordinary. Maria had come to speak to me about what he had done: arrest her twice and falsely charge her with serious crimes.

Both times Peter arrested his wife, he claimed he was the victim. First, he falsely claimed she tried to hit him with her car (and that she nearly hit their daughter at the same time) in the parking lot of a police station where they were temporarily required to be to exchange custody of the child. Next, he falsely claimed that a month or so later she tried to run him and his minivan off the road. These were well-crafted stories for a man trying to demonstrate that his wife was unfit for custody of their child. They cast her as a violent felon, an impulsive and unsympathetic hothead who endangered her own child. The consistency of these fictions created the illusion of credibility: By twice accusing her of trying to hurt people while driving her car, Peter

knew that the similarity of the two separate accusations supported credibility.

Maria was forced to pay bail for each of the two felony charges.
She was tense when she came to my office to hire me to represent
her in criminal court. As she told me her story and we talked
through the process and what was at stake, she eventually broke
down and started weeping. She knew that she would have to win
both criminal cases in order to have a fair fight over child custody and child support in family court. It was a lot to ask from a
system she wasn't sure she could trust.

As I sat in my office talking to Maria, I thought about another
cop's wife I had represented. She, too, had been arrested by her
cheating husband during a divorce. Her name was Zoe, and
her husband was having an affair with a female police officer. He
and the female cop arrested Zoe and provided matching false
statements against her. To bolster their story, they also arrested
and falsely accused Zoe's innocent, docile brother, who was present for the estranged couple's brief argument and backed Zoe's
claim that there had been no crime—they needed to neutralize
him as a witness for his sister.

Like Maria, Zoe had gone to family court with a family attorney to resolve her divorce, custody, alimony, and child support
issues at the same time she was separately fighting her criminal
case in a different courthouse. From representing Zoe, I knew
the quid pro quo offer that would come next for Maria in family
court. The husband, accompanied by his FOP lawyer, would use
the criminal charges as leverage in family court. Either the client
or the lawyer or both would suggest or state outright that the
wife's criminal cases would be dropped in exchange for the wife
giving the husband the terms he wanted in family court on child
custody, home ownership, child support payments, or alimony.

It is strictly unethical for a lawyer to manipulate criminal
charges in order to influence a civil proceeding, especially if the

charges are false. It is a bunch of crimes for anyone to knowingly push false charges, to get others to lie in court, to provide false information to police, to obstruct justice in any way in any court proceeding, or to falsely imprison someone else, even for a few hours. And, law aside, it's unconscionable to do these things to the parent of your child, your intimate partner, no matter how estranged.

Maria was in my office and crying again a couple of months later, after going to family court. The scumbag move was back. I confirmed her hunch that the trade-off her husband wanted was essentially extortion and also unethical, if his attorney was involved. I stared at the conference room table quietly for a moment, feeling the weight and consequences for the rest of Maria's life if we lost in such a fixed game. I had to keep her spirits up. Without conveying the obvious irony, I told her to trust the process. We went to criminal court to do battle.

In criminal court, Officer Acevedo produced no independent witnesses to support either arrest. First, his daughter destroyed one case when she said that Maria never attempted to or even accidentally came close to hitting anyone. Then Officer Acevedo's own father blew up the other case. He testified that Maria had not tried to run the minivan off the road. He quickly moved on in his testimony to argue passionately for his son Peter and him to have more custody of the child, as if we were in family court.

After two victories in criminal court, Maria and I, as her lawyer, filed a civil lawsuit against Officer Acevedo, a couple of supervisors, and the city. We asked for money damages, just as we had when Zoe won her criminal case and filed her lawsuit. But this time I also asked for a change in how the Philadelphia Police Department did its business. I asked for injunctive relief—a policy change moving forward—that would require high-level scrutiny of arrests orchestrated by police officers of anyone close to them. It wasn't a perfect safeguard, given that the blue sometimes covers for its own—it would be easy enough for the vengeful cop to get another bad cop to the make the arrest—but it was an improvement. And it was what the next Zoe or Maria or their kids deserved: protection.

The city agreed that Maria should get some money, but it flatly rejected any change in policy. With some real or feigned regret, the city attorney explained there was just too much politics around renegotiating the safeguard we sought into the FOP contract. The FOP would never support it, so the city refused to try to negotiate it. They would pay more instead. Maria needed the money and accepted it.

Maria's and Zoe's stories are about ordinary human frailty and individual abuse of power. The perennial forms of police corruption are all about abuse of power: Dirty narcotics officers either start out corrupt or become corrupted by greed and power. They steal money, drugs, assets. They steal overtime compensation by aggressively illegal tactics that keep them busy testifying in court, including illegal stop-and-frisk and illegal car stops of anyone driving while Black. Dirty narcotics cops brutalize, physically abuse, and sometimes sexually abuse people who are subjected to their power when they raid properties or search and arrest them on the street. They lie until their tongues are tired in court to profit from and to cover their own crimes. Some resell the drugs they steal. All dirty narcotics cops eventually end up as allies with some drug dealers against others because those alliances are how the dirty narcotics cops get their profitable information to use against their drug dealing partners' competition. For some slimy cops, a narcotics assignment is too tempting to resist. For honest cops stuck in a narcotics assignment, the pressure to go along and cover up can amount to a threat on their lives.

And these are not the only stories of a jaw-dropping institutional vacuum of accountability. How can a city or a police department that doesn't fix this engender trust in the community? Why would a vulnerable victim of crime come forward? Why would a blameless witness trust police not to shift blame? Who

will a police force that elevates bullies attract as applicants besides bullies? What will stop officers from leveraging their gov-
ernmentally given power to mistreat their ex-partners, like
Maria and Zoe? And in a culture that tolerates such conduct
against significant others who resist, what can we expect to happen to people they never loved, people who have no such significance and resist?

It was the autumn of 2015. Khadijah Costley White wrapped
her hands around the handlebars of the bike she was pushing past
City Hall. The bike was slightly off-balance, its basket lightly
weighted with the vegetables and fruit she had just bought two
blocks back in the giant train shed that has housed Philly's great
farmers' market for over fifty years, the Reading Terminal Market.

She was pushing the bike past traffic, pushing it across cross-
walks, and getting ready to ride home where there was less traffic when she spotted a wall of police, mostly bike cops, blocking
the entry doors of the cement-and-glass cereal box that is the
Municipal Services Building (MSB). Scores of mostly quiet people, many older, were facing the police in the chill air, obviously
precluded from entering its glass doors. Frank Rizzo's statue
was there, thirty yards away from the doors and facing the same
direction as the officers, away from the building and toward the
public. And then Khadijah remembered why the public was there.

The pope was coming, so the city wanted to "clean up" by
banning the feeding of homeless people in public. There was an
outcry from church groups and other do-gooders over the ban,
including many whose congregations and groups viewed helping the homeless as their duty. Many had done it for years. Liberal Catholics who were waiting on a visit from the most vocally
anti-poverty pope in recent memory were also offended at the
city's hypocritical embrace of the pope by pushing the homeless
away: loaves and fishes; take all you have and give it to the poor—
that stuff. The outcry forced a public hearing, which the city
scheduled on its turf, in a room in the MSB that was too small for

the public, the size the city wanted. Government doesn't like dissent. But, where it's unavoidable, government prefers dissent in a smaller room holding fewer angry people, especially when there are cameras. So government limited public access to the hearing, which effectively divided the public and conquered the many people who were stuck outside. Between the increasing darkness, decreasing temperatures, and lack of bathroom access outside power's hallways, most of them would leave without the news media ever knowing they came.

Khadijah had spent most of the day, and almost every day for months, in seclusion, typing her Ph.D. thesis in communications for the University of Pennsylvania's prestigious Annenberg School. She was tired that late afternoon, but also happy knowing that the next day was supposed to be a break from her monkish life, a celebration. In a public ceremony, Khadijah was set to receive a Women of Color at Penn Award for outstanding achievement as a graduate student from the hand of a local celebrity news anchor. Khadijah's mother, sister, and others were just arriving from out of state to attend the ceremony. She felt a good, home-cooked meal was in order. But, as she saw the gathering of people between Frank's back and the MSB, she also felt that a brief stop to encourage those waiting to get in, whose cause she shared, was in order. Given her communications talent, maybe she could persuade police to relent a bit—bathroom access, a warmer interior space where people could wait, a bigger room for the hearing, whatever she could do before going home.

Governments like to talk about cleansing, and cleanups. Beware when they use those words to talk about what they want to do to human beings. That night, the city was feeling pretty good about its last so-called cleanup of Occupy protesters and was ready for more, having swept the encampment of a hundred or so Occupiers from the plaza around City Hall close to a year prior, ostensibly to rebuild the plaza—the outgoing mayor's pricey legacy project. The city's police sweep of tent-camping and day-tripping Occupy protesters and a few homeless people became known as "eviction night." Police arrested and the Philly DAO prosecuted dozens of random people at City Hall on misdemeanor charges for nothing and next to nothing—a professor, a union president, many young activists, and Khadijah, a frequent day-tripper with Occupy who supported their cause of economic equality. I first met her in a room full of "eviction night" clients before trial. She immediately made the top of my short list of best witnesses to call at trial if necessary. She was a verbally brilliant, joyful, churchgoing, radical graduate student whose future appeared limitless. At trial, they were all found not guilty without her having to testify.

As she pushed her bike past Frank, toward the line of cops holding their bikes in front of the MSB doors, Khadijah was feeling pretty good, too, about her progress on her dissertation, standing tall during Occupy, the trial acquittal that kept her résumé intact, her family's visit, a nice dinner, and the award the next day. She talked to people and went to the police line, where the officers were holding their own bikes. Smiling, she tried to cajole, charm, joke, and tease a couple of the reassigned, stony-faced narcotics cops holding bikes on behalf of her varied but increasingly irritated allies behind her.

Some police specialize in protest. Philly has a unit called "civil affairs." But the bike cops Khadijah met were mostly narcotics cops, who are not ideal peacekeepers for protest. Narcotics policing attracts a personality type and breeds a culture, like any other unit. Narcotics officers' work is more physical than verbal. Many narcotics cops view themselves as warriors doing battle with an enemy on dangerous ground, a culture that is one more pernicious legacy of the failed war on drugs. If warriors are scared, they hide it. In public at least, they need to win, to control and dominate the situation. Their first impulse is not to turn the other cheek, to de-escalate, or to listen when protesters question government authority with free speech. Anything less might suggest weakness to the "enemy." Often, they are less trained in free speech than they could be. Their daily work involves chasing and catching drug dealers, some armed, who are actually breaking the law, unlike peaceful protesters who usually are not.

Unexpectedly, the police line lurched forward and away from the building and toward Khadijah and the rest, who were mostly stationary. A police bike entangled with hers. An officer kicked at her bike. One officer angrily told her to step back, but her bike was caught, her basket full. She put her hand on the officer's handlebars to disentangle the bikes while saying she hadn't moved—that he had come at her. And then another officer threw her bike down, spilling her groceries away from the basket as she turned and reached toward her bike. In the commotion, the commanding officer lightly stumbled when his heel caught on a step behind him as his officers advanced at his command to push the crowd farther back. Khadijah was yanked off her feet and over and behind the police line, cuffed on her wrists, and arrested. Police grabbed her by a couple of fingers; for a moment, she felt like her fingers were being pulled off. At first, she yelled "You're hurting my hand!" Then she screamed, "They're breaking my fingers!"

The first I heard of Khadijah's being locked up was a desperate phone call from her family. They wanted her out of custody ASAP, ideally in the few hours remaining before the award ceremony. I knew there was no way to jump the line of people waiting twelve to thirty-six hours for a bail hearing. Khadijah's only chance to make the ceremony honoring her was for the city to drop her case immediately, even if they revived it later. I reluctantly placed a call to someone I'd known slightly for years, a city official, who was a bureaucrat and wouldn't care about Khadijah or her family, but might see the value in avoiding blowback in the press over an iffy arrest of a rising star set to receive an award that day.

I knew the bureaucrat I called was particular. He dressed precisely, frequently adjusting his collar or tugging his tie to make it vertical and smooth, sometimes even tucking his tie into his pants while seated. A year earlier, he was sandpaper in Occupiers' ears, circulating and speaking dismissively to protesters who weren't thrilled with his pro-government suggestions for their protest plans. After a few weeks of the Occupy encampment had passed, he went from suggestions to threats—walking around hinting that an incoming police commander wouldn't tolerate Occupy's encampment as the city had so far. When he said it to an activist social worker and Occupier I knew, born in Dublin during the Troubles, she responded: "You wee man, why don't you go supervise yourself? We're doing just fine regulating ourselves, thank you very much."

I called the bureaucrat and began to explain. He didn't recognize Khadijah's name or the details of the arrest I was trying to describe at first. I explained the urgency of Khadijah's getting out of jail, whatever happened with her case. In between smacking sounds from whatever food he was eating, he said, "Oh, you mean the one with the big mouth." He said he was a witness to the event and would testify against Khadijah at her criminal trial. He didn't say what criminal thing she had done meriting his testimony, other than that she had a "big mouth." He rejected even trying to do anything to get her to the award ceremony on time. He also didn't mention there was video of the incident, taken by hard-to-spot city cameras mounted high on the walls of the MSB, which housed his office. The call ended. I later learned that at some point he watched the video, if he hadn't already watched it when we spoke. Within a few weeks, he did nothing to stop the video from being recorded over "automatically," before any of us knew it even existed.

The award ceremony came a few hours later. Some of Khadijah's family watched in the auditorium as her best friend, Maryan, a history grad student, received Khadijah's award. Miles away, she was seated in a jail cell with a splint on her throbbing hand to straighten out her broken finger, thinking about the acceptance speech she had already written. I found out later that when the audience learned where Khadijah was and why she could not attend, they cheered.

Unless police violence is on video or is witnessed by, well, let's say a pope who is willing to testify, it is mostly unaccountable. When there are broken bones, scars, or temporary but visible injuries more explanation might be required to show that police force was legally justified, but there are ways. When force is not justified, some of the blue sometimes use baseless criminal charges, phony police paperwork, and untruthful testimony to explain away their own mistakes, misconduct, or crimes.

Police paperwork written at Khadijah's arrest said she was the aggressor—vegetables, fruit, bike basket, and all. She harassed police, then assaulted them with her bike, and intentionally used her hands to push the giant, white-shirted commanding officer in the chest—supposedly the same zero-tolerance commanding officer the MSB official told Occupy was coming. According to police, Khadijah's push made the giant commanding officer fall. He avoided injury only because the people behind him caught him. That's what the city and the police said; those were their words, in essence. And the Philly District Attorney's Office said the government's words were good enough, as usual, and turned them into criminal charges against Khadijah that threatened her future, for the second time.

Video that the city couldn't erase said something else. Fortunately for Khadijah, someone was recording people waiting outside the MSB when her fictional crime was said to have happened. Against the gleaming white expanse of the commanding officer's shirt, the image of Khadijah's deep brown hand pushing him would have been stark. But the video proved her dark hand wasn't there, just as her supposed harassment, aggression, and assault weren't there. The commanding officer's "fall" looked like a stumble that came as his heel seemed to catch on a step. Other things were missing from Khadijah's case as well: a valid arrest;

a legal reason to break a finger Khadijah urgently needed to type her dissertation. And there was no reason to lock her in a cell awaiting a bail hearing while her fretful, disappointed family watched her award presented to the air. The charges were fake. We won her criminal case, again.

Then we sued the city and the police in federal court for their violence and their plot to maliciously prosecute and convict Khadijah for things she hadn't done. Khadijah's jury for her civil lawsuit consisted mostly of white people from politically conservative rural or suburban counties, as do most federal juries in the Eastern District of Pennsylvania. The jury heard the police version and the testimony of the city official who said Khadijah had a "big mouth." When I questioned him, pushing hard on why the video he controlled and saw within days of the incident was passively erased on his watch, his irritated defensive answer was "I'm not a detective." Some jurors who had been studying his face looked down. Others looked away.

Khadijah testified while we played the video repeatedly and slowly, punctuating her testimony with moments in the video. The jury saw that white expanse of the police commander's shirt, untouched by a dark brown hand every time the video was slowly replayed. They didn't look away; they chose to believe their eyes, which confirmed Khadijah's words. She was a truly great witness. We won. And the darkness of her skin helped persuade a white jury, for once.

What police did to these women was not just a reflection of ordinary human frailty or mundane evil. It is symptomatic of a lack of accountability in policing that enables it and much worse. Heinous crimes have been committed by people who have operated within or close to law enforcement and hid behind its shield. The Golden State Killer is a prolific serial rapist and serial killer whose decades of bloody crimes started while he was a police officer and continued after he was fired for what should have been a clue: He was caught stealing dog repellent and a hammer from a hardware store.

Civilian Ted Bundy served on an anti-crime commission, where he learned about gaps in law enforcement information sharing in the 1970s. He planned traveling murders with that knowledge and committed them wherever he went until his capture. Extraordinary evil and depravity are able to flourish in law enforcement where there is unaccountable power. It is emboldened by a culture that allows more mundane evil—the abuse of wives and lovers and contractors and business partners and drug dealers, drug users, and anyone else whose lives and rights stand between immoral officers and their selfish goals.

But the problems in police accountability go beyond individual evil: They also stem from the structures and incentives of our police departments and in American laws that allow and embolden deception and disrespect for the individual rights our Constitution is supposed to guarantee.

Consider, for example, how a Philadelphia police officer gets paid and promoted on patrol: The police department calls it "activity." "Activity" comprises certain kinds of actions recorded in a patrol officer's daily logbook. Supervisors are trained to demand a lot of it. A pedestrian stop, pat-down, search is an activity. Or stopping a car and searching it and/or its occupants. But you can't just stop and search a car—police need a good, constitutional reason to do so. But if they follow the Constitution, they won't make as many stops or searches, and their activity numbers will go down. Eventually, their supervisors notice and require them to "articulate" reasons and make more stops. Lost in this system is the good policing that goes with a patrol officer stopping into every business along a commercial row until the business owners start to confide, or developing relationships on every block with neighbors who keep a close eye on everything that happens there. Those things aren't counted as "activity" even though they stop crimes from happening and solve crimes when they do.

Promotions and pay depend on having high levels of activity. Many officers make tens of thousands of dollars per year through overtime; some officers make more money in overtime (and far more than any government lawyer in the room) than they do from their regular pay. "Articulating" what happened can mean adjusting the truth to improve a case, giving a constitutional story that justifies an unconstitutional search, or including your fellow officers who witnessed nothing in the case so they, too, can feed from the overtime trough. A few lies about what happened in the street mean five police officers get paid overtime to show up and testify in court. It's a win for profit, not policing or justice or truth. An honest cop once told me, "In the academy, they told us do what you want then articulate the reasons later. That's what they taught us." This becomes a culture of testifying to win cases (or "testi-lying" as almost everyone in the courthouse calls it), for money and promotion and for self, which is rationalized as necessary to protect the public from terrible people (predominantly poor people and people of color) whose rights don't matter and whose supposed threat justifies stealing from taxpayers to pay unjustified overtime and other extra compensation to police.

American law and the courts have at times also quietly endorsed deception by police in ways other countries don't tolerate. For example, American detectives are permitted to lie to suspects during interrogation for investigative purposes, sometimes to disastrous effect. Virtually every homicide defendant I met during my career in criminal defense who signed a confession of some sort told me the same story, even though none of them knew or were in communication with the others. Detectives had told them that if they signed the statement they would be released from custody, where they could fight the case "from the street." None of them fought the case "from the street." It was a lie. They were all then held in jail with no chance of bail under state law, as the detectives well knew they would be. Many of those homicide defendants disputed portions or the entirety of their statements, claiming it was not what they said.

It is a fact that 25 to 30 percent of convicted people who have been exonerated by DNA evidence that established they were completely innocent confessed to the crimes they did not commit (or even witness in nearly every case). How does a truly innocent person who never even witnessed the crime or the crime scene confess to the specifics believed to be true by the detective who is conducting the interrogation? How do the detective's ideas become the defendant's entirely false words? Every one of the defendants in the 1989 Central Park jogger case confessed to details of a rape and beating they didn't do and hadn't seen. Their confessions clearly reflected what detectives knew or incorrectly surmised. The confessions told the story of how the detectives imagined the crime. After years of these young men's incarceration, the actual perpetrator was connected to the crime by DNA and explained what really happened, a starkly different truth to replace the confessions' fiction.

All of this misconduct needs a reckoning. But how? What does accountability look like for detectives who turn innocent people into puppets, manipulating them to falsely confess to crimes with details spun from the detectives' imagination? What are the detectives' consequences when they essentially kidnap innocent people with coerced and phony confessions, while letting real perpetrators go free, sometimes to hurt others, and usually forever?

The answer we provided in our campaign was straightforward. When the facts and law support it, accountability means charging police with crimes, as you would anyone else. It means being transparent about troubled officers, as the Constitution and basic fairness require. And that means keeping information on troubled officers who threaten the integrity of the system and providing that information to defendants and their lawyers. It would be a step in the direction of true justice: Sharing the *Brady* information would prevent innocent people from being convicted and, just as important, prevent guilty people from getting their convictions overturned because we hid the information that the law required us to provide. We weren't going to let the Philly DAO cheat anymore. Our campaign supported the modern movement toward "open-file" discovery, in which prosecutors essentially open their entire files to the defense.

It would mean using our power to lift up the best police officers by knocking down the worst ones, and holding them accountable. That kind of accountability would shift the system. Prosecuting bad officers not only stops graft and corruption but also allows the larger system to heal and remake itself, so that routine corruption is no longer so routine.

A virtuous cycle would be put into motion, replacing the vicious one that came before. Hardworking, decent police officers will tell you that dirty, abusive cops make all police less safe, make their jobs harder, and degrade their profession, which in turn makes the community less safe. Bad cops chill the flow of information from community witnesses, reducing officers' ability to prevent and solve crime. The best cops have always hated dirty cops. They will tell you that their union dues shouldn't go to protect cops who commit crimes on the job. Our campaign was about supporting police who followed the law by doing what our oath would require if we won: keeping our promise to prosecute police who were all about breaking the law. And that is exactly how prosecutors always should have had the backs of the good cops and everyone else.

# CHAPTER 8

# Prosecutor Integrity

*Shut your eyes*
*Trust in me*

—Kaa the Snake, "Trust in Me"
from *The Jungle Book*

E very day, when criminal proceedings start in jurisdictions
all over America, lawyers stand up to identify themselves
first and then identify their clients to the judge and on the court
record, by name. Criminal defense lawyers state their client's
first and last name: "For Jack Smith." Prosecutors identify their
clients. They say: "For the people."

There are a lot of people. It is uniquely the prosecutor's job to
represent everyone in that jurisdiction, including Jack Smith.
And it is uniquely the prosecutor's sworn oath to seek justice for
the people. Seeking justice for everyone moving forward presents its challenges. Prosecutors weren't there when a crime occurred, no matter how committed, persuasive, or certain they
may be. They do not necessarily know what uncertainties, mistakes, motivations, biases, or games may be in play. But they
should be trying really hard, all the time, to find out and to get it
right, because that is what justice requires.

Zoe's and Maria's stories are about police integrity, but they invite important questions about the many prosecutors whose hands touched their files. No, the prosecutors were not eyewitnesses to the alleged events that were the bases of the charges. Yes, the prosecutors had spoken to the police officer husbands who were bringing the charges against their own wives and had heard the officers' versions. No, the prosecutors had not spoken to the defendants or their witnesses and heard their conflicting versions, as usual. But a prosecutor doesn't have to know everyone's version of an event to spot a motive.

The prosecutors who handled Zoe's criminal case and Maria's two criminal cases knew up front that the supposed victims in these criminal cases were estranged husbands who were police officers sophisticated in criminal proceedings, that they were going through divorces with the women they accused, and that the estrangement and divorce activity began before the supposedly criminal events occurred. They knew the accusers and defendants had young children together. They knew that family court proceedings involving child custody, child support, and alimony were under way. But none of the prosecutors who handled Zoe's and Maria's case files slammed on the brakes to take a closer look before we all found ourselves in a courtroom where police officers were testi-lying and getting carved up by a criminal defense lawyer's questions they couldn't answer and witnesses they couldn't refute.

It was nothing new, unfortunately. By the time I ran for district attorney, I had a sackful of stories about prosecutors whose necks must have been sore from looking away from obvious problems in cases or who, in my opinion, had tried to actively conceal facts and evidence that damaged their cases just because they wanted a win that bad and didn't care how they did it. I can tell those stories without spitting because their tricks and lies and constitutional violations and unethical conduct didn't work. I will probably never know about the dirty, illegal tactics that worked.

When I tried my first death penalty homicide case, the defense was identification. I was arguing there was a reasonable doubt whether the defendant, my client, was the killer in a homicide by gun. The evidence established already that the victim and defendant knew each other well. I had planned to use two prongs of an attack on the prosecution to show the defendant did not kill the victim. They were (1) that the killer had shot the victim at close range, giving the victim the opportunity to see his killer; and (2) that the victim communicated to a police officer that the defendant was not his killer just before he died.

I was trying to establish part 1 by evidence of gunpowder stippling. When a gun is fired, stippling is caused by the burning gunpowder that flies forward, out of the barrel of the gun, and lands on anything in its path for a few feet before gravity drags the burning particles down to the ground. When that burning powder lands on skin or clothing, the particles often attach and burn on that surface. The victim's clothing and body had clear stippling, indicating the shooter was within only a few feet when he fired his gun. I needed part 1 to set up part 2, which was the testimony of a police officer who spoke to the victim as he lay dying and asked him, "Do you know who killed you?," to which the victim shook his head back and forth, in a motion the police officer said meant the victim was saying "no."

First, the prosecutor presented a police firearms expert who surprised everyone but the prosecutor by telling the jury that burning gunpowder particles travel great distances—thirty feet or more, contrary to the science we all knew and the testimony of other firearms experts who testified in the courthouse daily, including before the tall, imposing, and dignified judge who was presiding. The judge, James Lineberger, was a senior, Black ex-military officer and an ex-prosecutor who had also been a criminal defense attorney. As soon as he heard the expert's nonsense, he loudly coughed "BULLSHIT!" and called a recess in the trial while the jury left the room laughing quietly and covering their smiles. After the experienced prosecutor sputtered for a while over the scam her witness was perpetrating and the judge's unorthodox way of exploding it to get justice, the judge called the jury back in and advised them that they should disregard his outburst, which was caused by the firearms expert's testimony being "completely different than the testimony other firearms experts offer in this courthouse every day." The jury kept smiling. They got the point.

Second, the prosecutor presented the police officer who had spoken to the victim just before he died. Rather than have the police officer testify freely, she asked very specific questions designed to elicit very short answers. She got the officer to testify that the dying man "shook his head," without more specifics. That testimony, undisturbed, said nothing. A shaking head could be a paroxysm of a dying man. It could be a head shaking up and down, as if to say "yes," which police paperwork made clear was not at all the meaning of what the officer had seen. It was left to me to get the police officer to provide the specifics necessary for the jury to understand that the officer was testifying the victim had said "no." The jury properly found a reasonable doubt and acquitted the defendant, no thanks to the prosecutor's cynical efforts to conceal the truth. That experience was not isolated.

In another homicide, a prosecutor presented a jailhouse snitch—an inmate who was claiming to have heard the defendant admit guilt in the homicide while they were both in custody. Jailhouse snitches are notoriously unreliable. Many of them read the newspaper or steal another inmate's criminal case paperwork or work family and law enforcement contacts to harvest enough details about a crime so that they can fabricate a confession story that contains enough specifics about the crime itself to sound true. Jailhouse snitches do their snitching for the usual reason, to get reductions in charges and jail time or better treatment in custody. Unsophisticated juries often credit jailhouse snitches more than they should. Even so, some jailhouse confessions are real.

The prosecutor should have told me that this jailhouse snitch was a "frequent flyer," a jailhouse snitch who had testified in multiple cases against multiple defendants, but she didn't. My client's family had heard that the jailhouse snitch testified in another case involving another shooting in the neighborhood, and got me the name of that other defendant. I obtained notes of testimony confirming the jailhouse snitch's testimony from that other trial, which had been prosecuted by one of the prosecutor's colleagues. I kept reminding her to let me know if the jailhouse snitch had testified in other cases as a prelude to raising the issue with the judge. She repeatedly put me off, indicating she knew nothing about it until she got wind of the fact that I knew better. Mid-trial, she showed up with the notes of testimony I already had.

It turned out the jailhouse snitch was such a "frequent flyer" that he had magically accumulated three jailhouse confessions for the prosecution to use in three separate murder trials being prosecuted by the prosecutor's small, elite, and close-knit circle of homicide prosecutors.

The jury appeared to be taking the snitch's testimony about my client's supposed jailhouse confession seriously at first. That all changed when they learned through my cross-examination that he was so persistently helpful to the same entity that was prosecuting him, the Philadelphia District Attorney's Office, on so many different homicide cases. He just kept collecting confessions from people he barely knew. On closing argument, I referred to him as a "confession vending machine" who would give the prosecution any and as many jailhouse confessions as they wanted. Many jurors smiled. The jury didn't buy the supposed jailhouse confession.

Those are just a few of my own experiences on heavy cases—but I and the courthouses of Philadelphia were full of stories about illegal and unscrupulous prosecutors failing at their treacherous games. And we were full of stories from less serious cases about ugly and inappropriate instances of prosecutorial discretion that don't meet what the people mean when they talk about integrity.

Sam Chu was a fifty-year-old Asian immigrant I represented on charges that he stole back a bunch of money that was stolen from him. Chu allegedly photoshopped some cashier's checks to make them appear worth a couple hundred thousand dollars more than their actual value. He gave them to a laundry machine supplier who had ripped off Chu first. The money was even, but only Chu got charged.

It was unsurprising that Chu would be charged with crimes, even though he was a hard worker and good family man, had kids in college, and had no prior criminal record. But when it became thoroughly documented and crystal clear that Chu was stealing back from the laundry supplier the same money the supplier had stolen from him a few years earlier, the prosecutor should have hit the brakes. Yes, there was clear evidence Chu had engaged in an economic crime. But it was against a criminal who'd victimized him with a similar economic crime first.

My repeated efforts to obtain a diversion of Chu's case, an outcome that would have made him accountable in some fashion but avoided a conviction, was not well received by the Philadelphia DAO. I was told "no" curtly, then rudely, by prosecutors who kept insisting Chu pay back the thief who had stolen equivalent money from Chu in the first place.

The laundry equipment supplier had already gotten away with his theft due to the passage of time and little on the part of law enforcement in helping Chu, for whatever reason. Perhaps the laundry equipment supplier believed stealing and getting away with it is the same as earning money, so he tried to use the criminal process to make Chu give it back. Chu was lucky. At trial, we won his case before a judge who smelled the rat in the room and was unwilling to let criminal court be used by prosecutors hell-bent on helping thieves get their stolen money back.

And then there were Jed, or Dinosaur Man, as we called him, and Mr. Kirk, a schizophrenic homeless man who renamed himself at trial. I met these two severely mentally ill men about twenty-five years apart. Mr. Kirk was my client in my first felony criminal trial before a judge as a public defender. According to police, he had banged on the windows of a house while yelling scary things until a window broke, to the obvious dismay of the homeowner, who was inside and called police. Mr. Kirk was arrested on-site and charged with very serious high-level felony charges—burglary and criminal trespass, among others.

When I visited him in jail, Mr. Kirk told me he sometimes talked to people he could not see. Although he could see me, he still was not a great communicator and told me things that were vague and sometimes contradictory—for instance, that he'd been arrested while trying to save the homeowner. With no real treatment available for him, and no way to get out of jail because he had no money to pay bail, he was in danger of languishing there for a long time despite the fact that nothing in the case or his history indicated he had a propensity for violence or that he was inclined to break into places to steal things.

I tried to get him mental health treatment and housing rather than a conviction on serious charges, but the prosecutor—or more likely the prosecutor's supervisor—wasn't hearing it. Felony guilty plea and jail time or try it, I was told. With no other pathway, we tried the case before a fairly conservative but experienced judge whose career had been as a prosecutor.

I called my only witness, Mr. Kirk, not knowing exactly what he would say. He had told me a couple of versions. He took the stand like he was moving underwater, overly polite but wild-eyed, with his jail clothes in disarray, before testifying to the most complete and interesting version yet. Mr. Kirk explained to the judge that he had been walking on the block when he realized there were devils inside the house and that the devils had put the house on fire, so the people inside had to be saved. He repeated that the people had to be saved and then stopped, staring at the judge from the witness stand. The judge was guarded, watching him carefully. With great sincerity, my client slowly said to the judge, who was Black: "Did you know, Your Honor, that I was the first Black captain of the starship *Enterprise*?" The judge laughed, announced a short recess, stepped off the bench to smoke a cigarette, came back, and threw out all the original charges while devising a mechanism to push the captain toward housing and treatment.

Jed, a white man in his sixties, was even more impaired but no less lovable. His records indicated he had a severely low IQ, in the 40s. His brother hired me and tearfully told me Jed had never been educated in the southern state where they grew up. The brother explained that Jed believed he was a dinosaur. Jed was charged with felony assault on police in a confrontation outside a schoolhouse. Police suffered no serious injuries in the incident, but Dinosaur Man was badly beaten, his nose broken, among other injuries. At first glance, the case smacked of the unintended mess I frequently saw when militarized police responded to mental health calls. Serious injury to the mentally ill person routinely resulted. Often the injury coincided with criminal charges against the mentally ill person. Some police believe charging a person they've injured with crimes will protect their careers from disciplinary scrutiny or protect them and the city from lawsuits.

Before I visited him, it seemed to me Dinosaur Man would never go to trial, because the law did not allow it. Jed was not competent under the law to understand court proceedings, and it appeared, after three tests done months apart, he never would be. Jed was in limbo. There would be no bed available to him in our devastated mental health system. The charges were serious, and judges were reluctant to simply release him onto the street. So he sat for over a year in custody with no pathway to trial or a guilty plea that might resolve the case, and no mental health facility where he might be placed anytime soon.

Jed was housed in the mental health wing of the jail, where I expected to meet him at a table rather than in more restrictive surroundings. The corrections officers who guided me into the jail to see him smiled when they read my pass, which was inscribed with Jed's name. One of them told me he hoped I could get my client out. From seventy-five feet away, I heard a low growl that persisted until I took my seat opposite the slight man. I explained slowly that his brother had sent me, that I was a lawyer here to help him, and that I needed to talk about what had happened. He stopped growling and at first perseverated on telling me his name, covering for his difficulty in communicating.

Over the course of an hour he advised me that his encounter with police had been a showdown between himself, a dinosaur, and King Kong. Mostly he explained by standing and acting out the epic battle in slow motion and not very well, sound effects included. I knew things were going okay half an hour in when he was seated again and told me I was a stegosaurus, which I knew to be a plant-eating dinosaur. I disagreed, preferring to be a *Tyrannosaurus Rex*, a kingly carnivore, on the theory this might give me dinosaur dominance, or at least more persuasive sway with Jed should we disagree on legal matters in the future. He maintained I was a stegosaurus. We agreed to disagree on my dinosaur classification for the moment and moved on to the next topic. Most important, we agreed that his brother was a good man and that Jed would like to go down south with him. I knew his brother had arranged housing and treatment there—to begin fairly immediately—that was completely unavailable in Philly.

The arrangement worked. A truly memorable hearing with human growls followed. Somehow a harried court reporter recorded them during a release hearing before a compassionate judge. The court staff were at first bothered, and then transfixed. After the hearing, the brother, sufficient sleeping pills, and an Amtrak safely delivered Dinosaur Man to a better and freer future in the South. (An airplane was too much of a risk.) Sadly, Philadelphia prosecutors had done next to nothing with their considerable power and discretion to expedite this or a better outcome. Jed was neither dinosaur nor person to them during the year of his incarceration. He was just an inch of paper inside a brown file that kept coming across their desks from time to time, at taxpayers' expense.

But those stories don't answer the daunting question of how we fix the cases where those same tricks and lack of prosecutorial integrity worked. What do we do about the innocent people we've imprisoned and the guilty people we let get away? What do we do about more mundane abuses of discretion and power, about everyday but sweeping indifference to people who live with challenges? And what do we do about restoring public health systems that address these challenges more effectively than law enforcement and unjust custody?

Nothing in the prosecutor's oath to seek justice limits the obligation to the future, to seeking justice moving forward in time. The oath applies equally to cases from the past and to new ones. Some legal scholars and many traditional prosecutors emphasize finality—the importance of a conviction being final, with no further litigation allowed forever—as if the systemic and the bureaucratic convenience of not looking back were more important than justice and the lives affected. It isn't. Finality and closure? For whom? For bureaucrats and public officials, or for the people criminal justice should serve?

Finality and the prosecutor's oath to seek justice collide when crimes remain unsolved or when innocent people remain in jail. Prosecutors must solve and prosecute cold cases. Prosecutors must exonerate and get people out of jail whose convictions lack integrity. It's a heavy obligation to fix injustice in the past and in the future, especially when those involved are still living. In a perfectly just world, that obligation to seek justice goes on forever: Innocent people deserve their reputations back, even after they are executed or die in jail; guilty people who escaped accountability deserve the ignominy they avoided in their lifetimes, commensurate with their crimes. Even as an unattainable ideal, the commitment of our justice system to correct its mistakes, to constantly try to do better, is essential to public trust, which is at the core of a functioning system.

In 1693, William Penn wrote in *Some Fruits of Solitude*: "To delay justice is injustice." For survivors and victims of unsolved serious crimes, there is neither closure nor trust in future safety when a criminal goes free while the victims wait for justice. For the many people wrongfully convicted of serious crimes, their lives are destroyed one day at a time, often for decades, while waiting for justice. The lost time will never return. But in some ways justice delayed gets a bum rap. Justice denied is a whole lot worse.

The obligation of the state to provide information helpful to the defense is known as the *Brady* requirement, from the name of the U.S. Supreme Court case that requires disclosure. Prosecutors also have a special obligation to reach out to local police for any information that could help the defendant, even if it is not yet known to the prosecutor. Obviously, this is needed so constitutionally required disclosure doesn't become a shell game. But *Brady* violations are just one reason why prosecutors' offices need robust conviction integrity units.

The history of exonerations, especially those where the innocence of the exoneree is considered scientifically certain based upon DNA evidence or other factors, instructs on the pressures and motivations for prosecutors to do wrong. Exonerations of innocent people frequently involve the most serious criminal matters, especially ones that are hard to prove, where cheating may be the only way for a prosecutor to secure a conviction. Exonerations of the innocent also frequently occur in cases that were heavily covered in the press when they were tried, most followed by the public, and therefore are cases of the most political significance for ambitious chief prosecutors and the ambitious trial prosecutors they promote. In these important cases, a trial prosecutor who is convinced a defendant committed the crime, or who doesn't much care, feels pressure to win by any means from within the office.

In a traditional prosecutor's office, it's the most aggressive and winningest trial attorneys who get the promotions, the raises, and the offers to handle the most serious cases. Many become supervisors, trainers, mentors, and recruiters for the generations of young prosecutors who follow. Awards and promotions and raises are seldom given for dropping prosecutions where a prosecutor's careful review of evidence and further investigations show serious doubt that a charged defendant's guilt exists but there is no other, identifiable perpetrator to blame.

But the pressure to win every case, no matter its validity, comes from outside the office as well. Victims' and survivors trauma in these cases can be overwhelming and understandably affect the prosecutor. Victims and survivors who are convinced of a defendant's guilt—and who are energized by their grief, loss, and trauma, which historically have been inadequately addressed—can become a separate form of pressure to win. The groups that support victims and survivors can play a similar role as well. Even prosecutors who repeatedly handle terrible crimes, peering at crime scene photographs and blood-soaked evidence, dwelling on extraordinarily cruel details as they formulate their arguments, experience trauma that can cloud their judgment.

With all these pressures and incentives to win, what happens then when new evidence arrives that calls into question the prosecutors' initial certainty of the defendant's guilt? New information will be judged as either helpful to the prosecutor's theory, and therefore accurate, or unhelpful and therefore unreliable, inaccurate, and worthy of concealment or the shredder. No one likes to admit they were wrong, or even accept it. At times, prosecutors are so attached to their theory of the defendant's guilt that contrary information looks false to them or barely registers. Such bias, often called confirmation bias, can take over a prosecutor's judgment with disastrous results if the prosecutor considers strict rules on disclosing evidence to the defense to be flexible or non-binding when the prosecutor thinks they are an impediment.

Which lands us on the biggest problem of all. Our society's ethics are mostly utilitarian, and so are our prosecutors' in a system requiring strict adherence to rigid rules—procedures—that we call due process and that guarantee fair trials capable of separating the innocent from the guilty. Utilitarian ethics are flexible, bendy even: The end justifies the means. Sure, we as a society claim to be rule followers. And we follow rules when we feel like it, like the ones you'll find in the Bible or the Koran. But what about when we don't feel like following the rules? The highest rule most Americans actually follow is that the end justifies the means, so we should do what's necessary to get the result that is right, or at least that we think is right. No wonder we love the Dirty Harry films and the ubiquitous crime fiction narrative of bad guys caught by good guys who don't let absolute rules get in their way. It's Dirty Harry and the fascist ideal rolled into one. Dirty Harry has another calling—in a courtroom, at the prosecutor's table, wearing a suit. Such prosecutors think they're fighting fire with fire, failing to understand that justice is a tinderbox.

Even before I ran for DA, I knew the DAO had what it called a Conviction Review Unit for a few years. It consisted of a chief attorney, an assistant attorney, and an occasional administrator. Rather than try to fix past injustices, the DAO's Conviction Review Unit merely existed. One iteration of the unit was so underachieving, that appeared to be its purpose. Word among the defense bar was that the single exoneration that occurred during its existence was not the unit's work. That exoneration came from another prosecutor in another unit in the office, who unearthed overwhelming evidence of a defendant's innocence. That prosecutor's supervisor didn't want his unit to be stained by actually exonerating anyone, so the Conviction Review Unit was made to go to court and carry out the exoneration. After the Conviction Review Unit's chief was given other work in the office, he left behind hundreds of unopened letters written by inmates claiming their innocence in a filing cabinet. Some of the postmarks were years old. The outgoing chief blandly commented that it wasn't his job to read the letters.

We know that establishing innocence or guilt to a scientific certainty is often an impossible task, especially in a city like Philly that has chronically underused forensics. Scientific certainty via DNA or other compelling forensics is ideal, but is not available in most criminal cases.

The system recognizes that uncertainty is real in criminal justice and even dictates the conviction of people when there is some doubt, so long as that doubt is slight and does not rise to the level of reasonable doubt. The existence or absence of reasonable doubt is the key to the jailhouse door: Reasonable doubt means the defendant gets to go home.

But what if a reasonable doubt or maybe a whole lot more than a reasonable doubt shows up long after a seemingly accurate conviction at trial, even if there is no scientific certainty of innocence? What if, due to new developments—new evidence, old evidence that was hidden at trial, new scientific methods that were unavailable before, or new information that undermines witnesses—the conviction cannot stand because it now lacks integrity and always will? The answer must be that the conviction is reversed and the person who was convicted goes home. Integrity and a just system require it.

It can be overwhelming to handle current and future cases while simultaneously reconsidering cases that are unsolved and past cases where the conviction may lack integrity. But it is a prosecutor's timeless oath to pursue justice in a way that is also timeless. And going backward and forward in time to do justice is crucial for a system badly in need of restoring trust.

# CHAPTER 9

# Lisa Taught Me Politics

*But I still haven't found what I'm looking for*
*But I still haven't found what I'm looking for*
—U2, "I Still Haven't Found
What I'm Looking For"

Long before I tried politics, I gave up on it. Growing up during the Vietnam War, Watergate, and the assassinations of almost every single leader who made us hopeful, I viewed most politicians as mediocre narcissists, less capable of leading than most people I knew. The corollary theory of my harsh view of politicians was that their one truly extraordinary skill must have been getting themselves elected in the locked-up clubhouse of politics. They must have had some keys we weren't issued. How else could we explain the democratic elections of such uninspiring people? How else could we explain democratic government at the service of power and money rather than people? From the day I met Lisa through the first decade of our careers, I never imagined either one of us would run for anything. Lisa and I followed the news and voted habitually, but we viewed politics like the weather: Politics happened and we adapted. And then Lisa showed me how to change the weather.

Twelve years into our careers, Lisa told me that she wanted to run for judge in Philadelphia. She had been working as a civil rights lawyer representing individuals in employment discrimination lawsuits. I didn't expect the news and was not very supportive at first. By then, I had spent twelve years in courtrooms with Pennsylvania state court judges of that era who had little in common with her or her values. I believed they might hold her accomplishments, work ethic, independence, and idealism against her. We knew nothing about getting elected, and we had kids in grade school, had just finished paying our student loans and had no real savings, and had no obvious political contacts. The idea of a novice taking on the seemingly all-powerful party in Philadelphia felt to me like a long shot.

But Lisa had her reasons. Even in law school, she'd read cases to figure out whether a judge had made the right decision. She viewed the law around employment discrimination as being pretty good, but often found the judges applying it were unfair and reluctant to see discrimination even when the facts showed it. She said all she and her clients wanted was a fair shot. They wanted a judge who was balanced and open-minded, who listened to both sides before making a decision. If she won, she could make sure that, at least in her courtroom, the scales were even.

She lost that campaign—in a close election with the full force of the dominant party pushing against her. But she had cracked the code of Philly politics. She ran a second time two years later and won easily. To understand how that is possible, you have to understand Lisa—which is to say, you have to understand how the seeming redoubt of political power can fall to a good idea with an ardent, crafty, principled messenger.


In May 1987, Lisa and I skipped our Stanford Law School graduation ceremonies. We had to get to the East Coast in a hurry, where we could make a few bucks proctoring the Pennsylvania bar exam course that was about to start in our new home, Philadelphia. I had sold my motorcycle a week earlier for a few hundred dollars, a sputtering, oil-burning Honda 550 Super Sport that I'd bought from a San Francisco junkyard and, with the help of a friend, fixed up enough to get around. Lisa and I needed the money to pay the bills. The day before we left, Lisa packed up what we hadn't already sold or put on the curb as I sat on my toolbox disassembling a floor lamp we had bought a year earlier at a secondhand store and had rewired together. I stuffed the lamp's glass shade with clothing and wrapped the outside in a blanket. At least when we got to Philadelphia, we wouldn't need to buy a lamp.

The next morning, we loaded up as the sun rose and the fog burned away. The long lamp parts went on the floor of the back seat of Lisa's two-door econobox Mazda hatchback. We flattened the rear seat, which turned the car's trunk into one big moving box. The lamp base went under piles of stuff in the trunk. We covered the pile with blankets, got in the car, closed the doors, and left the home we'd made together as law students.

Our first turn was out of the parking lot of the run-down, two-story stucco apartment building where we had been living in East Palo Alto. Our neighborhood was the epicenter of murder and heroin dealing in the Bay Area at that time, a sandy grid of little one-story houses covered in peeling, light-colored paint, with grassless yards. It was the rent we could afford. We crossed the bridge over the 101—as always littered with blown trash—which separated East Palo Alto from Palo Alto. On the Palo Alto side of the bridge, where the techie millionaires had already begun to dig in, the road we were driving was immaculate. We headed up University Avenue through the taller palms and past manicured yards, the semi-arid landscaping and small mansions maintained by our mostly Mexican neighbors back on the east side. University Avenue led straight to Stanford. With the California sun above the palms, we detoured to take one last lap of the school's iconic oval drive, lined with towering palms, before Lisa would steer us back east, toward Philadelphia.

The oval, as usual, smelled of the nearby eucalyptus groves, and as we took a last look I remembered my first trip to Stanford. A little more than three years before, I had visited the campus for the first time at the end of a cross-country road trip in our old Plymouth Fury. My brother, a college friend of mine, and I camped just off the oval in an A-frame tent that we hid behind hedges and eucalyptus trees for the couple of days we were there. Each morning we took the tent down, sneaked it as discreetly as possible into the trunk of the car, which was parked at the oval, and found our way to a shower in the open athletic buildings' locker rooms. We were a little rough from the road and drew some attention, but campus police and preppy students let us be for the most part. The weather and campus were glorious.

I didn't meet Lisa on that trip. We first saw each other on the third day of law school at a packed mixer for new students in a dorm basement. Almost none of the class members knew one another yet, but that didn't stop their measuring whatever there was to measure, working on a pecking order, and forming tribes—as if we would all perish if there were no outsiders to distinguish from the insiders. Pretty quickly my vague dream that this would be a gathering of mostly like-minded future public interest lawyers evaporated.

I was an hour in, mildly disappointed. I looked around and was wondering how much more I could take and what conversation to strike up next, when I saw her. She was looking around, too, maybe tired or also disappointed. I kept watching from a distance. She had gray or blue eyes, freckles, auburn hair pulled back. She was wearing a woven silk batik top from somewhere else. I couldn't place where. The rest of her clothing was worn denim. I was rapt even before she caught my eye. Strangely, when she did, I found I was already smiling. Stranger still, she seemed to brighten a little and smiled back at me. She walked over, holding my eyes. I looked at her for a moment, trying to cipher whether we were really responding the same way to the people in the room. I took a chance:

"They're not all who you thought they would be, are they?"

She paused. "No. Not really. Why do you say that?"

"I spoke to one whose family owns all the oil in Oklahoma or something."

"Yeah. A lot of name-dropping."

"Where are you from?"

"All over. I'm an Air Force brat, so all over. And I just got back from the Peace Corps."

"Where? I'm jealous."

"Thailand."

We talked until the mixer ended. Within days we were friends, taking study breaks together in the law library that usually lasted longer than planned. A couple of days later I fixed her bike's flat tire in five minutes. Broke skills. She made me a better dinner than I could make. Our study breaks at the law library were filled with sunny political talk and rookie critical commentary on what our classes revealed about how the law skewed the game in favor of wealth and power and against marginalized people. Some of our more corporate classmates grinned when they overheard bits of our self-righteous talk. We didn't care. By November we were together.

Lisa had left rural Thailand right before law school, but it would be awhile before she was really back in the States. For a few months, she couldn't shop in peace in the posh Palo Alto grocery stores. We would lock our bicycles, go inside, and face redundant rows of cans and boxes, different brands of the same kinds of food. For a while, it overwhelmed her.

"You okay?"

"Too many choices. Too much."

"What do you mean?"

"Who needs all this? We didn't even have a grocery store. We didn't have fifty kinds of everything. People just had enough, even if it took more time. It was fine."

Thailand was not Lisa's first time living as an outsider in another culture. From ages six to eight, she lived with her family in Kabul, Afghanistan. Her father was the pilot to the American ambassador at that time. Her two years in the Peace Corps came after college. She was the only American living in the village of Chonnabot. Most of her days were spent working in villages of houses built on stilts, surrounded by rice paddies. She traveled among sixty villages in her zone. Each village faced different challenges and reflected a slightly different culture. She got to them on her putt-putt motorcycle, teaching nutrition to subsistence farmers. Every village had its *poo yai ban*, literally its village big man. In theory, the *poo yai ban* ran the town and was the key to a Peace Corps volunteer's access to the people; custom required deference, which Lisa gave. Lisa always met the *poo yai ban* first, bowing respectfully with her hands joined in a prayerful pose. But she soon learned the villagers held the power, not their supposed leader. In fact, the *poo yai ban* ran things when the villagers allowed it. The lesson was clear: Establish trust with people above all else, no matter how long it takes and by whatever route, and they will come around—even on something as central to their lives as their food. She learned to speak Thai. She tolerated the fingers of the Thai matriarchs feeling the texture of her hair, even the one who tried to rub freckles off her skin claiming they were dirt, while opining to the other women that Lisa was blind because her eyes were blue. Even after Lisa reminded the Thai women that she had arrived on a motorcycle, they tested her vision by holding up fingers for Lisa to count, just to be sure. Lisa ignored their racist comments about other South Asians, for example the frequent Thai claim that eating

Vietnamese food caused infertility, despite Vietnam's ample population growth. Lisa ate with appreciation whatever the village people served her, even if it was more and different food than she wanted, including the insect larvae and silkworms that were local delicacies. Connecting with people in the villages was a rewarding grind, the price she gladly paid to save villagers and their babies from the dirty water and dietary gaps that caused fatal diarrhea, iodine deficiencies, and other diseases of malnutrition. Gaining people's trust was what it took to win.

Sometimes Lisa and other American Peace Corps volunteers in Thailand would meet on the weekend in Bangkok to speak English and reconnect for a brief escape. Evenings were spent in the red-light district. There was no cover to pay to enter the bars. Drinks were cheap and there was good music. Sometimes Lisa would listen in on sex workers in Thai, venting their amused contempt for their European customers.

She completed her law school applications with a manual English-alphabet typewriter she found tucked away in a village hospital. When her Peace Corps service ended, she took a break before law school by trekking solo for three weeks in Nepal, despite the dangers. After Afghanistan, Thailand, and a childhood of moving to new schools every couple of years, she knew whom to walk with and when it was necessary.

Now, three years later, Lisa and I were driving away, leaving law school behind. We hit the highway on our five-day drive to Philly in a car full of what we could carry, excitement, high hopes, and quiet fear. We had a couple of tapes for the drive. One was U2's *Joshua Tree*, which was just out. The album was an Irish band's idea of America, especially of the open American Southwest, where we were headed first.

U2 was a nostalgic favorite from my college days. I had never heard of them before I saw them play for a hundred or so people at the International House at the University of Chicago on their scruffy first American tour. That was about six or seven years before we started our drive east. I think the concert was free and the band was just looking to warm up for paying gigs in clubs in Chicago and elsewhere over the next nights. All four of the band members and most of us in the crowd were about twenty years old, standing on a tile floor—no lights, no stage, no alcohol—with nothing separating us, awash in sound. The show's DIY theatrical peak came when Bono used a pint glass to throw water through the air and onto the small crowd as if he were carrying out a vaguely religious rite or foreshadowing his later stadium theatrics. I remember making fun of them and their prospects after the show. Twenty-year-olds do that to avoid thinking about their own chances of success. But the band grew on me and I followed every album they put out through college, usually by helping to wear out someone else's copy.

The other tape was more obscure: Michael Hedges, a brilliant twelve-string guitarist and singer who would die ten years later when his car skidded off a cliff on a slick California road. The soundtrack of our seemingly endless, beautiful coast-to-coast trip became U2's *Joshua Tree*, including its anthemic, aspirational "But I Still Haven't Found What I'm Looking For," and Michael Hedges's intricate guitar, most memorably on his version of Bob Dylan's "All Along the Watchtower," which asserted the lyric "There must be some kind of way out of here," even as we were driving away.

When we graduated from law school in June 1987, the financial aid officer quipped that we were "at the top of our class in student loan debt." Our classmates were being pursued by big law firms that offered them perks like moving expenses, signing bonuses, and immediate pay at five times the salary Lisa and I were going to get. Our salaries wouldn't start until September, after we survived the summer and hopefully passed the Pennsylvania bar exam. We were among the 10 percent or so of our law school's graduating class who were pursuing public interest law; the other 90 percent were headed for big firms that represented power, at least for a while, often with a pit stop at a judicial clerkship.

Our big-firm classmates and even some members of our family weren't shy about criticizing our decision to get expensive, fancy degrees with fat loans that in their view were incompatible with public interest law compensation. Parents, even adventurous ones, are supposed to steer their kids away from risks. And ours were good parents. We repeatedly heard, expressed in different ways, that we would need to soon "grow up and get a real job." Some of our corporate-bound classmates joked about how soon we would "sell out," missing the self-descriptive irony in their own words. But we smiled through it all; we thought we would find what we were looking for. We had been side by side since we met, and still were as we drove east, looking through the same windshield.

Lisa's years overseas, as well as her life as a school-hopping military brat, would serve her well when she decided to run for judge, a truly foreign adventure. She had no political background and no Philly connections. There were about sixty different political fiefdoms in the city, like the villages she had visited. They're called wards. Each ward had its ward leader, its *poo yai ban*, who fronted power when the power was actually with the ward's voters if they chose to take it. Some ward leaders helped her. Others she went around to get to the people. When Lisa visited each ward meeting, she knew how to endure invasive comments and unnecessarily familiar touching. There was that neighborhood's food to appreciate, even when the stainless chafing dish of beef in gravy looked bland, slippery, and silvery gray. She already knew what was required to win.

She was a great insurgent candidate who could talk to anyone and disarm a room one stranger at a time. Her years of representing employees and workers in civil rights matters provided material for easy conversations with committee people in a working-class town. Her lack of political connections and experience hurt but also meant that no one held a grudge against her and no one took her candidacy as seriously as they soon learned they should. On the campaign trail, she left nearly every room better off than when she came in. Very few candidates can claim that.

My reputation for representing protesters and criticizing people who kicked them around—especially our politically powerful DA at the time, Lynne Abraham—militated against my taking any public role in Lisa's campaign for fear it would hurt her. It helped that Lisa's and my last names were different, so our connection to each other was not widely known in political circles.

During Lisa's first run for judge, she figured out that in Philly, judges are elected by voters who know virtually nothing about the candidates. Knowing that became key to our guerrilla campaign strategy. We knew voters wanted to elect fair judges despite knowing nothing about the many unfamiliar names. We had to get their attention in a few moments and make our pitch, a role the political parties' people usually played. The Democratic Party's power in a Philly judicial election at that time was its ability to extract money from candidates with the promise that the party would push certain candidates on election day through its vast network of ward leaders and their minions, known as committee people. The party's committee people—its poll workers—were indeed ubiquitous, and of wildly varying ability. The judicial candidates, almost always political novices, cheerfully paid the party tens of thousands of dollars and relied on the party's promises of election day support that the party sometimes broke, especially for candidates who weren't insiders, who weren't connected, or who hadn't "paid their dues." Lisa—who spent her whole career helping marginalized people—hadn't paid her dues by the party's standards, wasn't connected, and was no insider. As expected, the party did not support her. More than one source claimed that the boss said: "She cares more about civil rights than patronage!" Even as the party was declining to support her on election day, it hadn't yet grasped how strong she was becoming without their help. We formed a rebel army of our own volunteer poll workers for election day to give her a chance.

After Lisa schooled me on the realpolitik of how the party steered the vote—and got me intelligence on every ward where her record might appeal to the voters—I grew intrigued, and then slightly obsessed. In the evening, when the boys were occupied or sleeping, I quietly reviewed oversized computer printouts from the election commission's obsolete printers that itemized vote totals by polling place. We prioritized high-turnout locations before enlisting Lisa's satisfied clients, her family and friends, fellow lawyers, and our many activist allies to try to do a better job than the party did of steering voters on election day.

I became her invisible field organizer. Key to our plan was matching volunteer poll workers to places where they could be most effective. It mattered that our volunteers were persuasive, verbal people who believed in Lisa, rather than party functionaries pushing candidates they barely knew for the few dollars they were paid. I held sessions for novice poll workers to role-play the twenty-second pitch they would make as voters walked up to the polls. Since we were up against the party, with its much greater resources, another key to our plan was secrecy. The party boss had connections to Kavanaugh Printing, the major union print shop in a town where union printing was required in politics. The legend was that the boss's connection to Kavanaugh allowed him to divine the candidates' political strategies, their funding, and their plans from the orders they placed for campaign materials with the shop. To avoid giving up our plans, we printed our campaign literature at a different union print shop, Curtis's Printing, which was not connected to the party or its boss, hoping they wouldn't know what we were doing and might think we weren't even trying.

I had learned from my activist friends about limiting the damage that any one spy, one leak, or one mole could cause. Our volunteers didn't need to know how many other poll workers we had, where the others were being placed, or even who they were. In the days leading up to the election, I spoke to them myself, one at a time. They didn't even need to know exactly where they were going until late. They got their unique packets of materials (printed maps, campaign literature to hand out, emergency numbers and instructions) delivered to them at the last minute.

The first time Lisa ran, the party beat her only by exceptional effort. One week before that election, the party boss figured out she was on track to win without official party support. She had gained the support of some of the more powerful independent ward leaders and most of the unions based on her having represented workers for years. Some of them must have talked. Even in some wards that opposed her, some of the more independent committee people were defecting, offering her help when the ward leader wasn't looking. The party boss worked the phone for days right before the election to make her lose. Some of her support in wards and labor called her to apologize for backing out on their promises of support. It was nothing personal—the boss just needed to elect candidates the party had selected to be their insiders, and who had paid for their insider status in free work, generational connections, money, and unquestionable loyalty that extended the reach of patronage to their judicial staff— or all of the above. The boss needed to show that candidates who won had followed his party's rules, a notion that she would have dented by winning without the party's support. The party's funding required it; so did its patronage.

Two years later, Lisa ran again. But this time the party supported her from the beginning, mostly to make sure its weakness was not exposed but also because she had remained diplomatic the last time around, even when she'd been targeted and was denied a win. The party wisely preferred to embrace her candidacy the second time rather than see her and her army gain strength and win without their support. She had laid a foundation of support the first time. She was just too damn strong on the campaign trail, and her novice ground game was too big and too stealthy for the party to be sure it could beat her again. If the party opposed her, it risked discrediting its main asset: the illusion of its unassailable power. The party knew that maintaining the public perception of dominance was its highest priority. Even with a promise of party support, we saw no reason to sit back on election day. Three times as many volunteers as we had at the polls previously showed up pushing for Lisa, to the surprise of the party leadership. Many of them were organizers or activists or lawyers who were organized in groups with humorous, dramatic names they selected, like "Quaker Death Squad," "Flying Monkeys," and "Pants Brigade." Lisa won by a wide margin.

By jumping into an election political insiders said she had no business winning, Lisa was able to probe the weaknesses of a corrupt and sclerotic system, and test her theory that it could be outsmarted and beaten. It was a thrilling discovery: We weren't chained forever to a broken system. We weren't stuck with apparatchiks. Maybe democracy could work in our favor. And the code to victory we cracked on her first try wasn't even all that complicated. We just had to learn a few key lessons to apply the second time she ran:

Lesson 1: Any dominant political party's power is mostly perceived and therefore highly vulnerable to insurgent candidates who connect with people.

Lesson 2: Being a supposedly unelectable outsider can be an advantage, if it means your chances are underestimated, your tactics unknown, and you have no old beefs with political insiders.

Lesson 3: Let your book of business be years of helping others with no expectation of anything in return, and you might get something in return. Voters can smell public service for powerless people that's selfless and real rather than performative.

Lesson 4: Check your nuts and bolts, novice. The local party is called a machine for a reason. It wants you to believe that what it does is complex, opaque, and beyond the ken of a political novice to deconstruct. But it's not hard to figure out which polling places attract thousands of votes and which polling places attract less than a hundred. It's not difficult to focus resources on the high-turnout polling places where the characteristics of the voters make traction for a particular candidate possible. There are decent people everywhere, including many of the people within the party structure, who are open to someone new once there is a meeting. And it's not that hard to match persuasive supporters and persuasive literature to the polling places where they best match the voters.

Lesson 5: Believe voters want to pick and vote for candidates they believe will do a good job. That's why most of them bother to vote. You or someone they trust just needs to persuade them with a credible message that resonates.

Lesson 6: Be creative and unexpected. The local party has shown its routinized tactics in election after election, but your newness means it hasn't seen yours and may have no idea of how you can exploit the flaws in its own tactics. Let the dominant party and your opponents figure out your moves too late to adjust. This means keeping your strategies very close and very quiet. It means zagging when they think you're going to zig.

Lesson 7: If you can avoid it, don't make it impossible for the dominant party to offer support. Remember: They want to support winners. But don't trust that support enough to give up your secrets or pull back on your own support.

**Lesson 8:** Don't campaign like a politician, for God's sake. Answer questions directly. Speak your truth. People hate politicians.

Every one of these lessons would guide our campaign for district attorney almost twenty years later, when the weaknesses in the dominant party were even more apparent.

# CHAPTER 10

## Victims *and* Survivors

*I've got scars that can't be seen*

—DAVID BOWIE, "Lazarus"

Thirty years of representing criminal defendants taught me how to try a case, and how to see the dirt in the dark corners of a traditional prosecutor's office. But it didn't teach me as much about the needs of victims and survivors, who are just as often used as helped by traditional prosecutors. Even though I didn't spend much time with victims as a defense attorney, I knew something about the needs of victims and survivors before becoming DA. What I knew came from becoming a victim of violent crime in my private life, from things that were first illuminated for me in moving shafts of light.

I was slashed in the face about fifteen years before becoming DA, a couple hundred feet from my old law office, in a little grid of narrow historic streets and alleys in the center of the city, less than ten minutes' walk from City Hall. I was cut at the end of being assaulted and robbed by two people who had just smoked crack or maybe meth in the alley behind where I worked, on my way to my parked pickup truck to drive home.

It was early afternoon on a sunny Saturday in summery weather. I had just finished meeting with a new client, Matt, a cheerful "train kid"—a modern hobo—whose neck and arms were tatted up. In his early twenties, Matt had joined the train-hopping subculture for adventure. The day I met him, he had been charged with assaulting a police officer and trying to get his dog to do the same.

The incident happened in the lot outside the same church where I would later perform "Clampdown" with Sheer Mag during my campaign. A two-day, all-ages punk festival was going on in the basement music venue. The music promoter had hired a gang of white crew cuts who called themselves Fuck Shit Up (FSU) to be security for the event. After the first night, some of the train kids and others who attended claimed that a member of FSU had raped a woman who was attending the festival. As tension built between festival attendees and FSU, police were mingling with FSU, whose look and demeanor and supposed purpose at the venue were similar to their own.

At one point, an FSU security guard accused an unarmed train kid of carrying a weapon. The train kid was threatened, searched, and humiliated with the help of police, who must have believed there was a weapon. The train kids were increasingly incensed about the disfavored treatment they and other attendees were getting and the free pass on the rape allegations that FSU apparently enjoyed. Arguments and minor scuffling broke out between FSU and some of the attendees. No one was injured until a mountain of a cop—who had seen nothing of what had happened earlier—drove up suddenly in his patrol car and began cracking train kids' heads with his police baton.

A documentary photographer took more than fifty serendipitous photographs of the incident. She had been following the train kids all day and happened to be on-site when the incident occurred. The photographs indisputably showed that Matt was innocent, which is what a judge ultimately found at trial when Matt was acquitted. I remember Matt and that case for a few reasons, including Matt's amazingly good fortune that there were photographs of it all. Matt was a strong kid, the son of a bricklayer, and could have done me some good in that alley. But we parted paths two minutes too soon.

As we parted, I was thinking about the ironic duality of Matt's position in the case. He was a defendant, but he was also a victim of egregious police misconduct during and after his arrest. His girlfriend, a slight train kid, had it worse. She was a victim of life-threatening police brutality. Both were victims of obstruction of justice and false statements to police by a police officer, and at least Matt was a victim of perjury by a police officer. The fifty-plus photographs proved that the massive three-hundred-pound ex-boxer cop had hit Matt's girlfriend with his baton across the bridge of her nose so hard he knocked her out cold, and permanently changed her profile. An ambulance was called. The photographs showed that police dragged her sprawled-out body and concussed head along the pavement before the ambulance arrived, which had the accidental effect of riding her shirt up to her neck, exposing her breasts while she lay unconscious.

In the midst of this chaos, the photographs showed Matt, understandably concerned, talking to the giant police officer while holding his placid pit bull mix by a leash. The photographs are sequential. The first shots show that Matt is talking, but not yelling. He makes no effort at a punch or a push. He never makes physical contact; there is no struggle. The dog is docile, with four paws touching the pavement, mostly facing away from the police officer and never even barking at or moving toward the officer. The story the police officer told was a lie: He claimed Matt attacked him and sicced the dog on him. The officer probably had nothing against Matt, but he had created his own reason to lie.

The real motivation for the assault charges was to dirty Matt up as a witness against the officer's extreme brutality against Matt's girlfriend. The dirty, tattooed train kids—with their asymmetrical hair, frailties, and unconventional lives—appeared powerless, which makes them exactly the kind of people most likely to be victimized by the kind of cops who like to hurt people who are different from them and lie about it. Many, including Matt's best eyewitness at trial, are Black and brown. All of them, like all people perceived as powerless, are marginalized.

Matt's fear and anxiety around his outrageously unjust prosecution abated when he was acquitted. But his girlfriend didn't fare as well. Her face was changed. She had a permanent depression at the bridge of her nose and who knows what else. No healthcare. She didn't remember much of the incident and never made it to court to testify in support of Matt—they had split up and grown apart, it appeared. But Matt's trial and acquittal came over a year later. On that particular sunny Saturday, I had just met Matt and heard his compelling story and learned that his mother lived in New Jersey at 45 Shades of Death Road before we left my office and parted ways. "Why forty-five?" I asked him. He responded: "Forty-five is the house number. The road is Shades of Death."

It all happened so quickly. I was heading for the little street behind my office, where I'd parked my pickup truck, to drive home and cook a nice weekend dinner for my boys. Lisa was in Georgia for a couple of days, attending an educational course for judges on the history of American law. I walked by two skinny people sitting hunched on the steps of the rear porch of a building fifteen feet from my truck. They were smoking some kind of drug through a straight glass pipe.

I casually told them not to smoke drugs there and kept walking. I was too comfortable. Fifteen-plus years into my career, I had dealt with a few thousand people who suffered from addiction. I was used to being direct with them. I had talked to people on that same porch more than twenty times who were sleeping it off or in withdrawal or jonesing to buy drugs but too broke or panhandling. I would ask where they were staying and suggest where they could get food, a shelter bed, or treatment if they showed any interest. Until that day, there had never been a problem. But until that day I had never spoken to two people who were in the middle of smoking meth or crack or coke or whatever through a glass pipe. It was a mistake.

They didn't move or say anything after I walked past them. Just as I was getting ready to open the driver's door and get in, I noticed they hadn't even reacted. I got irritated and said, "Look, you can't smoke drugs here. Do you want me to call 911?" while I reached for my bunch of keys to get into the truck. It was another mistake. Immediately one of the two skinny people was off the steps moving quickly, as if to talk, but walked past me, turning me around. From the corner of my eye, I saw the other one still seated but fidgeting with his pants cuff or sock. As I turned to the first one, the second one ran up from behind. They attacked from opposite sides, each becoming more aggressive as I defended against the other.

As I kicked and turned and threw punches, the back of my heel caught on the curb. I tripped and fell backward. The second one swung his arm as I was falling and must have cut me. I never saw or felt the blade. As soon as I hit the ground, they both stopped and stared for a moment. I wondered why they had stopped. The first one looked horrified. The second one's look was colder. He grabbed my phone off the ground. They both ran.

I got up slowly. I was completely alone on a beautiful, breezy afternoon with shafts of sunlight moving on the pavement. The world was silent except for some birds chirping in the swaying trees. My right hand was bleeding a little and swelling from the fight or maybe the fall. Still, I didn't feel any pain. As I got up, I reached in my pocket for my phone even though it was gone. I looked down and saw splashes of blood intermittently hitting the asphalt, but the flow wasn't coming from the torn-up skin on my hand. I remembered that Lisa was out of town and my kids were home by themselves.

I stumbled out of the alley and walked the couple hundred feet back to my law office to find a mirror and a landline. Heavy bunches of blood drops followed me across the black pavement and brick sidewalk, across the hardwood floors of my office, and onto the white tile floor of my office bathroom, where it began to pool around my shoes. I started to panic, thinking that if my neck was somehow cut, I might bleed out before getting help with no one else in the office.

When I looked up and into the bathroom mirror, I saw what looked like a mouth above my left eyebrow. The left side of my face was sagging with gravity, my brow peeling away from my skull. In disbelief, bewildered and shaky, I knelt to keep from passing out and then got back up. I tried to push the cut closed. I was standing in front of the mirror, heart racing, breathing heavily, when I heard the front door open.

Scott, a lawyer who rented space from me, was coming in the building. He had stopped by the office to pick up a file for court on Monday. He spotted me through the open door of the bathroom, quickly turned around, and came back in. Scott calmly directed me to skip calling an ambulance, and to walk with him immediately the couple of blocks to Jefferson Hospital Emergency. I walked with him, my hand clamped over my brow, blood dripping between my fingers and guttering down my forearm to gather at and drip from my elbow. Pedestrians stared or covered their mouths. Homeless people winced and pointed. Some wore the same look of horror I'd seen on the face of the attacker who hadn't cut me. Even medical staff sat up and quietly looked when I walked into the emergency room.

Inside the ER's automatic doors, I knew they wouldn't let me bleed out. I began to calm down. Faces bleed. It might not mean permanent injury. It was just a question of damage. Not knowing how bad the injury was or how long I would be in the hospital, I didn't want to scare Lisa and have her come home just yet. I didn't want to scare the boys, then eleven and thirteen, by telling them over the phone what had happened to me. And I knew they would call Lisa immediately if they knew the truth. Maybe I would be stitched up and home soon.

Still, I needed to let my boys know I'd be late. I couldn't call them myself because I would never be able to hear their voices and stay composed, even if I didn't tell them everything. My distress would be theirs. They would have no answers yet and no one to comfort them. Scott took charge again. He called my boys and told them something had come up at work. I would be home later, not sure when. It might be awhile. I couldn't hear them, but I could tell they weren't saying much. They didn't know him. I knew this weird, vague news coming from an unknown voice would be strange to them. They would wonder why I wasn't calling. What about dinner? Was something wrong since I didn't call them myself, like always?

In the first few hours at the hospital, detectives came to see me, while bits of sand and gravel from the street were being plucked and washed from my wounds. I overheard doctors discussing whether or not I might have lost nerves that control the eye. Given the precision of the cut, doctors figured it came from a razor blade. The detectives asked me what I, a mid-forties man, was doing on a Sunday afternoon in an alley in that part of Center City, which really meant the part commonly known as the gayborhood. I explained that I was a lawyer, that my office was located there, that I had just seen a client before walking from my office to the alley to get in my truck to drive home and feed my kids. And then they had me explain it again.

They asked why my wife wasn't at the hospital. I explained she was out of town. They looked at each other. They slowly asked who was with my kids. I said the oldest was a teenager, his brother was almost a teen, and they were fine at home. More questions about why I wasn't in a suit. It's Saturday; I'm representing a broke client for a low fee, mostly as a favor for people we knew. I saw no need to say more about the facts of Matt's case to police. Then we got to their questions about my key ring, which was lying next to me on the gurney. It was a carabiner that had a few rings holding a bunch of keys on them for various doors in my office, for my house, and for my truck and car. The carabiner holding keys must have meant something to them. Why the carabiner? they wanted to know. What were the keys for? And so it went. They kept asking why I was "standing on the corner" where the assault occurred. They either hadn't heard what I said or were clearly implying my story was false—that I had nowhere to be or that I was looking for drugs or a hookup or maybe that I was a john who had done battle with a sex worker. Every time they said I was "standing on the corner," I corrected them, repeating that I had just left my office and walked past the corner, on my way to my truck to drive home. Finally, I reminded them "I never stood there." They stared at me. Months later, when I saw the police report, it simply said what the detective wrote: that I was "standing on the corner."

The detectives were professional in demeanor, and their words were mostly polite. Part of their job is to test what witnesses say, as they should when the story is odd. But their bias was clear, the reason they perceived my story as odd. Their overt suspicion about what I told them was rooted in the fact that I was in Philly's historically gay neighborhood, on the weekend, casually dressed and carrying my keys in a way that they didn't.

Having grown up broke before becoming a suit, I already knew that if I had gotten cut wearing professional clothing in another part of town on a workday, the detectives would have reacted very differently and doubted nothing I said to them. But, as they asked questions and I answered them, I silently wondered how much worse I would have been treated—by police then and prosecutors and defense attorneys later—if I had been a victim who was Black or brown or gay, or suffering from addiction, or homeless. How would I have been treated if I were a woman who was sexually assaulted or beaten by someone she knew during an era when those crimes somehow were suspect or didn't matter enough to law enforcement? The list goes on.

I had gotten just a taste of violence and just a taste of what it must feel like to be a victim from a disfavored, marginalized group who was engaging law enforcement. How much worse would it have been if I had been a victim whose status was criminalized, in addition to being disfavored and marginalized? What if I were a drug buyer who got cut by a dealer, or a sex worker who was cut and robbed by a supposed john? A dealer or a john who got cut? Would the police have helped me or arrested me or both? What if I had been an undocumented immigrant? Help, jail, or deportation? What would have been the consequences of being a gay victim of crime who sought help from the criminal justice system in the times when their sexual activity was still a crime and gay bars and gatherings were rousted by police at will? And what if I were all of the above—a victim marked by marginal status, criminal status, and foreign status all at once?

Historically, the answer has been that if you are an outsider victim who comes marked by a disfavored status, you don't report the crime because you fear the system won't protect you. You fear the system will not protect you the same way it protects insiders, as you deserve. It might even come after you, so you don't trust it enough to engage. And so classes of pariahs for criminals to victimize without consequence come to exist. Serial killers and serial rapists have chosen to prey on sex workers and other marginalized people to avoid detection and its consequence. In America, criminals single out undocumented immigrants to rob, knowing that their robberies won't be reported because undocumented victims and witnesses will fear deportation if they go to court and testify. The situation doesn't get safer for anyone when victimized undocumented immigrants can't engage the criminal justice system, so they buy guns on the street to protect themselves or to deter further crimes against them and their community. They carry those guns on their twelve-hour work-days as they move in their vans full of tools.

Because I appeared less privileged than usual the day I was cut, the detectives heavily scrutinized what I said rather than confirming the details: that I was a lawyer; that my office was around the corner from the crime scene; that my truck was a few blocks away, still parked right next to my blood as we spoke; that hastily abandoned drug residue and paraphernalia remained on the nearby back porch; that my home address confirmed why I would be driving and to where. An hour after interviewing me, the detectives said the details of what I had told them checked out. I thought they looked slightly disappointed that their sala-cious backstory wasn't true. They left and I stayed.

On that gurney, I was alone again just like in the alley, and far away from my family for hours. A nurse told me that doctors had ordered more testing done for possible eye damage, nerve dam-age, a broken eye socket, concussion. Testing was good, but it would take some more hours. At least when I told my boys ev-erything, I would have answers and would probably be home. I knew that no matter how bad the damage, it could have ended much worse

Eight hours and a lot of expensive imaging later, I was in-formed there was no orbital fracture, no nerve damage or evi-dence of concussion. In the middle of the night, an ER resident gave me more than twenty meticulous internal and external stitches and released me onto the street. Cool, pitch-black air and the sound of crickets hit me when I passed the hospital's auto-matic doors around three A.M. Exhausted, jumpy, and in pain, I made my way past staggering people, sex workers, people who were selling or buying drugs after the bars had closed. Some turned and looked. Walking under a streetlight, I caught my re-flection in a storefront. Light shone off the fresh white bandages on my head, my arm, and my splinted right hand. A sling for my arm was rolled up and hanging out of my back pocket, making me an obvious target. I tried to disappear by avoiding people, switching sides of the street, reversing and changing my route when I saw people until I could discreetly get to the poorly lit alley where my truck was still parked. When I made it a short block from where I'd been cut, I peeped around the corner to make sure no one was there. Keys in hand, I jogged to the truck, looking down for my blood on the pavement. The alley was too dark for me to see. I unlocked the door and jumped in the driver's seat, closed it, and locked it as fast as I could. My shaking hand found the key slot. The old truck started with a growl as I turned on every light I had but the domes—headlights, high beams, and fog lights as if I still needed to be invisible as I steered. The truck's big wheels rolled over and down from curbs as I slowly maneuvered around bollards, telephone poles, and dumpsters that had rolled out of position and were impinging on the narrow lane of travel. I turned onto another narrow alley to get to Twelfth Street's two wider lanes, parked cars, trolley tracks, and streetlights. Controlling the truck and being surrounded by its armor reduced my fear as I headed home, wondering how best to break the news to my kids in the morning.

The attackers were never caught. No fingerprints or DNA were pulled from whatever drug paraphernalia remained or my stolen phone, which was discarded a couple of blocks away and recovered by a pedestrian the next day. As far as I know, law enforcement didn't try to lift prints or gather DNA. I never knew whether the people who attacked me took the phone to rob me or took it to stop me from immediately calling the police. Either way, without being able to break the phone's security code, they had no use for it.

Weeks later, the detectives did offer to have me go through mug shots of the usual suspects. My view of the attackers was brief, mostly peripheral while I was spinning around, fighting. They wore hats very low. I barely saw their faces and saw noth-

ing distinctive. Even their races and approximate ages were uncertain: One was olive-skinned, the other paler. Deep in their
addiction, they had slim physiques and generic oversized clothes.
I declined, knowing from the event I had seen too little and
knowing a decade into my career that there was less chance of a
correct ID than a mis-ID. I was unwilling to risk an innocent
person going to jail.

For a couple of years afterward, I mostly avoided the corner
where it happened, although I passed close by every workday.
When I had to walk by, I would give it a wide berth as if a bull
could come charging off the back porch at any time. Sometimes,
when the afternoon light was a certain way near where it happened, my heartbeat would pick up or my hands would shake. That
was then. The scar has faded and blends with the other creases in
my forehead now, and in some ways so has the memory.

I have thought for fifteen years that the blade was probably
meant for my jugular or my eye and only missed because I was
falling backward over the curb. Drugs you smoke don't improve
your aim, if the razor was aimed at all. At first, the idea of bleeding out alone in shafts of sunlight moved by a benign wind in
trees full of singing birds, of leaving my young sons without saying goodbye, was just overwhelming. I knew my wife would have
struggled, but been okay. My boys grew up and moved out, and
those feelings mostly went away. I can smile about it now and
joke that my daily existence since I got cut is my afterlife, a second chance for someone who believes in second chances. I'm
okay, but I know my experience was nothing then and is nothing
now compared to what victims and survivors of far more serious
crimes endure when, and after, the crime occurs. And I know that
the criminal justice system often fails them in ways that are easier for me to feel in the aftermath of my own attack.

During my career as a criminal defense and civil rights lawyer,
I sometimes spoke to victims and survivors of crime during the
course of an investigation, at court, or after being sought out. On

a few occasions, I was hired by victims or survivors of crime to represent them when they felt the police, the prosecutors, or the courts would not get them justice. And on many occasions I represented people who believed that law enforcement, usually police but sometimes prosecutors as well, had victimized them. The victimization they described was serious—broken bones and scars, concussions, severe sexual harassment and abuse, inadequate and biased or corrupt investigative activity, and unlawful incarceration.

From my talks with victims and survivors before becoming DA and from my own victimization, I knew that survivors and victims are truly individual. They need and want different things, but there are patterns. They want information. Some want to know why the crime happened. They want details of how it happened, the sequence of events. They want to find the mistake, imagine a different step in that sequence—to envision how a different step would have prevented their loss. They need to stop blaming themselves and their loved ones. Sometimes they want to hear what was endured, although it's something they have already imagined, with dread, for too long.

They want the perpetrators caught, and every forensic tool used to catch them. They want specifics on the perpetrators. They want to know why the perpetrator harmed them, at least to get more information about the motive for the terrible act— drug turf, money, disrespect, jealousy, dominance—or, more broadly, to be informed about the life of the person who committed the crime—addiction, mental illness, childhood, prior criminal record if any—for their own reasons. They want to know that the perpetrator will not harm them again or others. They want their loved one's loss to accomplish something good in the world. They want or they reject help with trauma they admit or deny is real. They want closure. Some want retribution, punishment, revenge. Others do not, believing that their wounds will not be healed by wounding others. Often their relationship with investigators gets rocky; often it's excellent. Some feel abused or manipulated by police or prosecutors; others feel well served. Especially when their loss is recent, sometimes they just want you to listen and to say nothing for a long time, which is about the most difficult and the loudest thing you can say back in a silent room.

During my career in court as a criminal defense attorney, I gleaned how emotionally difficult it must be for a prosecutor to get close enough to victims and survivors to help them, while remaining distant enough to be objective and to keep their oath to do justice for everyone. Prosecutors aren't supposed to be saviors or avengers. But I understand the prosecutor's temptation to play savior for one victim and their family, to the exclusion of all else. Defense attorneys are tempted to play savior, too. But "savior" isn't part of either side's job description; neither side can afford to ignore their limitations or let their professionalism and objectivity slip away. Prosecutors are generally untrained in addressing trauma, which is best handled by trained victims' services advocates, at least until prosecutors become well-trained in trauma and can help the victims' advocates out.

In a truly serious case, the traditional prosecutor's toolbox for victims and survivors contains only a few tools: obtaining convictions on the highest possible charges, maximizing years of incarceration, and attaining the death penalty are the primary metrics for achieving justice for victims. Trials understandably focus lawyers on the crime itself rather than on society as a whole. Victims and survivors understandably sometimes focus on their loss and the crime itself. Too often, traditional prosecutors have come to view themselves as lawyers for victims and survivors, whose job is to pursue whatever their clients say is fair. Prosecutors, whose job is to uphold the law, need to remember that the law recognizes that victims and survivors are so obviously biased from their connection, love, and trauma, that they are never permitted to be the judge or to serve on a jury in the case where they or their loved one was harmed. Often, they are excluded from serving as jurors on unrelated cases that are merely factually similar to the crime they endured.

Sometimes, traditional prosecutors have become the agents of their victims and survivors for even worse reasons: It's good politics, with the complicity of a cynical press, which is important if your chief prosecutor's first priority is their political career rather than the slow work of preventing victimization in the future.

In Philadelphia, where for decades chief prosecutors' true north has been politics, I watched as assistant district attorneys openly claimed to be lawyers for victims and survivors in court and on the record, which the law makes clear they are not. They are supposed to represent the people, to be for the people. But, for the sake of politics, they left that job—to represent everyone in Philadelphia and to seek justice—to be done (or not) by judges and defense attorneys and juries. The politics is simpler and press coverage more favorable for prosecutors when they simply ask the families of victims what they want. Death penalty? Okay. Drawing and quartering? Okay. A decade in jail or twenty-five years for a drug-addicted burglar's violation when no one was home? Okay. To be served in a jail with no drug treatment available? Okay.

Taken to its extreme, this type of prosecution and its fawning press coverage are harmful frauds perpetrated on victims and survivors who don't deserve to be hurt more. When families insist that a lower level of murder is really first degree as a way of expressing how much they value their loved one's loss and their grief and outrage, prosecutors can either tell them the truth and persist in prosecuting the lower charge, or lie to them and pursue an unjust first-degree charge that they know a judge or jury should reject. The fraud is complete when the prosecutor blames the judge or jury for an actually correct but supposedly unfair outcome. Victims and survivors then leave the criminal justice process having been deceived by a prosecutor into feeling cheated by a judge and jury who did their jobs. By telling victims and their families the truth from the start, prosecutors can ensure that victims and survivors understand that the system actually worked.

We also need to make sure marginalized people can come to us when they are victimized. We should not prosecute sex workers for what they do, or people who suffer from addiction whose only crime is possession of drugs, in part so they can safely report crimes committed against them and can testify for one another when something happens. And we need to provide public health solutions to help them turn away from a life of addiction or sex work because their lives have value, and because doing so makes for fewer victims. We should specially handle cases involving undocumented people so that they can participate in the system with less fear of immigration consequences.

The challenge for justice in our adversarial system is that it can appear that "justice" is not in anyone's job description. Defense attorneys speak to their clients, learn about their lives, and see the frailty and humanity in them, even when their clients have committed terrible criminal acts. Defense attorneys are seldom allowed to and seldom do speak to victims and survivors and their kin outside of a courtroom, except when they are testifying. Prosecutors speak to victims and survivors of terrible crimes and see the frailty and humanity in them, especially when they have suffered a terrible criminal act. They are seldom allowed to and seldom do speak to defendants and their kin outside a courtroom, when they are testifying. The result in our adversarial system is different knowledge and different loyalty, an inadequately informed other-ization of the opposite side's most directly affected party.

Ironically, the people who would never be permitted to serve on a jury or to judge a terrible crime are exactly the ones who wrestle behind the scenes with what justice should look like for the victims, survivors, defendants, their families, and society as a whole. Prosecutors and defense attorneys never get to be on the jury or play judge in a case they handled, even later in life when they have different jobs or retire. Because of their bias, loyalty, emotion, and trauma, victims, survivors, defendants, and their kin never get to serve on a jury or be the judge in a matter that directly affects them. This is as it should be in a rational system that is trying to be fair to everyone.

There is no higher calling for a criminal justice system than to focus holistically on what works to prevent future victimization, by doing justice for everyone. That's a special challenge in an adversarial system where, de facto, the prosecutor's sympathy lies with the victim and their antipathy is directed to the accused. But the job of the prosecutor is to achieve justice, and that means representing all people in their jurisdiction, which means doing what defense lawyers take no oath to do. Prosecutors, consistent with their oath to seek justice, have to break the adversarial cycle when it comes to the people involved. From the point of view of the state, a just outcome means justice is achieved for all parties in the courtroom and everyone else in society. If the prosecutor's job is done right, there will be more compassion and more prevention, and in the end we will have fewer victims.

# CHAPTER 11

# Progressive Prosecutor

*You're gonna have to serve somebody*
*Well, it may be the devil or it may be the Lord*
*But you're gonna have to serve somebody*
— BOB DYLAN, "Gotta Serve Somebody"

Everywhere I campaigned, in public or in smaller meetings, people wanted to know why and when I chose to run. What was my awakening after so many years? And how did I hope to bring change to the highly entrenched culture of the Philadelphia District Attorney's Office if I was elected? To me, both questions were asking the same thing.

My years of studying social justice movements in order to defend protesters in court had led me to believe that great social justice movements in America often take about thirty years to succeed, which I defined as winning major battles that achieve their primary goals. The war almost always goes on. In 2017, I figured the movement for criminal justice reform was still in its first decade, with many tumultuous years to go before it could claim success. In any social justice movement attempting to fix and rebuild broken, entrenched institutions, culture change is required and achievable only if personnel embrace the change.

Often that requires new hires, as I was repeatedly reminded on the campaign trail. Before we could convince voters we were serious about changing office culture in the Philadelphia DAO, we had to understand and be transparent about how we hoped to change DAO culture.

About 70 percent of the DAO staff and 80 percent of its lawyers were white in a city that was roughly 40 percent white. The people who got locked up in Philly were mostly Black and brown; so were most victims and survivors. The DAO didn't resemble Philly in its racial demographics. But that was only part of the self-satisfied, homer culture of the office that we hoped to diversify and make more reflective of the world that criminal justice engages if we won the election. We wanted life experiential diversity, as well as geographic, linguistic, religious, intellectual, age, gender, and sexual orientation diversity. We wanted all personality types. We also wanted experienced mid-career and late-career lawyers whose idealism and expertise drew them to us. The DAO staff we hoped to work with if we won needed to understand and reflect their client: the people.

On the campaign trail, I told people I was interested in attracting lawyers whose career experience, life experience, or studies showed they were open to questioning the traditional prosecution approaches of the past. The kind of lawyer who was set on locking up even more people for even more years would have a few thousand traditional prosecutors' offices where they could work to make mass incarceration even worse. But they wouldn't be working in the DAO in Philly if I was elected. The people we would want to recruit would be change agents whose vision was to improve the world to make it more humane and just.

People didn't necessarily know what progressive prosecution was as we campaigned. We were educating, evangelizing, proselytizing. We campaigned by telling people what we were about— and it was working: We convinced voters that we were nothing like traditional prosecutors, which was what they were hoping to hear in most Philly neighborhoods in 2017. Popular culture around criminal justice had shifted.

We recognized the inevitable, slow twist in the history of prosecutorial politics. In my thirty-year criminal justice career, the moral high ground had shifted completely with the catastrophic rise of mass incarceration, the enduring decline of crime in America, and the writing and scholarship around it. In the early 1990s, the prevailing notion was that defending people charged with crimes was immoral. As a young public defender from 1987 to 1992, I had my morality questioned repeatedly by all kinds of people who often asked how I could defend "those people." But by 2017, time had flipped it. I knew that Philly voters were rightly questioning the morality of prosecuting "those people" in traditional ways. We would need to answer their question.

The answer was something I had lived and learned during my career. Progressive prosecution filled the space abandoned by the compassionless power of traditional prosecution. We had a case to make that progressive prosecution was like all sacrifice for others in public service: Its goal was to positively change the lives of the people served, something traditional prosecution had failed to do. In a number of cities around the country—Chicago, San Francisco, and Seattle, to name a few—it was already under way. It was time for Philly to catch up, to combine great power with great compassion.

At the level of culture, America was ready for a serious discussion about criminal justice reform. In 2018, the legal scholar James Forman, Jr., won the Pulitzer Prize for his 2017 book *Locking Up Our Own*, a nuanced and unflinching history of how and why Black politicians, community leaders, and others assisted in pushing the war on drugs, which backfired into the mass incarceration of Black people. Forman won the prize in the same year as Kendrick Lamar, the first hip-hop musician ever to win the Pulitzer. Lamar won for *Damn*, the album that followed his 2015 Grammy-winning album, *To Pimp a Butterfly*, and the track it contained, "Alright." "Alright" became a Black Lives Matter anthem for a while, at least. The fortress was feeling a shift—two Pulitzers, one for telling a lesser-known and self-reflective story of mass incarceration, the other for a voice from the heart of the world mass incarceration created.

Forman is a brilliant writer whose book is equally brilliant. He clerked on the U.S. Supreme Court, and walked away from the fortune he would have made in big law if he had wanted it. Instead, he chose to work for little money for eight years at the most prestigious public defender's office in the United States, the Public Defender Service for the District of Columbia. While there, he lawyered for poor defendants in criminal matters and founded a school for juveniles who were in custody. James is the son of James Forman, Sr., the civil rights leader whose youthful image appears frequently in 1960s-era black-and-white photos from the movement, sometimes standing right next to Dr. King. The elder Forman is known for his radical and strategic work with the Student Nonviolent Coordinating Committee (SNCC), Black Panthers, Freedom Riders, and others throughout his career. He was at Selma, Birmingham, and Albany among other places when it mattered. In later years, he was an academic. Writings from throughout his career live on. And he was a highly regarded strategist, always focused on the win.

That culture shift, however, did not mean everyone was gravitating toward progressive prosecution. There were loud voices in the community and academia that contended prosecutors' offices, like jails, were beyond redemption. Paul Butler, an ex-prosecutor and law professor, was one of those voices arguing that idealistic people should not become assistant prosecutors. In a traditional prosecutorial system, the training, supervision, policies, and culture would either corrupt them or expel them. They could do more good as public defenders. He had a point. As long as the prosecutor's office was run by the traditional status quo, I agreed.

But I felt completely differently about an office run by a progressive chief prosecutor who was committed to achieving criminal justice reform inside and outside the office. And thirty years in the trenches eliminated any notion that the dogged and capable public defenders I respected and admired were ending mass incarceration or improving prosecutors' other practices. The data was undeniable: They weren't, no more than I had during my criminal defense career. We had to do what was necessary to win.

My campaign made me rehash my own decision to run for district attorney—my own belated, almost desperate awakening to the fact that my life's work for individual clients was buried in an avalanche of incarceration I had no way to address.

Was it moral to prosecute "those people"—to be a prosecutor, even a progressive prosecutor? To me, the answer was yes. If anything, given the decades of failure by dedicated people to change prosecution from the outside, my question was: Was it moral to let a traditional prosecutor prosecute "those people" when a progressive prosecutor could take their place?

It needs to be said: Don't be too virtuous to win. It's okay to win. This is a discussion I used to have with activists I represented all the time. I would meet with them in a large group. There was always the coolest one, the one with the literal or figurative beret and the fist in the air, the one who was outdoing everyone else, more-radical-than-thou. And that one was going to have the best social life with people who were already in the room. But that was usually not the person who had been arrested fifteen or twenty times and had fifteen or twenty years of experience and knew that when you actually are winning, you have to know how to solidify that win by reaching over to your enemy and embracing your enemy.

The reality is that I was asked a bunch of times to run for

judge as a Green Party candidate (no thank you), to run for DA as a Green Party candidate (no thank you). And it was no thank you for an obvious reason: I wanted to win. Dramatic and virtuous failures have their place, but what's wrong with winning?

What I used to do as a defense lawyer was go into a courtroom, walk up to a prosecutor who didn't agree with me, and say, "Please, please, please . . . come on now, let's do a reasonable thing here." And the answer I would get most of the time was "no," because I was talking to somebody who didn't agree with me about anything on the planet or in history.

What would it have been like all those years if I had done the same thing but the prosecutor I approached was me? Even though the prosecution and defense have different obligations and do not completely share information, the outcome between me as defense lawyer and me as prosecutor would have been a lot better for justice. Because the reality is that the locus of power is generally the prosecutor, even more than the judge or jury. And yes, a dedicated public defender can sometimes dunk over the head of the prosecutor, getting justice from a jury on something like a question of proof beyond a reasonable doubt or innocence. But there are a lot of things criminal defense lawyers just cannot wrestle from a jury and cannot wrestle from a judge—unless they bring their values along and become prosecutors, in which case they can do these magical things.

My wife has this expression, which she started using only after she became a judge: "Ta-da!" She uses it to mean that, like a fairy princess, a judge has a wand and gets to wave it and say "Ta-da!" and magically make justice happen. Well, that's what judges can do some of the time. And prosecutors do the same, only they have a lot more magical power to do justice: "Ta-da! We are not pursuing the death penalty in this case." "Ta-da! Don't pursue the highest charge." "Ta-da! Reopen that cold case." "Ta-da! We're not okay with excessive sentencing." That's power. That is not theoretical power. That is real, magical power to do justice. And that's power that I didn't have working in the criminal justice system as a criminal defense attorney, standing outside the DA's office, banging my head against the wall, and trying to persuade a bunch of prosecutors who are beyond reason and will just keep carrying out a philosophy that is antithetical to justice.

So I decided I couldn't keep doing what I'd been doing on the outside of power, as a criminal defense attorney. I could feel virtuous and pure doing criminal defense on the outside, maybe even put on my figurative beret and put my fist in the air when no one was watching, or I could run for district attorney, try to win, and if that worked I could just get it done. I decided at fifty-six years of age, let's just get it done. Let's just change every broken thing that we can, knowing we can't change everything.

The criminal justice system in America is rooted in slavery, racism, and social control as much as it is rooted in anything we can really call justice. Internationally unprecedented mass incarceration in the United States has been wreaking havoc on vulnerable communities for five decades. Stepping into a prosecutor's shoes means actually sending people to jail, and many of those people will be Black and brown and poor and troubled for all the structural and historic reasons we already know. We can't fix it all, but complete fixes are for absolutists and purists, not pragmatists who recognize that every minute of every life can be improved in ways that profoundly heal us all. Being a progressive prosecutor means you can improve justice because you have the power to change things. You will change things if you can bear the discomfort of holding and wisely using power.

Is the system itself—burdened by a grotesque track record of inaccuracy, bigotry, violence, and cruelty—so darkly murky that we don't know how to find a path to real change? Shouldn't we try? Isn't trying to be fair with our moral compass pointed north okay, even when we have to take action in the murk?

Consider a hypothetical example that unquestionably resembles thousands of actual crimes: The victim was his financially struggling family's hope and pride and just days away from leaving town for college when he was robbed at gunpoint in the parking lot of a fast-food place where he was working his after-school shift. The young shooter and some other, older teens took the victim's car keys and could have left with the stolen car and done no further harm. Instead, they began to taunt the victim while he lay prone and submissive on the ground. The young teen shooter then stood over the victim and shot him to death.

The example is complicated by the reality that we treat juveniles, especially younger ones, differently from adults in our criminal courts. The U.S. Supreme Court and the latest neuroscience are both clear that juveniles have immature brains and are therefore less capable of consequential thinking than fully grown adults, but also more capable of rehabilitation. Juveniles are both less culpable for their actions and more capable of improvement. That was the state of the especially immature hypothetical teen who pulled the trigger. The victim's brain was all over the asphalt. You could hardly find a more sympathetic victim; you could hardly find a more immature offender for such a terrible crime. Neither one of their two families would ever be the same.

What does justice look like in a system where juvenile jurisdiction often ends at twenty-one years of age and where juvenile jails (which we call "placements") mostly try to rehabilitate but often fail, and where adult prisons mostly don't even try to rehabilitate? In other words, what does justice look like in this terrible case in a system that cannot competently look after the victim's rights, the young perpetrator's rehabilitation, or the community's safety? Whose interests matter more or less? Where is the balance? The life of the victim was sacred and needed an accounting, an act of justice. But wasn't there also something sacred in this barely teenage defendant who had, in an instant, ended his victim's promising life and so much of his own life that night? For how many years should a prosecutor try to send this child away—and to what place should he be sent? What should happen in that place?

I don't know exactly what justice looks like in that case without doing more homework, just as I don't know for many other cases like it before doing the work. Defendants do not walk into a courtroom with a number on their foreheads that tells us the sentence they deserve on a truly serious case, or any other case for that matter. Experienced prosecutors are used to spitting out a number of units of time—years, months, days—that reflects their gut, which usually means how they were trained and mentored and brainwashed by more experienced, traditional prosecutors. We know that approach is exactly how we got mass incarceration, and it was almost never based upon criminological science. Can't we do better than that, even when we don't have all the data and science we would like, and even though deciding on how much time in custody is enough is a murky task?

My answer is that seeking justice means doing your homework first before making tough choices among the possible outcomes in an imperfect system. First, you gather as much useful information as you can get about the killer's life, the victim's life, the other people involved, the night, and everything else that matters. You will need some school records on the defendant, prior testing of various types, family information, prior law enforcement contacts, drug and alcohol use, addiction, psychological records if any, responses to treatment. You may need to order new or additional testing, and to hear from some experts.

Try to find and discern each piece of that information like someone peering through fog to spot and interpret objects that are far away. Which factors suggest the possibility of more rehabilitation and less future danger? Which factors suggest *less* rehabilitation and *more* future danger? What mitigates the criminal conduct? What aggravates it? Being thirteen years old mitigates more than being a juvenile of sixteen or seventeen because it shows extraordinary immaturity in considering consequences, and even greater potential for rehabilitation than an older juvenile. Shooting the prone victim to death when the robbery was complete aggravates. The negative peer pressure and influence of older participants mitigates. The killing of a victim who played no role in initiating the violence aggravates. Consider the input of the survivors and the crime's terrible impact on them and society. And so the looking goes. There is no point scale to fit into a formula, except maybe the one derived from the CDC's Adverse Childhood Experiences (ACE) Study, which measures such factors as witnessing violence, sexual and physical abuse, neglect, extreme poverty, and so forth. And no point scale alone will ever solve such a complex puzzle.

Once the work is done, there are options to consider. Does the case belong in juvenile court, where jurisdiction will end in most states at a particular age? In Pennsylvania, for example, that age is twenty-one, so a young teen's potential period of rehabilitation, monitoring, and incarceration would end in no more than eight years for a terrible murder. What juvenile placements or institutions offer a real shot at rehabilitation, given the specific needs of a young teen? How effective are those placements and services within the juvenile system in reality—not just in their shiny brochures? Or does the case belong in adult court, with the potential for a much longer sentence? The juvenile defendant would not serve time in adult jail until reaching adulthood. Is more time warranted? In some circumstances, there might be potential for a combination of a juvenile sentence and an adult sentence. No matter how hard we try, there are some things we just can't see with certainty in this murk. But we try to see them all, because specifics matter, like lives.

What I do know for sure is that someone has to make the decision. Someone has to look closely into that murk, and struggle with the imperfect options we have. It really matters who that person is. That person could be a prosecutor who believes that people change and who is committed to human dignity, rehabili-

tation, and the wise use of resources to increase safety by preventing future crime, someone whose expertise and sensibilities
are like those of James Forman, Jr. Or it could be a less thoughtful and knowledgeable, punitive prosecutor who believes the
world is binary, inhabited by unchanging saints and monsters,
who is committed to revenge, retribution, and a false notion of
safety based on endless incarceration rather than using resources
to prevent future crime. These two prosecutors have different
visions of justice that will lead to different outcomes. The story
of mass incarceration in this country is the story of one of those
people's errant set of beliefs and values triumphing over the other's. It's the story of what happens when you build a whole system on those values, and the human costs of that system. Lawyers
in criminal justice can try to hold powerful roles as judges, legislators, or even well-established and respected criminal defense
attorneys later in life.

There is an opportunity cost that goes with rejecting being a
progressive prosecutor. Aren't critical thinkers and compassionate people who understand our history and who struggle with
the weight of taking others' freedom exactly the ones we need to
make those decisions? Isn't power that knows when to stay its
hand the kind of power we want? Don't we want reflective people blessed with self-doubt?

There is also great value in defending people who are charged
with crimes, especially as a public defender. We need both prosecutors and defenders who are attached to working hard for their
clients within the law, to truth, to accuracy, and to fairness. Justice requires the symbiotic excellence of defense attorneys and
progressive prosecutors, whose adversarial work is also profoundly complementary in achieving justice so long as it never
becomes adversarial to the truth. But prosecutors have more
power.

These were the thoughts I revisited, explained, and reconsidered as the campaign wore on. At one point, I even reconsidered

my choice to run for district attorney. I quickly landed here: No matter how uncomfortable and how murky the view, isn't it important and helpful to the marginalized people you propose to serve—the survivors, victims, witnesses, defendants, and all the people who are less directly involved in a criminal case—to be the one in the fog, looking for answers and solutions you actually hold the power to achieve in that murk?

# CHAPTER 12

# Difference = Power

## *The Campaign*

*You are now about to witness the strength of street knowledge.*

— N.W.A, "Straight Outta Compton"

I have been talking about my people and my nascent campaign as being made up of outsiders. People who are "different" from some notion of normal. But what does being different really mean in politics? Most of us have been told that being an outsider, being different, is a problem, a deviance. But what if it turns out that the majority of us are different, at least according to the people in power, just in a million, splintered ways? And what if all of these different people actually align in lots of ways, especially against whoever and whatever decided to tell us what normal means and that we were different? What if our difference is not really from one another, but from the people who gave us that label?

The question of whether we different people—we outsiders—make up the majority and can come together is essential, because majorities win elections. Which means that those of us who are called different—again, we outsiders—have the power to win every election if we are together. I spent my campaign inadvertently finding people who are different and realizing that, when difference is aligned, it equals power.

Right after my announcement, a Philly journalist wrote about the bad bet that was my campaign. He called me a "liberal unicorn." The head of the Fraternal Order of Police told the press that my candidacy was "hilarious." He didn't enlighten the press about our two decades of combative history, and his bottomless support for officers acting under a cloud of suspicion, including while I sued them. But he wasn't wrong, either. Their point was the same: My candidacy, as we had succeeded in defining it with our platform, deviated far enough from their status quo expectations in politics to make it a joke.

At their worst, traditional prosecutors supported a fascist fantasy: Merciless leaders stamp out crime by sweeping away the individual rights they swore to uphold. The Philly prosecutors elected in my lifetime weren't that bad, but nearly all of them had beaten the drum of punishment and retribution until it broke. And that familiar thumping sound won elections and reelections, over and over. But as the ninety-eight-day campaign started, it quickly became clear that this time around the voters wanted to hear something else. A lot had changed, and quickly—I'd sensed the change growing over my time in the legal trenches. It had been thirty years since I began my career and about twenty-eight since my first jury trial, in 1989. Things were different.

In 1989, MC Hammer and his Aladdin pants were dancing up the charts. I was twenty-eight years old and two years into my legal career. Lisa and I had just gotten married on a budget. Pennsylvania's Quaker traditions allow marriage by any four witnesses, clergy or not. Given we were a union of Catholic, Protestant, and Jewish parents, we had enlisted our parents to marry us in a lovely, low-dollar ceremony that summer. Siblings cooked and catered the meal. A public defender clerk DJ'ed. And then, after a driving honeymoon in Canada, we went back to work as struggling, baby public interest lawyers.

Not long after, on the day of my first jury trial, I walked into a dreaded calendar room in old City Hall carrying my public defender's office file for my case under the arm of my suit jacket. Calendar rooms are courtrooms where a judge assigns cases that are ready for immediate trial to other judges. The process magnifies everything good and bad about judicial power. Too often, calendar judges divvy up cases in ways that will expedite their conclusion but have nothing to do with evenhandedness, equity, justice, or restraint. Guilty pleas go to kinder judges; jury trials on serious cases go to hammers. Don't try your case and lose.

When I walked in, the giant courtroom was jammed. Defendants who were out of custody and their families filled the gallery seats of the courtroom. My client was locked up. Lawyers socialized and talked business standing around the periphery. Inside the bar of court—the wooden rail that separates lawyers and judges from observers—there was a room made of oak and frosted glass windows. It looked like the DA's trial chief, the judge, and the court officer who would call the list of cases were all together in the back. When they came out, I didn't see any defense attorneys come out with them. Maybe there were some inside, but I wasn't one; I was outside. The law and rules of ethics require that when one side meets with a judge on a matter of substance about a case, the other side must be present as well. The group who came out assumed their posts on the lawyers' side of the bar. The judge took the bench and was reviewing files before his court officer called the room to order. An unfiltered Philadelphia assistant district attorney (ADA) I knew was spoofing defendants seated in the courtroom. He was complimenting their decoratively inscribed haircuts, mostly depicting lightning bolts or their initials. My client was in a cellblock a few floors away.

As the judge called the noisy courtroom to order, the ADA's next antic was to call out just low enough to be heard in the din of the room: "Put 'er in there, Your Honor!" The judge's eyes snapped back and forth, looking in vain for the source of the humor before moving on.

In my mind, this was more like a circus than a ball game, and I was the guy in the circus with the shovel who cleaned up behind the elephants. Judges and prosecutors were in the back, possibly in violation of ethical rules, and probably discussing which cases would go where. My ADA friend was blowing up solemnity and civility with pranks. And my hands were on the shovel because I wouldn't follow the unwritten rules that would have given me an advantage in that room in the late 1980s. They were:

1) Be a private attorney, not a public defender.
2) Be connected. Being an ex-prosecutor who could backslap the ADAs helped; being connected enough to be politically useful to the judge helped; and being related to either of the above helped in a nepotistic system.
3) Bribe the court officer in cash, and at least annually, in order to enjoy his assistance in manipulating you and your clients' cases to favorable judges. The court officer in the calendar room got one card after another during the holidays, always in sealed envelopes from what I saw.
4) Plead your clients guilty almost all the time in a system that required lots of guilty pleas, so your occasional trial request would be grudgingly tolerated.
5) Be old. Young defense lawyers who asked for jury trials were like dogs soiling the carpet, deserving of immediate consequences they would remember.
6) Validate that the defendants are all guilty, and subhuman. No matter how severe your case, cheerfully exchange niceties about weather and sports and pretend everyone is acting ap-

propriately even when things get wild and weird. Remember
this is commerce and you are a mercenary or should act like
one, even as a public defender. Convey that your clients are
little more than business to handle before an afternoon of
golf.

I was breaking all the rules. I was a young public defender,
connected to and politically useful to no one, who knew what was
up and was repulsed by it, and who was too self-righteous to hide
my disgust. I demanded a jury trial more times than they wanted
to hear, so I got consequences. That day and over a period of
months that followed, five separate times when I came into the
calendar room and asked for a jury trial, I was sent to the same
punishing jerk of a judge, despite there being many other quality
judges whose courtrooms were available. Each time, when I was
told to go to Volo's courtroom, there would be an amused gasp
from the other defense attorneys in the room, relieved that their
cases were safe from the infamous judge.

Deusdedit Volo (or Dee Volo) was close to seventy, but his
age-defying jet-black hair formed a pile on his head like soft-
serve ice cream left over from the 1950s. He was a World War II
veteran, an "American hero" according to the regularly assigned
young prosecutor in that room who strangely emulated Volo's
style and mannerisms. Volo wasn't my hero. In a saga of five jury
trials, he loudly dressed me down in front of the jury and held me
in "contempt" in the presence of the jury in every single case.
The "contempt" charge was a fake—no real hearing, no sanc-
tions, no permanent record, no due process, and no real consequence to my freedom or career. Volo just did it for its theatrical
effect, to bash my credibility with the jury, to bully and distract
me, in order to undermine my client's defense. To Judge Volo,
actual guilt or innocence was not the point; the point was to stop
people from exercising their sacred constitutional rights to try

their cases—because trying cases takes a lot more time than pleading people guilty—and to furiously punish their lawyers. To Volo, the jury trial was worse than the crime. And the system had picked him and his courtroom to teach people like me that lesson.

I remember standing before him, a senior judge, cloaked in his black robe, sitting two and a half feet above me, and feeling his anger rain down on me. When Volo wasn't calling me out for "contempt," he would call me up mid-trial to the side of the bench farthest from the jury and berate me while lightly punching his fist into the judge's bench close to my face. The jury could not see what he was doing, and the trial transcript would never record it unless I was crazy enough to inflame him more by putting it on the record. I wasn't. I would glare through his tirade and mostly keep my mouth shut. But the flailing he delivered daily had its effect. I was exhausted by the end of each day, my suit soaked in sweat, looking at another night of light sleep before the abuse started up again the next morning.

During my second trial before Volo, I was in the hallway outside his courtroom, standing with my back to the courtroom wall. Thurgood Matthews, a tall man ten years into his distinguished career as a Philadelphia public defender, walked up in an open, long wool winter coat with a case file under his arm and fedora worthy of another Thurgood. Thurgood Matthews was unquestionably named for Thurgood Marshall, an earlier graduate of the same great law school Matthews attended, Howard University's School of Law. Marshall was arguably the most important lawyer of the twentieth century before he became the first Black justice on the U.S. Supreme Court. He was still serving on America's highest court the day I met his namesake in the hallway.

Thurgood Matthews cracked open the sash of the giant City Hall window across from me and began smoking a cigarette. I was shy in the face of the local public defender legend and gave him space.

He looked out the window and asked, "Is he in there?"

"Yes."

"What do you have? How long's it going?"

"Oh, a drug case that probably finishes today. Another jury trial. They keep sending me here."

He took another drag and glanced over at me. "They'll do that. I have a shooting trial right after yours. Follow me if you want. I'm going to put that motherfucker in the stroke zone."

Surprised, I looked up from the tile floor. Thurgood inhaled once more, snuffed out the butt, adjusted his long coat, cupped the fedora in one hand around the back of its brim, and used his other hand to yank the courtroom door wide for effect. He went straight in. I quietly opened the door five seconds later, slipped into the courtroom, and stayed in the back.

Thurgood was down front—coat still on—standing and waving and pointing at full height, hollering while Volo stood behind the bench on his platform, shook his cane, and yelled back threats. My eyes were wide as I watched the good fight for another minute. Then Thurgood turned and calmly marched out while Volo ranted and fumed, his face red and his eyes popping. I didn't know exactly what the fight was about—some pre-trial issue that ticked off Matthews. But Thurgood proved that Volo's intimidation game was easy to provoke and nothing to be feared. Unwittingly, Thurgood had taught me to expose this judge's raging unfairness and corrupt power in open court. From a distance, I could see that Volo unhinged wasn't a pretty sight and would actually help me with some fair-minded jurors who perceived his malicious bias. His intimidating tactics didn't seem so insurmountable; I was losing my fear.

It was even harder for jurors than for a young lawyer to be unafraid when they interacted with Volo for the first time. Judge

Volo's initial interaction with a jury was not at the trial, where a newly schooled lawyer like me might expose his claws by becoming its target. It was at jury selection, where Volo would crudely ridicule any potential juror who asserted a reason for not serving on the jury. As usual, truth and justice were not Volo's issue. He bashed members of the jury pool as a deterrent to stop others from shirking or legitimately avoiding jury duty. He made potential jurors afraid to talk about work obligations, family illness, childcare issues, prepaid and planned vacations, and religious objections to serving as a juror. When he attacked one potential juror, many of the others laughed at the ridicule, either as kindred bullies or just to get along before he got to them. But many did not.

I still remember my face burning as Volo cross-examined and berated a middle-aged Asian woman who quietly said her religion did not allow her to sit in judgment. I noticed that some other potential jurors laughed. I immediately imagined my mother, who graduated from Bible college, attended seminary, and was a tent evangelist in the Midwest in the 1940s before she married a secular Jewish man. She would have been out of her seat, telling that judge what she really thought. Like my mom's, the juror's faith was real; she had the details to support it. After Volo humiliated her for minutes, he allowed the Asian woman to be excused from the jury, but smiled when he angrily ordered her to attend the trial and sit in the gallery anyway every day until it was over.

Volo had no right to make the woman, or anyone else, go to his courtroom and watch a trial after being disqualified from jury service. It was servitude; he did it anyway. My jaw muscles tightened, but I said nothing about this patently illegal treatment of a woman of faith, or what was clearly implied by the venom this World War II vet spat at a dignified and principled Asian woman. I reminded myself that she wasn't my client.

There would be other fights during this trial between Volo and
me for my client's benefit that the jury to be formed from this
group of prospective jurors would witness. Fighting Volo now,
and in front of them, would be a mistake. I quickly marked on
my sheet which potential jurors looked upset or uncomfortable
with the judge's rotten conduct. Over the next couple of hours,
I put as many of them on the jury as I could. Fairness seemed
to be in their gut. I had a good case and needed fair people on
this jury.

Eventually, after seeing what happened with Thurgood and
the Asian American woman, and after being in Volo's courtroom
so much, I calmed down enough to figure it out. In any society
there are some bullies and sadists, some people who claim power
to wreck others. But they are not most of us. Bullies offend most
of us. Once I grasped that, I won more than I lost in Volo's room.
The key was to pick the most decent jury I could and expose its
sensible members to Volo's raging malice and his bias against
defendants, defense lawyers, and anyone else who would not be a
conductor on this infernal railroad. Those jurors' own sense of
fairness would rally to even the scales.

There was a case I tried before Volo about a dispute between
two bar patrons over money. They knew each other. The dispute
got spun as a robbery, supposedly between strangers. It seemed
like a decent case for the defense. I picked two lawyers to serve
on the jury, figuring the judge's undue process would offend
them. Picking lawyers for juries is uncommon, often unwise because they sometimes have too much sway over other jurors. I
then printed out copies of case law that supported my position on
legal issues I knew would arise in the trial. I anticipated the judge
would cut off my cross-examination of witnesses or try to cut off
my defense regardless of the law, as he usually did. When the
trial came, Volo cut me off repeatedly, as expected. Each time he
did, I held up copies of the case law and said, "But, Your Honor,
I have case law—" He would cut me off again, refusing to read it

as he erupted, and holding me in fake contempt again as I shot a look at the lawyers in the jury box.

The lawyers looked back, noting the judge's refusal to review my case law, as any fair-minded judge surely would have done, and his baseless claim of contempt. The jury acquitted on all charges within a couple of hours of starting deliberations on a Friday afternoon. Judge Volo was not happy. The foreperson, who read the not-guilty verdicts, turned out to be one of the lawyers.

The next Monday, I was at my desk reading a small article in the *Daily News* that reported Judge Volo had broken his leg in multiple places on the street that weekend. The paper said he had been the victim of some kind of attack by a prostitute. Senior attorneys did a little checking around. Their version was that Volo, walking in his neighborhood as he liked to do, came upon a homeless woman urinating and tried to kick her to oblivion. She moved and he fell badly. His right leg was broken in multiple places; there were no other injuries really.

For the next year, from time to time, I would be in City Hall when I'd see Judge Volo walking the halls, first in a giant cast and then in a brace from foot to upper thigh, stomping along like the mad captain in *Moby-Dick*. The "American hero" was usually trailed by a phalanx of obsequious law clerks and court officers, a deferential half a step behind him on the quarter-mile-long square that was the hallway nearest his courtroom. Perhaps he walked to rehabilitate his leg, or maybe to burn off his vindictive energy.

Not long after, Volo was stripped of his robe and removed from the bench permanently by the federal courts for forcing potential jurors to attend trials where their religious beliefs and other perfectly good reasons would not allow them to sit as jurors. Removal of judges from the bench is very uncommon. The federal courts spoke out about his lawless imposition of servitude on people who neither were compensated (even at juror rates) nor served any purpose in the trials. There would be no more contempts or guilties or not-guilties with Judge Volo. It was a singular distinction for a supposed "American hero."

Judge Volo wasn't unique. He was simply an extreme example of a culture sometimes uninterested in justice or truth in Philadelphia that I encountered regularly as a public defender and private criminal defense attorney early in my career, but that started long before my time. He was on my mind twenty-eight years after my first jury trial before him, when I decided to run. Judge Volo wasn't really the problem. The system was, and he was its distillation. The system had to change, which could only happen if we got to people outside the system and showed them how broken it really was.

After my February 2017 announcement, my first fundraiser was a low-dollar event at a batting cage called Everybody Hits. Its owner sported a 1970s mustache and was married to a young public defender. The event attracted a mostly young and mostly white crowd that drank local beer out of cans, flirted, and talked politics and music. A few nonprofit warriors and grizzled lefty union organizers who I knew slightly from protests or through mutual friends mingled among the crowd. After half an hour of mingling, I stood on the cage's cement floor with a long-wired mic in hand and had a conversation with this slice of the community. Hands went up with questions.

We started with weed. Do you support making recreational use legal? "Yes." A hum of approval and a few chuckles passed through the crowd. Will you prosecute marijuana use? "No. We have better things to do with our resources than punish people who are basically drinking beer at the end of Prohibition." Louder buzz. Some laughter. "And, by the way, the beer you're all drinking tonight is worse for you than cannabis." Louder laughter, this time with grins and some side-glances in the mix. The older labor activists were watching, impassive, but they stayed. Someone asked if the criminal justice system was racist. "Yes." Was it fair? "Not often enough. And especially not for poor people and Black and brown people." Were there too many people in jail? "Yes."

Before leaving, I posed for a picture with a bat over my shoulder that the owner instantly turned into a baseball card. Suit, tie, bat. I kept the card. Millennials with bills and student loans to pay pulled money out of their pockets in a humble batting cage and put together over a thousand dollars. It felt like a good night, and the people in attendance didn't look anything like most people at a traditional political fundraiser.

The primary campaign was dominated by public forums featuring the seven Democratic candidates. Sometimes the lone opposing party candidate joined us even though it was the primary election. The race was wide open. The dominant party's boss was loath to bet on a single horse with so many running and no favorite. The stakes were high at the forums, where we'd make our arguments directly to the public. The first forum was in a so-called business incubator, a giant converted industrial building in a mostly Black part of town across from West Fairmount Park, filled with offices and production facilities for start-ups. On the roof was an urban apiary, where beekeepers produced honey, which they bottled on-site. The bees supported the building's gardens. The forum took place on a wide-open factory floor used for trainings and gatherings. With its pillars, giant joists, and thick, worn wooden floors, the place looked big and beefy enough for a car show. In Silicon Valley, this kind of space would have been full of hyper-educated techies; in Philly, it was diverse and grassroots and wildly varied.

Only one other candidate had equivalent trial experience. The rest had worked in prosecutors' offices or, in one instance, had served as a judge but hadn't tried the hard cases we had been trying for more than thirty years: federal criminal cases, including long trials involving giant conspiracies, death penalty cases, homicides, and everything else. These were the kinds of cases that put you under pressure to stay on point. The experience helped. Aside from giving me some insight into how the justice system in Philly actually worked for real people, thirty years in court- rooms helped me to read people, to think on my feet, to block or dodge a punch, to avoid distraction, to tell a true story, and to stay focused on the people who make the decision and their reac- tions, whether those people are jurors or voters.

Lined up seven-wide in tall chairs, we listened to one another. After brief opening statements by each candidate, we were ques- tioned by the moderators. The other candidates mostly juked the questions to hit their repetitive talking points. Not wanting to give up a sound bite that would alienate any group of voters, they either said nothing or said two opposing things at once. Their evasive answers exemplified why people get so disgusted with say-nothing, forked-tongue politics. When I initially an- nounced my candidacy with the details of my full platform, it wasn't a one-time stunt; it set the tone for my whole campaign. I wasn't going to win by being vague. And politics were so side- ways that I realized I could distinguish myself from the other six just by answering the questions directly. Besides, I was fifty-six and my political ambitions were pretty much this or nothing; I was going to lock in, answer the questions, and win or lose on our platform.

The questions rolled in. I answered them. They were the same questions I was getting almost everywhere I went. Was the criminal justice system racist? "Yes." Were there too many peo- ple in jail? "Yes." Was there a problem with police accountabil- ity? "Yes, a big one." And what were the causes of these problems? That question required a longer answer.

The problem was our broken system—unjust criminal justice institutions, traditional prosecution, and traditional prosecutors. Every other candidate running had been a part of our broken system, whose worst manifestation was the Volos of the world. It would be one thing if the other candidates could prove they had worked to improve the system from within or that they had quit the system because they could no longer bear to work for one that delivered so much injustice. But that's not what happened. None of these candidates had written a memo in 2000 or 2006 or 2012 pushing for positive change in the system. They were content to serve a system that was known for extreme mass incarceration, mass supervision, stepping on the poor, convicting innocent people, not turning over required evidence, and manipulating and lying to victims rather than meeting their needs. As a candidate, you need to own your life's work. My life's work had been pushing against that system, not serving it. How had they done more than serve the life-destroying engine of our broken system?

I said all that at the panel and then shut up. After I got quiet, the other candidates got hot. The panel quickly shifted from seven candidates trying to differentiate themselves from one another to the six of them gunning for me. I was unexpectedly taking a lot of fire, but suppressing a smile. The other candidates' attention focused the audience on me and my platform. I had fully expected them to hit back by embracing conservative criminal justice themes. I expected the lite version of traditional "lock 'em up" law-and-order talk with its emphasis on scaring voters. Instead, one by one they asserted that they were progressive, too, just not a crazy progressive like me. They positioned themselves as more qualified, balanced, and moderate than me because of their prosecutorial experience, while offering few clear positions.

My platform was clear. The other candidates were punching me with the fact that I hadn't been a prosecutor, thinking that would get me out of the way for the real battle among them. But what none of us knew yet was that being a prosecutor, being a cog in this punitive machine, was no longer something a candidate wanted on their résumé. I was as surprised as anyone to see that my public defender history was my advantage. That shift of position and attention turned me and my supposedly extreme views into the other candidates' point of reference. Suddenly, they were all following our platform, timidly going our way.

When the forum was over, people came up to each of us, asking questions and mostly holding back their opinions. It was hard for me to gauge whether my straightforward, combative approach was turning off the public or animating them. An elderly, dark-skinned Black woman approached me, lightly pushing her walker. She was tiny. She tilted her head slightly, peered at me through her glasses, and said, "I noticed something about you. When they asked you a question, you answered it. You were direct. Direct. That's very important. You stay direct and you'll do all right." She looked me in the eye again for just long enough. I thanked her for her kind words and advice before she walked away. I never got her name, but I followed her advice in more than fifty forums over ninety-eight days. I stayed direct.

In my jumbled-up campaign days I found myself one Sunday afternoon at a storefront Baptist church in a neighborhood of row houses in varying levels of disrepair. There were tire shops selling used tires. The parked cars were older models. A couple of people had their cars' hoods up. Inside the church, portable chairs for parishioners were laid out in a few rows. I sat on a well-worn red velvet seat on a high metal stool, facing the audience. The microphone's amplification was punctuated by squeak and feedback. Behind my head hung a large sign that announced in big letters: THE DEVIL CAN'T HAVE MY FAMILY.

No more than twenty seats were occupied, mostly by older Black women wearing big, colorful hats, and their elderly male companions. I took it all in and wasn't sure why I'd been invited to speak. I was the only candidate there. This was not a church that I knew, nor was it connected to any of my friends in Philly's progressive clergy. And these might or might not be my voters. Having tried a lot of cases in Philadelphia, I'd found that older, churchgoing African Americans on a jury can view crime, even minor crimes, harshly. I'd been hired by a lot of them to represent a nephew or a grandchild. Many of them told me they disapproved of weed; of pants worn low; of hip-hop, social media, and overt sexuality; of skipping church. Many had experienced victimization from terrible, tragic crimes in their families. I was wondering how this churchy room might react to me and our pro-decarceration platform, but I was grateful for the invitation to appear solo and wanted to connect.

I began speaking while a few latecomers drifted in. A tall, beautifully dressed older woman who was wearing a yellow hat to match her outfit thanked me for attending and said the congregation had never been addressed in their church by an elected prosecutor or someone running to become one. She then asked me not to be offended by what she had to say next. I held my breath for what came next. "You need to understand that, to me, a prosecutor is like . . . a devil. The prosecutor is the one who takes the neighbor boy when he gets in some little trouble and gives him two years in jail. So he can't get a job. The prosecutor is the one we call for help when police are not treating the children right. And they do nothing. They do nothing. So we are here to listen to what you have to say, but you need to understand that to us a prosecutor is, well, like a devil. So we would like to know how you are different." As she finished her question, I was breathing and smiling. These were my voters, too. I was home. I began my answer.

The church door opened and I saw Russell, an old client, and his wife, Lydia, who had hired me to defend him a few years prior. He was a big, strong, and sunny broad-shouldered man of fifty who had been the on-site manager at a McDonald's for a couple of decades when he was charged with aggravated assault. He'd had no criminal record until he was arrested. He'd believed a security guard had mistreated his wife, lost his cool, and, with one punch, broke the guard's jaw in two places. She came in the church with him, beaming, and kissed my cheek.

He was facing three or four years in jail when I represented him. We tried the case to a jury, and got a not-guilty verdict on the main charge of aggravated assault, which carried a couple years in prison. He was found guilty of the lower, misdemeanor charge of simple assault and spent four months in jail, including some time served in jail earlier, right after his arrest. Lydia visited him every week. He got out and got his job back. His life was interrupted, not destroyed. He was smiling when he walked in and said, "We're so glad the pastor invited you. We asked him to do it; this is our church."

Small and large gatherings continued, often several in a day. Surrogates filled time when I was late or when my schedule was too full to allow me to attend a smaller event. My campaign manager, Mike Lee, told a story for the grassroots activist, organizer, and millennial crowd that he polished over time:

> So my wife is pregnant and we're expecting our first child. When I'm home, which is more now, I watch a lot of Animal Planet, which I probably would have done anyway, even if she wasn't pregnant. I love Animal Planet. I saw this show about penguins in the Arctic that I think says something about why we are all here.

At this point some of the listeners usually got quiet and began to fold their arms and squint, unsure whether Mike's naïve affect and deadpan delivery meant a joke was coming or Mike was the next generation's Mr. Rogers:

> So penguins gotta eat. They're social. And they tend to gather together on an ice floe, surrounded by dark, threatening ocean. But they gotta eat. So usually one of them goes to the edge of the ice floe, looks in the water, and senses danger, which is true: orcas, polar bears, sharks swimming around just waiting for their own meals. Mmm . . . a tasty penguin. But the pen-

guin's hungry, too. Hungry for fish. The penguin's thinking
about it. The danger and the fish. Finally, he jumps in the dark
water. He's gotta get that fish. And, when he does, a little later
one by one at first and then all at the same time, the other pen-
guins jump in, too. Splash, into the water. Now they're in the
water, looking around at each other and looking for fish.
There's still danger, but there's less danger because they're all
together. And they're filling their bellies with fish.

Now, to me, that's a lot like this campaign. Larry's that first
penguin. He had something to lose, but he jumped in. We
watched and then jumped in, too. Except in our case, we
weren't hungry for fish. We were hungry for justice.

The laughter usually started in earnest around "Larry's that
first penguin" and filled the room around "hungry for justice." It
was a break we all needed from Philly's traditional politics.

Philadelphia is a ward politics city, or used to be. Each neighborhood has one ward leader for each major party, whose job is to
get out the vote through the assistance of the ward's committee
people. The committee people and ward leaders who are closest
to their communities solve problems for the wards' residents—
they ask the city to fill potholes in the neighborhood or sort out
local homeowners' and businesses' entanglements with the byz-
antine details of local government.

Ward leaders are unpaid by their party, in theory, although
some of them find legitimate ways to make a little money before
and on election day by getting out the vote. And the slippery
ones find less legitimate ways to make even better money by
lying to candidates, taking their money in exchange for the
promise of working all day to pass out their literature and persuade voters to vote for them, only to double-cross them on
election day and persuade voters to vote for someone else, with
different literature in hand.

On election day, the city's few thousand polling places see

streams of voters. The ward leaders' committee people stand outside the polling places and give out palm cards with high-lighting, bright colors, and short lists that tell the voters—their neighbors—which candidates the ward deems worthy. They also chat up voters as they go in to vote. The power of the chat is no joke among undecided or underinformed voters, especially when the committee member may have helped that voter with a problem that required some assistance from a representative, or when their kids attended school together or played together in Little League. Even though this kind of street politics in Philly is aging and evolving, committee people still matter. And for a candidate, courting ward leaders and committee people matters, too.

Halfway through the campaign, maybe forty days in, I found myself in a dimly lit bar in West Philadelphia around sundown. This was a ward event. Candidates were there to meet the local ward leader and his committee people at an open bar. Old-school 1970s and '80s music was blasting—the Temptations, James Brown, the Commodores, the Ohio Players, Kool and the Gang—while we candidates awkwardly made the rounds, introducing ourselves to the people in the room. The bar was serving mostly tallboy beers, shots, and malt liquor.

Four or five older Black women were sitting on a wide win-dowsill. I walked over and introduced myself. I had to say my name a few times as I tried to be heard over the music. One said, "Krasner? You're Krasner?" She looked over to her friend. "Who's that guy? Who's the civil rights guy? Are you the civil rights guy?" I said, "Yes, I've done civil rights work and criminal de-fense work for thirty years." The women looked at each other. One asked the other for an ink pen, got it, and circled my name on her printed list of candidates. She told the woman at the far end of the windowsill: "He's the civil rights guy." They ex-changed a look and nodded to one another. I thanked them and walked away. It sounded good.

All the candidates got their few minutes with the microphone. Two or three of them hit me for not having been a prosecutor. When they did, my campaign strategist Brandon Evans watched a woman open her purse, pull out a 3 × 5 card, and apparently write down my name. By her side, others were writing something on their candidates' lists at the same time. Much later, Brandon told me that was the moment when he realized we just might win, even though our traction was uncertain. We were doing okay in the wards, among people who followed and participated in local politics. But what about the unlikely voters, and not just the activists I knew? What about the political outsiders who hadn't marched and protested but who might come out to vote if they were excited?

Using a combination of old-school political craft like door-to-door canvassing and new-school tactics like mass texting and social media–based campaigning, which are particularly effective with young and Black voters, my activist friends were proving they did politics better than politicians. Doors opened for our canvassers. People responded to our texts. Our message was welcome, and we could feel it resonating. We were close, three weeks out. A supportive union, the carpenters, conducted a poll that had us basically tied for first, with a margin of error that meant we were first or second. It was our first poll of the campaign. The other leading candidate in the race had big support from centrist politicians, had raised a lot more money, and had announced his campaign several months before we did. But the poll said we were even with him. Our campaign was no longer "hilarious." The message was spreading.

With just six weeks to go, other candidates focused on paid media. Two well-funded contenders produced TV commercials attacking each other. It's likely their political operatives had written and produced the commercials weeks prior, when our campaign was not viewed as the threat it became. It's also likely that both candidates wanted to believe their money would turn into votes. Money was among their strengths, so they believed in it. One of them had spent $1.2 million of his own money on his campaign, while our campaign had raised a few hundred thousand dollars from several hundred donors. We couldn't afford television commercials. We watched the ads on television. I was intimidated by the other candidates' ability to pay for TV advertising and amused by the fact that, as the two candidates punched each other, they left us alone. They were hurting each other, but helping our campaign.

With twenty-one days to go, our campaign started getting support from outside groups. It helped. I hated the corrupting role money played in politics, but I had no way as a voice for broke people seeking local office to raise much money myself in a broke big city, especially with my platform. In a political game that too often works better for money and power than it does for marginalized people, outside money can level the playing field—at least until we change the troubled rules of the game.

In Pennsylvania, in 2017, the law allowed people or groups that were not coordinating their efforts with a campaign to spend whatever they wanted on attacking or supporting it. A political action committee called the Safety and Justice PAC, funded at least in part by liberal billionaire George Soros, decided to support my campaign. I didn't know it was happening. The PAC had already supported several other progressive candidates for chief prosecutor in other jurisdictions. Mailings, radio ads, and television ads were imagined, written, and produced without my knowledge or input from me or anyone else in my campaign. The PAC bought airtime without our knowing it. Members of the PAC were so meticulous about avoiding even the appearance of coordination between my campaign and their activity that their mailings supporting my campaign went to other houses on my block, but not to mine. My next-door neighbor was the first person to tell me there was a mailing. It was the first time I knew support would come at all, much less what it would say.

The first time I saw the mailing, I thought I was doomed. It focused on my work defending Occupy and Black Lives Matter activists. I was proud of that record. But wasn't my message radical enough already? Wasn't this a step too far, when polling showed we were so close? The answer was no. After the ads started, for the first time I found that people I had never met knew me before I entered the door for public forums. Some talked to me about our platform even before I spoke about it. Strangers wanted selfies before the event. Our message had already resonated. But the media ads and mailings were amplifying a solid message across the city. Momentum was building.

It was April 30, 2017, two weeks before the primary election. I was suited up and walking in the bright midafternoon sun to the front door of the district attorney's office, a place that looks directly at City Hall. I was by myself, walking toward the power that was waiting outside the office's doors. I didn't understand how much the power was going to help me, because the power was itself different.

Retired city council member Marian Tasco, at close to eighty years of age, was the power. Born in 1937 in the South, she taught school as a young woman but gravitated toward politics. She was a born political phenomenon from her early years for her command of the political army that first swept Black political power into office in Philadelphia, culminating in the election of Philly's first Black mayor, Wilson Goode, Sr., in 1984. Four years later, in 1988, Tasco was elected to the city council for the first of eight consecutive terms. She chose to retire in early 2016 and turn the city council seat—and, at least nominally, the ward— over to Cherelle Parker, a mentee she had embraced as a teen, ever since spotting Parker's fiery eloquence during a high school oratory contest.

Marian Tasco is a diminutive, charming, affable woman known for her lifelong love of dancing the night away and lack of interest in candidates' connections. But she was mostly known for the power of her political influence, usually wielded to help vulnerable people, and mightily exercised as the ward leader of "the Mighty 50th Ward," which under her command became the city's biggest single vote-generating ward. Marian and her 50th Ward were also the persuasive leaders of a coalition of several of the highest-turnout wards in the diverse, liberal Northwest section of the city.

The sidewalk outside the Philadelphia District Attorney's Office on a sunny afternoon was Tasco's deliberately provocative choice for a press conference, her polite way of telling everyone exactly how things were going to be.

One after another, nearly every prominent elected Black and brown woman politician in the area came to the stage in brightly colored suits, many in heels. They were dressed in pink, yellow, white, teal, baby blue—like a flower garden in full bloom the day before May first—a bold contrast to the male politicians who were staying noncommittal in their suits of navy and gray. The women, and the message they were about to send, were hard to miss, which I'm sure is exactly what Tasco planned.

As the women spoke, briefly and forcefully, one by one, their reasons became clear. Two had been schoolteachers. Many were mothers. All of these elected officials had answered the late-night calls of their troubled constituents when tragedy struck their families from both ends of a gun. They knew where the people's money belonged—in prevention, meaning education mostly, but also in treatment and economic development that could beat back poverty. Increasingly, public resources had been hijacked to pay for jail cells, and they wanted it back. They wanted to lock up people who did vicious things, but even then they wanted the process to be accurate and to be fair. They had lived the reality of criminal injustice and racial injustice, had seen it in their homes,

their families, their classrooms, and the lives of their constituents and sororities and places of worship. They wanted change
and had decided to use their power now rather than hold back in
an uncertain election for district attorney, where most of the
male politicians were unaffiliated.

My task was to say little during the sunny sidewalk press conference, which I achieved, as one powerful woman after another
endorsed our campaign, lauded our dedication to fairness, and
commended our platform with superlatives as proof of why Philadelphians should vote for me. In Philly politics, this was nuclear
power. Not only was the Mighty 50th and its coalition of wards
on board, but a big and influential swath of Black sorority power,
church power, and community power was there, planting its
brightly colored flag at the very door of the district attorney's
office.

I didn't see what was happening behind me, but was later told
that several DAO employees had trickled out the front door and
stepped into the press conference, not realizing what awaited
them. Most of them hurried off as they exited. A few smiled and
stayed.

A few days before the May 16, 2017, primary election, I was
standing in the dark outside the entrance to the First Unitarian
Church on Chestnut Street near Twenty-first, a liberal church
that has a rich history in an affluent, mostly white part of town.
There were Black Lives Matter banners hanging on the church's
Victorian Gothic gates, facing the sidewalk.

The church was designed in the late 1800s by Philadelphia's pre-
eminent Victorian Gothic architect, Frank Furness. Frank was
a wild man, a Civil War hero for the Union whose uniform was
pierced in battle by three different bullets that somehow never
wounded him. Like his personality, his brilliant architecture was a
jumble of tension, strength, and variability. He disassembled and
reassembled old motifs in ways that pointed toward movements in
design yet to come: form follows function, Louis Kahn, skyscrapers.

In the late 1800s, Furness designed six hundred buildings, mostly in Philadelphia, many of which have since been destroyed. He designed this Unitarian church for his father, William Henry Furness, a famous and prominent minister. Frank carved into the church's stone front several images of a flower turning toward the sun, each in a different position, as if turning its stone petals to follow the sun's actual motion along the axis of Chestnut Street over the course of a day. His father deserved statuary.

Frank Furness's father, the Unitarian minister William Henry Furness, was a friend of Ralph Waldo Emerson. A prominent theologian, William Furness wrote books about Jesus that rejected the notion of miracles, including the notion of a miraculous birth. But Reverend Furness is best remembered as a strident reformer and committed abolitionist. During his life, William Furness's opposition to the Fugitive Slave Act resulted in President James Buchanan discussing indicting him for treason at a cabinet meeting. Abolitionist senator Charles Sumner recovered in William Furness's home after suffering a severe beating by South Carolina congressman Preston Brooks for his abolitionism. And William Furness was a featured speaker at a public gathering of Philadelphians on the date and time of John Brown's hanging for Brown's assault on Harpers Ferry, where two of John Brown's sons died trying to capture weapons that they hoped would supply a slave revolt. The crowd that day was divided between white racists from Philadelphia and elsewhere and Philadelphians—many Black—who sympathized with Brown. The event was a near riot and an unlikely triumph for Philadelphia police, who managed to keep the peace.

In more recent times, the Center City Unitarian church had become a genteel, progressive, and somewhat diverse congregation known for its activist events and for allowing large, alcohol-free and therefore all-age punk and rock concerts to take place on a full stage in a basement so cavernous it accommodates several hundred people.

I loved the church, but it was punk that brought me there that night, so close to the election. The band Sheer Mag, which had just grabbed a four-star review in *Rolling Stone* for its debut album, had invited me to come and speak at their show, as long as I also performed a Clash song of my choosing. I chose "Clampdown" a week earlier so they had time to rehearse.

The Clash were in my musical pantheon, and "Clampdown" was my favorite, with its persistent refrain of "I'm not working for the clampdown / No man born with a living soul / Can be working for the clampdown." It's a scorching, defiant refusal to collaborate with an oppressive government that brings the "clampdown" on people regardless of the consequences: "The judge said five-to-ten, but I said double that again / I'm not working for the clampdown." Or at least that's what I thought it was about in college. I caught its spirit, but the song's English references were lost on me. I later found out it was about the programming of English youth into factory workers who are forced to wear "blue and brown" to work. I assumed "blue and brown" somehow referred to "brownshirt." Close enough.

Standing in the dark outside the Furness church, I looked west and mused that from where I stood I could almost see the University of Pennsylvania's Class of 1923 Ice Rink. Sometime in the early 1980s, I saw the Clash play live there, maybe ten blocks west and a block south on Walnut Street. The underappreciated opening act that night was the great Peter Tosh, who was murdered not too long after, nasally intoning "Legalize It." He was a good choice to open for the Clash, who followed with their sometimes reggae-influenced punk. They came onstage in an ice rink wearing white workmen's overalls for a few thousand wildly appreciative fans who enthusiastically confirmed that they were the only band that mattered.

Sheer Mag let me onstage early to speak to the sold-out crowd of six hundred or so standing, mostly white hipsters, as a decoy for what would come later. If the crowd thought I came to speak, they wouldn't expect me to come onstage later and sing. When I took the stage to talk, the crowd was friendly and loud in greeting me, so I took a chance and told them to be quiet or I'd lock them up. They laughed. I spoke for two minutes about mass incarceration, interspersing without attribution a few snatched lyrics from "Clampdown" into my argument that they should vote in a few days for our campaign. A few young Clash lovers smiled broadly when they recognized the lyrics. Most listened, but didn't catch the references to an earlier generation's music. Others were just talking and waiting for me to get off the stage so they could hear the band. Sheer Mag was great, and so deafening that I ran outside as soon as they started playing, in hopes of preserving my hearing enough to be able to sing (more like yell) when I returned to do "Clampdown."

Temporarily protecting my ears didn't help much. When I finally went back onstage, I couldn't really hear above the crushing volume of Sheer Mag and the roar of the surprised crowd. Tina Halladay, the lead singer, and I stared down toward the edge of the stage, both of us reading the handwritten lyrics scrawled in block letters on a sheet of paper taped to a massive speaker. She had just learned the lyrics that I had forgotten long ago. I hollered away, but because the event was being livestreamed, I deliberately stopped singing when we hit the lyric "Kick over the wall, 'cause government's to fall / How can you refuse it?" I was, after all, asking people to vote for our campaign so we could take over government from the inside, not literally make it fall. I didn't think I needed that sound bite right before election day, even though I could have explained it as a metaphor for government being taken over democratically by the people in an election.

Four days before the only election day that mattered in Philadelphia in 2017, I was embracing just a little caution about what I said and did, even if only in the middle of performing a song that none of the other candidates would have dared sing or yell, written by a band they didn't love and performed by another band that hadn't invited them to perform it anyway. My caution about delivering those lyrics felt awkward, like a slight retreat from the campaign's spirit.

"Clampdown" is a song about rejecting imposed uniformity. It's about knocking down a system that should fall because it crushes people who are different, a system that lived in American courthouses through people like Dee Volo. That kind of government should fall, and no one born with a living soul should work for it. But in my travels through the city—from the churches to the hipster hangouts to the ward events to the steps of the DA's office flanked and lifted up by elected women who knew that even within government they were different, I'd seen that people who are different have all the power they need when they align.

I'd seen that government can do something other than clamp down. It has the potential to do the will of so many different and aligned people. If government couldn't be changed by outsiders using the tools of democracy, if an election couldn't destroy the clampdown, then maybe revolution was our only option. But I had seen a path to something else—a fulfillment of the idea that different kinds of aligned and mutually supportive good people were everywhere, just like the members of a Philly jury, and the ones who wanted something better could build their own government that would fight for justice. They could build government, not just tear it down. Without necessarily knowing one another, these "different" people in their splintered groups were already together on criminal justice reform. And in the most unlikely, often seemingly powerless corners of the city, we just kept finding them.

# CHAPTER 13

# Protest Clampdown

*You have the right to free speech*
*As long as you're not dumb enough to actually try it*
 —The Clash, "Know Your Rights"

Power does what it wants, but it doesn't always win. It's not always easy to see this. When I was a kid, I watched on television as Chicago law enforcement officers abused their power during the 1968 Democratic National Convention. Police were rioting against peaceful protesters. Anti-war demonstrators were met with violence and hundreds of bogus arrests, all organized and supported by the city's authoritarian mayor, Richard Daley. The lesson for the nation was clear: No matter how illegitimate power is—even when it undermines the law and the Constitution—it can't be stopped. Power does what it wants.

But over the years I started to wonder: What if "power does what it wants" is the chorus that power wanted people like me to sing? Maybe power does what it wants because we believe—and accept—that it can. And what if unrestrained power sets loose its own destruction by animating and radicalizing good, ordinary people to stand against it on the streets, in jury boxes, in voting booths, and then inside the institutions that hold that power? Could all those people attacked and arrested for speaking up be hardened into a new force that takes power back for the people? I know of at least 420 people who can answer that question. Philadelphia has its own legacy of unchecked power being abused at a national political convention.

It was a hot night in late July 2000. Philadelphia was hosting the Republican National Convention, which was on track to nominate George W. Bush for president of the United States in several days. I was thirty-nine, and our two boys were nine and seven. Lisa was preparing for her second run for judge after her impressive near win the year before. If anyone had told me then that in seventeen years I'd be running for district attorney, I would have laughed. If anyone had told me how consequential that year's Republican convention would end up being, I would have cried.

In the end, Bush won the election even though Al Gore took the popular vote. Bush became president through the electoral college and the help of the U.S. Supreme Court, in a partisan decision that has besmirched the reputation of the court ever since. And then in quick succession the president most voters did not choose faced the shock of 9/11 and left us with the ill-considered Iraq War, the barely vetted Patriot Act, a very conservative Supreme Court justice, and the seemingly endless so-called war on terror that survive his presidency even as I write. The country has never been the same.

But that was all still ahead of us. That night in July 2000, I was walking up a hilly, tree-lined street, parked up with older cars, balancing a case of local Stoudts beer on my shoulder. I was headed for Not a Squat, also known as Not Squat and Knot Squat, a group residence for activists and lefties, to share some beer with my people. I had selected the beer with care, in part because it had American flags on the box and was local—from Adamstown, Pennsylvania. Juries liked that kind of thing. If law enforcement was taking surveillance pictures for some cooked-up trial, I would give them some good photos of me carrying a flag-covered box of a quality local Pennsylvania brew. Let them put that in evidence for a Philly jury to see during a trial.

In 2000, which many called Y2K, the Republican Party held its convention in Philadelphia, then and now an overwhelmingly Democratic city. They called it the Republican National Convention (RNC); my people called it R2K.

City government wanted to bring in the locally deeply unpopular Republicans but was worried about what the world would think of their city if it was roiling in demonstrations. Actual freedom of speech in the cradle of freedom might repel tourists, especially the ones coming for the convention. For months, efforts by activists to obtain permits for public speech had been thwarted by city government, which unconscionably agreed to give Republicans and the RNC first dibs on the use of all public space. The ACLU was litigating. Protesters of many stripes were frustrated by the city's one-sided restrictions, but they eventually settled for a miles-long march down Broad Street under a scalding, midday July sun as their best opportunity to be heard, at least until they collapsed or quit from heat exhaustion. Neither the city nor the RNC appeared worried that protesters would fail to complete their march.

Three days before the convention and before any protests, a city official whose job description included protecting civil rights said he heard a municipal judge—and former Philly police officer—tell a university classroom that there was a plan to detain protesters until the convention was over. Judges aren't allowed to do that. Judges are supposed to be impartial and separate from law enforcement. They can't make plans with law enforcement, especially not plans for a preemptive strike to keep people from exercising their sacred free speech rights.

The First Amendment to the U.S. Constitution strictly protects free speech from preemptive suppression because the loss of that illegally suppressed speech can never be restored. When speech is allowed, speakers can be held accountable for anything illegal they might do after the fact. When the city official overheard the judge's comments, he was so alarmed that he talked about it. His words made their way to members of the press, who should have been outraged at a possible governmental plot against free speech. Instead, they were only mildly interested. Even with the judge's gaffe, the police were giving off signs that they planned a crackdown on free speech. The police commissioner at the time, John Timoney, promised "fisticuffs" for protesters. The mayor called protesters "idiots." District Attorney Lynne Abraham promised harsh prosecution.

Protesters had spent a month painting signs, building papier-mâché creatures, and constructing parade floats, storing them in a giant warehouse that belonged to a sympathetic union carpenter, in preparation for the march and other events. There was a float built on a flatbed truck of a boxing ring where protesters playing Gore and Bush would mud-wrestle. There was an "Elephonkey"—a Republican elephant copulating with a Democratic donkey—to show the collusion between the parties. Anti–death penalty protesters mounted scores of six-foot-tall white cardboard skeletons on poles to represent the people executed in Governor George W. Bush's Texas at the unprecedented rate of around one execution every nine days. The Kensington Welfare Rights Union was piling up banners and signs about poverty and homelessness. A protest troupe who dressed as the wealthy elite were painting and stacking tongue-in-cheek pro-Bush signs and preparing their Gatsby-era costumes—including tuxedos, fake furs, and long gloves for holding long, circa-1920s cigarette holders in one hand and BILLIONAIRES FOR BUSH signs in the other. Environmental protesters built and painted floats and signs against global warming. Other protesters opposed globalization, police abuse, racism. They all had reason to be hopeful that they would be heard in what was expected to be a close presidential election, and reason to be concerned that they would not.

I got consistent reports from different people that there had been surveillance by local and federal law enforcement on and off all week at the various groups' houses in the area, as well as at a couple of social justice nonprofits in the city. Everyone was planning to protest, but what would be the response? One collective house, Fancy House, at Fiftieth and Christian, reported a sighting of beefy white guys with short hair knocking on their door, vaguely claiming to be city inspectors. Spiral Q Puppet Theater, an arts collective dedicated to doing art for "pageantry" (meaning marches, parades, and protests, usually) was raided by Philadelphia police. Nothing criminal was found, of course, but the raid was unjustified and intimidating.

Not a Squat was at the epicenter of activist group lodging in Philadelphia, in the 4800 block of Baltimore Avenue. It was Philly's best-known activist group home at the time, including to law enforcement, who were obsessed with the crimes they imagined were occurring inside. In truth, the people of Not a Squat were mostly interested in peaceful action to promote good causes, free speech, punk music, and vegan food while they lived their own way, partly off the grid. They shared the neighborhood with other group houses of a more or less political nature. Some had been around since the late 1960s. Fancy House, at Fiftieth and Christian, was a sixteen-bedroom reconfigured funeral home, complete with a coffin lift, only two blocks from Not a Squat. Sebulba, Killtime, and Stalag 13 were other group houses and warehouses that served as occasional underground punk music venues and gathering places of the West Philly activist community.

The occupants of these group houses varied, but there were some modes of dress in common. Many wore heavy Carhartt work pants—the ones held together by rivets, with two thick layers of canvas over the knees. Carhartts were ideal for living in a poorly heated warehouse or doing heavy construction (or for their original use—working in coal mines and the kind of factories that don't exist in the Northeast anymore). Black was a favorite color in West Philly. Bicycles put together from cannibalized, worn parts were the primary form of travel. Bike transport meant carrying locks, sometimes a thick chain wrapped twice around the rider's waist, or a mini-U lock that fit in a pants pocket. Carabiners linked water bottles to backpacks that were covered in cloth patches and stickers that said things like THERE'S NO GOVERNMENT LIKE NO GOVERNMENT or BREAK THE SYSTEM or FUGAZI. It was a practical, post-apocalyptic look.

That July was not my first time visiting Not a Squat. In fact, my business card was stuck on the inside wall by the front door in case anyone needed a lawyer to repel one of law enforcement's occasional paranoid investigations. Some of the Notsquatters I had represented more than five times; a few I didn't know. I wanted to see them on the eve of all the trouble we sensed the city would bring to peaceful protest. We gathered in the way that friends and neighbors gather on reports of a coming hurricane. I brought the case of beer to share.

I counted many of the occupants of the group houses as my people. I was drawn to them and their often remarkable work, but their lives differed from mine. I was a married homeowner with kids and a professional degree who agitated as an outsider working within the system. My getting arrested by protesting with them made no sense, especially since I knew they were better served by my lawyering than by my arrest. In turn, they respected my idealism and appreciated my support. They were well-intentioned skeptics who viewed society with a critical eye from outside the system and chose to live differently and plot positive change on its margins, at whatever cost to their own freedom or future. I fondly rejected the idea of being one of them. They were, in aggregate, a group of practical-minded dreamers who offered me a tantalizing sense that fundamental change was possible—but they also offered cautionary tales about dreams deferred. Some of them have gone on to truly change the world. Others in their orbit changed nothing and fell apart.

Kathy Change was one of the activist community's presiding spirits—one I never met and one who fell apart. Born Kathleen Chang in 1950, she had gone through two suicide attempts, two universities, and one marriage by the time she landed in Philadelphia at thirty-one years of age. She was an actress, performance artist, and activist, the daughter of Chinese intellectuals who had emigrated to escape Mao. She lived in one of Philly's Powelton Village–area group homes in the early eighties and became well known for dancing and performing with colorful political flags on the Penn campus and doing a weekly performance in front of the giant sand-colored pillars at the top of the Philadelphia Museum of Art steps. She cartwheeled with spinning bright flags that were visible for hundreds of yards from the various scenic roadways and pedestrian sidewalks that surround the art museum's entrance. The acrobatic visuals were a common, cheerful, and mysterious riddle in my peripheral vision from a moving car when I happened to drive by alone or with my family during the baby-seat years. I only remember seeing them on sunny days, usually on weekends.

In 1996, Change hoped to start a non-violent social transformation (she founded her own "Transformation Party") in which workers would democratically take control of their places of employment. In letters she wrote to explain what she did next, she said she had concluded that the media would cover only violence, but she was unwilling to use violence against any other creature just to draw attention to her transformative ideas. So instead of harming another creature, that October she went to one of her usual performance spots on the University of Pennsylvania campus, doused herself in gasoline, and self-immolated while dancing and performing. A campus police officer used his jacket to wrestle her to the ground and extinguish flames that only relit. She died within twenty minutes. Despite her sacrifice, her Transformation Party never happened. Kathy Change's smoky angel is still looking down from the three-story heights of the group houses of West Philly when she isn't spinning flags, a sort of patron saint of sacrifice and protest. But whatever she hoped to accomplish by dying didn't get done.

Others got things done. Most of my West Philly people were extremely effective, despite first impressions. Paul Davis was one of them. Paul was inside Not a Squat that night in July 2000, and he was edgy. I'd represented him a dozen times in a decade, as a leader in ACT UP. He was wily and enigmatic.

My connection to his world as an AIDS activist and multitalented agitator started in the early nineties. When I first met Paul and his partner at the time, Julie Davids—who, like Paul, went on to do historic work around AIDS on her own—they had a fondness for black clothing, accessorized with dog collars. Paul's adventurous life since then has included years of pushing world AIDS policy in ways that worked. He has met with Kofi Annan. He has lived and been robbed by a machete blow to the head in Kenya, where his girlfriend, an infectious disease doctor, worked in the Kibera slum, and they moved AIDS policy in Africa. But his and his colleagues' greatest achievements started around then, the year of R2K, when they undertook saving millions of African lives and refined the art of bird-dogging.

Bird-dogging is the art of forcing candidates for elected office to face your issue at nearly every campaign stop, until they have no choice but to give you what you want. Paul's issue was to obtain generic AIDS drugs for Africa. He knew the disease would keep raging throughout the continent and the world unless the meds—which were completely unaffordable for Africans—became generic. He also knew that Africans were being protected even less than people from elsewhere by the world leaders whose countries had the resources to help. Neither presidential candidate supported the idea when their campaigns began, due to a combination of Big Pharma's big lobbying, as well as unspoken homophobia, racism, and generalized fear of the disease within the electorate. I knew Paul and ACT UP and his crew were brilliant, but even I underestimated what they could achieve through protest, information gathering, well-timed warnings, and just by persistently asking candidates difficult questions.

Paul got into campaign events almost whenever he wanted by being seriously inscrutable, showing up early, signing in, and tucking his ponytail into the collar of a white shirt. He wasn't one to give away all his tactics, but these were the ones I knew. His team was made up of old white ladies wearing Totes hats and young clean-cut College Republican–looking types, or apparent Bill Clinton wannabes—innocuous and virtually invisible people in a crowd. Their moment would come in the Q and A. Or, if there was no Q and A, they would create the moment: They'd find just the right time, stand up, and loudly but politely demand the candidate answer whether or not they supported generic AIDS drugs for Africa. They'd sprinkle in some press-worthy facts for assembled local journalists. The bird-doggers blended into the crowds at stop after stop in every state, all over the country. They were invisible until it was too late. They did politics better than politicians. They knew how to win without resources.

On one of his missions, Paul ended up onstage with a banner stuffed into a future journalist's clothing. He was within a few yards of the candidate and flanked by party officials who never questioned his presence. Mid-event, Paul and the future journalist unfurled the banner, which urged generic AIDS drugs for Africa, while other bird-doggers chanted in support. As with all good modern activism, the banner drop was complete when the unfurled banner's words were in the photograph that appeared in newspapers around the country the next day.

Paul and his crew kept on it and honed their bird-dogging

over a few years until they got most of what they wanted. It used to cost $10,000 per year to treat an HIV/AIDS patient in Africa. It now costs less than $100. An unknowably large number of African lives and other lives around the world have been saved. I've heard it's 26 million. Regardless, activists made it happen. Paul's outsiders, who had no money and no connections, took on both American political parties and forced them to support their cause by being more organized and communicating better than politicians could.

The day after I visited Not a Squat, phalanxes of Philadelphia police in riot gear arrived at the puppet-making warehouse. Helicopters circled overhead. Scores of mostly young people inside the warehouse locked the doors and engaged in a tense but peaceful standoff. Outside the giant warehouse the mood was both post-apocalyptic and festive as militarized law enforcement and the occasional activist engaged. From the street, a protester in clown garb loudly implored police who were walking on the giant warehouse's roof in SWAT gear: "Don't do it! Don't jump! You have so much to live for!"

Eventually, after some unsuccessful mediation by lawyers from the public defender's office and others, approximately seventy-five people were pulled from the warehouse, arrested, and loaded into prison buses that heated up like ovens in the July sun. The people were left baking in the buses for hours. Their backpacks and belongings were taken from them by law enforcement, searched, and discarded on-site. And their months of work—signs, banners, parade floats, and the Elephonkey—were broken up and discarded into city garbage trucks that pulled up on cue.

The city had a warrant for the raid, authorized by DA Lynne Abraham, whose antipathy for ACT UP, and nearly all other protesters, and their dramatic tactics was well known. But the warrant was signed by a young prosecutor named Dick Rubio, who would go on to become the city's managing director, work for a company that sold food to prisons, and then one day run against me and others for district attorney himself. In 2000, Rubio privately bragged that he signed the warrant because he was "a good American." In 2017, when we ran against each other for district attorney, he didn't brag about it. He would claim that he'd signed the warrant only because he was junior in the office and had no choice. Philadelphia activists hadn't forgotten. They effectively bird-dogged him on the issue at several events during our campaign. He started as a perceived frontrunner. His shot at becoming district attorney gradually slipped away.

Immediately after the puppet warehouse raid in 2000, an uncritical press provided misleading reports that the warehouse contained explosives and materials suitable for arson. These turned out to be nothing more than varnish, paint thinner, and other tools of the carpenter's trade. The press reported that city inspectors had determined the warehouse was a firetrap unsafe for the people who were arrested. City inspectors had shown no interest in the building for years prior. It was the kind of grimy, selective-enforcement tactic that the city had used for decades to carry out nefarious schemes—and the pro-law-enforcement press simply reported law enforcement's sneakiest claims as truth.

Finally, as further proof of the protesters' alleged criminality, the press reported that the warehouse contained lockdown devices. Part of that claim was actually true. There were lockdown devices, but their possession wasn't a crime. These homemade devices consisted of short lengths of white plastic PVC plumbing pipe just large enough to slip over the hands of two people, plus some other fittings like nuts, bolts, and carabiners that made it difficult for police to force two people's hands apart. Nonviolently locking down or locking on (to a fence or to another person) has been a staple of peaceful protest since before the suffragettes used it successfully in their efforts to gain the right to vote for women. It non-violently slows down arrests long enough for protesters to speak and be heard.

Between the earlier surveillance and the raids on Spiral Q and the puppet warehouse, we knew that the hurricane we'd expected had arrived. The judge's cryptic mention of a plan to detain people in order to silence their message during the most sacred of American democratic institutions—a presidential election—was real, and there was more coming.

I was in my office wrestling with a legal filing deadline when I got a call. The caller identified herself, said she was part of the R2K protest coalition, and asked me to drop everything and go to a police station to legally advise someone named John Sellers, from the West Coast. I didn't know John, but quickly found out he was part of the leadership of the Ruckus Society, an organization that teaches non-violent direct action to achieve social change. The caller said John had been involved in the Battle of Seattle, a famous protester-led shutdown of a meeting of the World Trade Organization the year before. The person on the phone told me John hadn't done anything illegal; he hadn't even been protesting when he was picked up. I missed my filing deadline for the moment because my gut said seeing John was more important.

John was sitting in a room in a police station, studying me and offering me a broad smile. Local police and FBI had already tried to question him without a lawyer present. My first thought when I saw him was that he looked like an Amish farmer, with his pale skin, broad shoulders, and intense blue eyes.

"What's your name? You're a lawyer?"

"Yes."

"Yeah? That's great. Well, show me some ID. Where's your business card? Because, so far, all I'm seeing are FBI agents and Philly cops, and now you say you're a lawyer." His broad smile was getting wider. I showed him my ID, but I hadn't grabbed business cards when I ran out to see him. He looked at the carabiner I used to hold my keys and smiled again. John knew carabiners. Among other adventures, like chasing Japanese whaling ships with Greenpeace, John had climbed skyscrapers, bridges, and giant construction cranes in Chicago, San Francisco, and Texas with his people to drop enormous protest banners about protecting the rain forest or ending deforestation or otherwise saving the planet. His colleagues included tree-sitters—people who climbed into the tops of sky-high old-growth redwoods and sequoias and set up temporary homes there in order to prevent loggers from cutting down the trees. Sometimes they lived up there for more than a year. Sometimes they got hurt or killed. I later learned that when he saw the carabiner on me, his suspicion grew that I was law enforcement posing as a lawyer and trying to get him talking with my keys on a piece of climbing gear. A busy, out-of-shape dad at thirty-nine, I didn't look like much of a climber.

"So, carabiner, huh? You climb?"

"Not really. I mean, I did a few years ago."

"Where?"

"Ralph Stover State Park a few times when I was young. And then the only real effort was a few years ago in Colorado."

"Colorado's a big state. Where in Colorado?"

"Uh. What's it called? Eldorado Canyon?"

"Yeah? What did you climb in Eldorado?"

"I mean, I just took some lessons. I wasn't ready to climb the Bastille Crack. Too old, too fat."

Apparently, that was proof enough. John stopped interrogating and got friendlier. He knew I was no serious climber, but had also decided from my self-deprecating answer that I probably wasn't a cop trying to get him to talk. He decided to trust me enough to have me handle his bail hearing, which was coming up in a few hours. John was adamant that he had done nothing illegal. He said he was in town to observe what happened in the next few days and to speak to the media about protest generally, the theory of nonviolent social change, and the specific issues that were motivating these RNC protesters. John told me he was arrested walking around Philadelphia in shorts and a T-shirt, no-where near any protest. He said he thought they just wanted him in jail for several days until it was all over. He was right.

At the bail hearing, John was given an outrageous and un-precedented $1 million bail for nonviolent misdemeanor charges, including obstructing the highway, disorderly conduct, defiant trespass, and conspiracy. In 2000, most people charged with rape, arson, gunpoint robbery, or aggravated assault with a fire-arm got less than $1 million bail. Million-dollar bail for a pile of misdemeanor protest charges was absurd. I immediately ap-pealed the outrageous bail in a telephonic hearing with a higher judge. She was ordinarily reasonable, but glaringly not so that day. That appeal failed. What the city bureaucrat claimed he had heard a judge say a few days earlier seemed to be on point. Was there really a plan to detain and silence protesters, including anyone law enforcement supposed might be their leaders, until Bush's plane left the tarmac?

Once future president Bush was gone, suddenly so were the exorbitant bails—reduced in sweeping ways. People who had spent a week or more in jail for no good reason were finally re-leased. I broke my own rule against having criminal defense cli-ents in my home, and invited a backyard full of protesters, including John Sellers, over to my house for food (including vegan barbecue), talk, and a little bit of work. John and I spent several minutes discussing his case privately in the living room. Out of the corner of my eye, I caught my seven-year-old son, Caleb, and his best friend peeking around the corner at us. Lisa later told me that she overheard Caleb in the kitchen, both hands holding on to his wide-eyed friend's shoulders for emphasis: "Do you see that guy with my dad? He's been to jail!"

John wasn't the only potential protest leader arrested with a million-dollar bail. But he was the first to have his charges thrown out in court. Months later, they were dropped by an honest prosecutor who had little choice on the day of trial because video told the story. At the time when police paperwork falsely claimed John was committing and leading others in a bunch of misdemeanor crimes, video captured him in a lengthy conversation with a national television news reporter.

I also represented Kate Sorensen, a union organizer who led marches around healthcare. She was given a similarly enormous bail after a similarly questionable arrest. Almost two years after her arrest, she and I endured a lengthy jury trial on more than a dozen heavy charges, including serious felony charges like riot, risking a catastrophe, and conspiracy, as well as criminal mischief and others. She was found not guilty of all but one misdemeanor charge of criminal mischief by an exhausted jury, and walked away with probation. Terrence McGuckin, a "half-million-dollar baby," was represented by another attorney and was convicted of nothing.

John, Kate, and Terrence were among the 420 people who were arrested and often given crazy bails at the RNC for nothing more than using their rights of assembly and speech to try to make the world better. The 420 arrestees were found not guilty at the absurdly high rates of 99 percent of all charges and 98 percent of all people. None of the 420 people did an additional day in jail beyond what their fixed, excessive bails had already caused. And all of their bails were lowered as soon as their free speech was erased forever, right after the Republican convention ended and Bush's plane was wheels up.

But these victories in court would take four long years, more than enough time for the U.S. Supreme Court to declare George W. Bush the winner of the 2000 general election. Enough time for W to ignore an early warning about the 9/11 attacks and for those attacks to come. Enough time for Dick Cheney to assume nearly presidential power and advise Bush to invade Iraq over phony "weapons of mass destruction" while Cheney's stock from his former employers at Halliburton grew enormously in value during the war. And it was enough time for anyone to wonder bitterly about the real cost of a preemptive strike against free speech at a national presidential convention and what difference that free speech might have made if it had been heard in such a close election.

By the time I was arguing the last of the R2K arrest cases, it was 2004. I was forty-three years old and had been a defense lawyer for seventeen years. Lisa was settled into her third year of being a judge; our boys were eleven and thirteen. That last case was the jury trial of Caleb Arnold and Curtis Rumrill, better known as Curt the Skirt after I began calling him that. Curt was a straight guy who wore skirts; Caleb was trans. Caleb and Curt the Skirt were arrested away from the puppet warehouse the day it was raided in 2000 by Pennsylvania state troopers who had gone undercover for days in the warehouse, posing as union carpenters. The phony carpenters volunteered to work on parade floats for days in order to surveil and lay various traps for protesters. They kept suggesting extreme, even violent activity, while the real protesters winced and eyed one another, trying to figure out how to rein in the newbies. The undercovers failed to foment violence or observe anything serious, so they settled for arresting whomever they could, including Caleb and Curt and others, whose actual and non-violent plan was to span a central city street in order to temporarily block a bus of Republican delegates on their way to the convention. If they succeeded in blocking the bus for a short while, the protesters would use the time to school the Republican delegates on board, and the public via the press, on criminal justice reform. Their tools were lockdown devices, signs, banners, and posters bearing messages. They carried a couple of gas masks in the event that they were teargassed by law enforcement. After loading their signs, posters, and other gear into a van driven by one of the undercover state troopers,

Caleb and Curt and others were stopped and arrested at the side of a road far from the location of their planned protest and away from the puppet warehouse raid that would happen the same day.

By the time we tried the case in 2004, it was four years after the arrest and I knew Caleb well. Caleb, born Calyn, had worked at my law office for a couple of years. They were the child of Colorado high-country farmers who were so alarmed by their child's sexual orientation during high school that they expelled them from the home for fear of Caleb's orientation spreading to their siblings. Caleb attended Mount Holyoke College and became an organizer, advocating around queer rights, mass incarceration, and animal rights.

After being arrested in 2000, Caleb did great work as a volunteer gathering video and witness information to assist other activists with their defenses in other cases, which is why I hired them a year later. Caleb soon became an efficient, sharp, and pesky employee in my law practice who was increasingly interested in becoming a lawyer and who knew how to argue. When Caleb was photocopying, the number of copies I needed was frequently in dispute. Caleb, like the Lorax, spoke for the trees.

By the time Curt the Skirt and Caleb went to trial, Caleb had completed two weeks of law school. We devised a scheme. Caleb would represent themself, sitting at counsel table next to me. Curt was another matter. He had no legal training and didn't want to represent himself, although he was handsome and personable. I thought if he spoke, he would go over well with the jury. He was musically talented, and would go on, fifteen years later, to get a graduate degree in musical composition. But, for now, he was going to trial. The scheme was that I would represent Curt Rumrill while simultaneously advising Caleb. It was traditional representation for Curt. It was hybrid representation for Caleb, an opportunity for Caleb to speak directly to the jury and convey their idealism during opening and closing arguments as well as while testifying, with my help on the technical aspects.

Caleb was starting law school, after all. We hoped the trial wouldn't end that.

The judge, D. Wayne O'Maith, had spent his life in the military before becoming a judge. He was a Republican and compassionate and fair on the bench. The Philadelphia District Attorney's Office, tired of already losing so many RNC cases, was determined to win this one. As usual, they had assigned a homicide prosecutor to try to crush protesters.

I showed up on the day of trial, having won case after RNC case in which I spoke about the theory and strategy of protest, the legacy of non-violent direct action and especially Dr. King, and the fact that most Philly jurors wouldn't even be serving on the jury but for protest. I brought into the courtroom several giant cardboard-backed black-and-white photographs of famous direct actions that recorded that history. There were photos of people locking down streets and using signs and banners for political expression. The judge quickly announced there would be no reference whatsoever to any person in history during the trial. I was stunned. There had been no timely written motion by the prosecution to exclude the history and theory of protest, not even a last-minute oral motion, and zero prior discussion with me. I was given no chance to argue the photographic exhibits' relevance and why they should be allowed. I knew the prosecutor had ordered trial transcripts from my prior wins for protesters. The judge's bizarre announcement that history wasn't allowed made me wonder if she had violated legal ethics and talked to the judge alone, or ex parte as lawyers call it. I slyly asked the judge if his requirement that I reference no person in history included all the defendants and witnesses.

The trial's start was funny but deeply troubling. Another defense attorney in the case flouted the ruling, repeatedly bringing up Frederick Douglass during the opening argument only to be ordered twice into the back by the judge and dressed down out of the jury's presence. The bewilderment on the jury's diverse faces suggested they were wondering what was wrong with mentioning Frederick Douglass. It was pretty good comedy, and I was happy to see my fellow attorney stepping up for a beating early because I knew there would be some beatdowns later for me. I could see the prosecutor's efforts to exile history from the trial were working with the judge but might be backfiring with the jury.

Both the judge and the jury appeared to be coming around to our side as they observed the slow accumulation of evidence. There were no weapons. There was no plan to commit violence. The defendants' tools were mostly words on banners and T-shirts, which the Constitution allows, plus lockdown devices and a gas mask in case police went wild. Both Curt and Caleb told their stories. The jury and I noticed the prosecutor's unnecessary use of purple latex gloves to handle ordinary evidence. In more than twenty years of trying cases, I had never seen anything like it. The evidence had been in storage for years; there had never been anything to test. Everyone agreed who and what was in the van, so why purple latex gloves? Was this an odd coincidence or a dramatic attempt to imply uncleanness or contagion? Why the latex gloves' purple color rather than ordinary white or beige? If the point was to dehumanize Curt for wearing a skirt and Caleb for wearing men's clothing, it was backfiring. The prosecutor's curious tactics peaked during closing arguments when she compared the non-violent defendants to abortion clinic bombers. The judge erupted, instructing the jury to completely disregard that kind of argument, which he told the jury was improper and had the potential to prejudice them. He growled again that the jury should completely disregard it.

During my closing, I argued that Curt could have put on pants and Caleb could have worn feminine clothing if they wanted to misrepresent who they were. But they didn't, which meant their testimony was good. And, despite the order not to mention anyone in history, Caleb and I got away with arguing to this typi-

cally diverse Philly jury that their jury service was impossible
without protest. With the exception of white men like me, every
member of the jury had the right to serve on a jury only because
of peaceful protest. Women's fight for suffrage eighty years prior
came from women locking themselves to fences, doors, and each
other as they peacefully resisted and spoke. Their vote paved the
way for their jury service. Black and brown people's jury service
came from centuries of struggle and passive resistance as they
raised their voices for equal rights, the Voting Rights Act their
efforts produced, and the greater jury participation they made.
As the jury left the jury box to deliberate, a number of them
made and held eye contact with the defendants or with me.

They had a verdict in less than forty-five minutes. The foreperson, Romeo, a Black musician and dancer who was very busy on
the bar mitzvah circuit, read the not-guilty verdict on each one
of the several charges for each defendant more loudly than the
last until he almost yelled "Not guilty!" on the final charge. After
the jury was dismissed, we spent a few more awkward minutes
listening to the aging judge explain to the defendants that he
would have given them probation if they were convicted and that
their idealism was commendable but should be channeled into
"more constructive" activities—such as pursuing graduate studies or working to change things as professionals. Caleb would be
finishing law school after all. The last of the R2K trials was finally over.

Half an hour later, Romeo walked over to me in the lobby of
the Criminal Justice Center on his way out of the building. My
poster boards of protest photographs, which had been excluded
from the trial for being historical, were leaning against a glass
window, not far from a trash can. They were useless now. After a
quick greeting, Romeo looked the poster boards over and told
me he wanted to show them to his daughter, who might want to
take them to her elementary school. He said goodbye, picked
them up, put them under his arm, and exited the courthouse

doors. Through plate glass windows, I watched as he made his way down the street through the early evening shadows of City Hall. His back got smaller and smaller as he carried history that had been excluded from a courtroom into the streets of Philadelphia on his way home.

Those four years representing 420 idealists broadened my understanding of the district attorney's power and how it could not only save or destroy people's lives but also change the course of history. When Philadelphia's district attorney Lynne Abraham decided to sucker-punch 420 people for nothing more than caring to improve their country by using their constitutional rights, she might as well have punched a mirror. Four hundred and twenty people were tortured in buses, in jail cells, and in their thoughts with the knowledge that a criminal conviction could not only land them in jail serving a sentence but, more important, ruin their ability to get jobs and pursue their futures in freedom. Some of them lived with this fear for years until they got their nearly universal dismissals and acquittals.

These 420 future leaders and I, and their circles of influence, would forever be radicalized by witnessing just how profoundly the criminal justice system had been corrupted and how much it needed to be reformed as we defeated that seemingly all-powerful system one case at a time. I had thought myself disillusioned before, but those four years of cases underscored for me that the criminal justice system was more about politics than justice. I had seen up close how the system would lock up anyone, literally anyone, for literally anything, and lie whenever convenient to justify it. I saw again that power does what it wants, but that doesn't mean it always wins. We won. And that history can't be suppressed.

I also understood, for the first time really, who was the linchpin of power in this corrupted criminal justice system. One person, more than any other, had enormous power that she wasn't using for the people. That was Philadelphia's chief prosecutor, its district attorney, who ordered her most elite, aggressive homicide trial prosecutors to put aside their homicide cases and relentlessly prosecute the protesters. It was the Philadelphia DAO, in league with other criminal justice system players, whose unjust tactics and abuse of power radicalized 420 people and, though I didn't know it then, planted the seeds for our 2017 election campaign.

# CHAPTER 14

# And Then We Won

*Time has come today*
*Hey*
*Oh*
*The rules have changed today*
— THE CHAMBERS BROTHERS,
"Time Has Come Today"

The legendary Saint George slayed a dragon and spared its next victim, a princess (of course). No more fiery breath. The Saint George I'd like to know becomes the dragon and breathes its fire for good, using its power to protect others, princesses included. No one yet has written the legend of George becoming the dragon or addressed the difficult questions it invites. How do reformers go from fighting something powerful and scary to taking its power to become its better self? On election day, those were the kinds of tough questions I hoped I would be given the chance to answer. We would need answers only if we won.

I went into the all-important primary election day, May 16, 2017, more preoccupied by the details than nervous. After listening to my campaign team's carefully worded input, I figured the next district attorney of Philadelphia, and the future of its criminal justice system, would be decided by a few hundred votes either way. Best-case scenario, we would win a close one after a very long night. If we lost, we would probably finish second or third. I still gave myself a 40 percent chance of winning, which wasn't too bad for a "liberal unicorn" and his "hilarious" candidacy. With seven candidates, the vote differences could be very small.

There is no way to drive, walk, hug, and handshake through every polling place in a city of 1.6 million people in thirteen hours. But on election day, we tried. The task was to be visible at polling places for news media, on social media, and to voters waiting in line and to encourage the legions of volunteers and paid election day workers over the arduous course of the thirteen hours when the polls were open.

Traveling in an unlikely, small convoy that consisted of one newer electric car and an old behemoth Chevy Suburban driven by my poker buddy Andy deLone, we were a mostly rotating crew of supportive volunteers and a few supportive elected officials who were the best matches for our targeted stops. We visited a dozen polling spots where my campaign strategist Brandon thought we were strong or where we even thought we had a shot. As the 8:00 P.M. voting deadline approached, we shot a social media video of me bouncing around in the car's back seat. I reminded everyone it wasn't too late to vote; we pushed it out. Most of the work that mattered had already been done, but we were doing every last bit we could, knowing that even in the final hour every visit or door knock or social media hit could be the decisive one in a close race.

My sons, Nate (twenty-six) and Caleb (twenty-four), were in town from New York and San Francisco, respectively, working polls. My mother-in-law, Sally, and her best friend, Ruth, were in from Nebraska, at a polling place that attracted a lot of seniors, drinking tea and serenely pushing that Sally's son-in-law deserved their vote. Sometime during the afternoon, I cuddled a golden retriever puppy that was plopped into my arms outside a polling place while campaign volunteers took pictures and spread them on social media in search of the dog lovers who hadn't voted yet. I didn't want to give the golden back. Holding the docile puppy was a strangely comforting respite. I was emotionally worn out, with hours remaining until the polls closed in a long day of electoral battle. I couldn't help but laugh an hour later, at a different polling place, when paid electoral workers for another candidate asked for our literature to hand out and put on our campaign T-shirts after learning more about the platforms of their candidate and ours.

I met people all over the city who made me hopeful that maybe the city was ready for change. I met a woman in her thirties who explained that her cousin was still unemployed after a youthful conviction. A young Black man told me he had thought of becoming a police officer until he was illegally stopped and humiliated. There was the middle-aged plumber who was the victim of a gunpoint robbery complaining that his requests for more information on the case had gone unanswered. In a more affluent part of town, I spoke to the parent of an autistic teenager who explained that her child's disability was misinterpreted by police, leading to an arrest and several traumatic hours in custody.

Our people were everywhere—campaign volunteers, activists, and volunteers with self-organized local groups named things like 215 People's Coalition, Pennsylvania De-Carcerate, and Reclaim. Our people were working the polls, working train platforms for votes, and following up on lists of likely voters for our campaign from people who had responded to the canvassing and the mass texting we'd done weeks before that had reached tens of thousands of people.

Around 6:30 P.M. we stopped by a polling place in South Philadelphia, a historically Italian and Irish neighborhood that Frank Rizzo had won heavily in the 1970s. Polls were closing at 8:00. We were spent; it was along the route to our Center City political headquarters, which would soon be our next and last car stop.

Until recently, the ward leader had been a powerful insider when he wasn't attracting the attention of the feds. I'd come there in the early evening to see how South Philly's polling places looked, but I didn't know exactly what to expect in a changing, old-line white ethnic blue-collar neighborhood known historically for its multigenerational hold on patronage, conservative labor, and ward politics.

As I sat for a moment on a cement retaining wall by the front of the polling place, I didn't see the old row-house South Philly coming inside to vote. I saw young working women carrying yoga mats on their shoulders. I saw hipsters pulling up on one-speed "fixie" bicycles. Lightly tattooed couples in their early thirties were socializing with one another on the playground while their toddlers played together.

In front of the polling place, I spotted the new ward leader who was a loyalist to the old one. His salt-and-pepper hair was slicked back, touching the collar of what turned out to be a poly-satin union jacket. I greeted him and he answered back, courteous but curt. And then we sat some more, apart, watching the same thing and I suspect coming to the same conclusions: The neighborhood was changing. It was still this *poo yai ban*'s ward, but these were not his voters. They were mostly young, mostly educated people. Many were working white-collar jobs. Many were dragging a bag of student debt. Some were young parents or parents-to-be, seizing the chance to live in the catchments of a couple of excellent public schools in an otherwise struggling public school system.

Like the generation they were replacing, they were mostly white. Unlike much of the prior generation that had left for New Jersey and nearby suburbs, these newer residents preferred life in a diverse, vibrant, affordable city to what was offered in the nearby New Jersey suburbs. This was not a hive of patronage workers or members of exclusively white unions. Some were artists; some were openly queer. Biracial couples showed up. Within a year, a former public radio journalist and mother of two young children would become the state rep there, beating out an old-guard candidate whose family connections and career as a detective no longer guaranteed him a win. And the state rep's husband, a small contractor and former welder whose day job was retrofitting aging buildings to make them more energy efficient, would become the new ward leader.

By 7:30, after fourteen hours of moving from polling place to polling place around the city, our dwindling caravan of campaign workers and volunteers finally returned to our campaign HQ, my old law office. It was time to gather ourselves for whatever came next. As I walked through the door, Jim Savage, the rock-eating, socialist ex-head of the refinery workers' union—also an ex-client I'd defended when he was arrested as part of Occupy Philly—gave me a crooked smile. He and Lauren Townsend, a key staffer and election veteran, were laughing and pouring whiskey, spilling a little on the rug—whatever that meant. I smiled back and went through a couple more doors until I found an empty office where I could write a few notes for a victory/concession speech, thinking I'd likely say pretty much the same thing either way, but I kept getting distracted by the laughter and noise. I changed my suit and my sweaty shirt and my tie. I was more exhausted than expectant, like a marathon runner who knew the race was finally over, whatever the clock said. For that I was grateful, as I was for all the help from people who understood how important it really was to take back power from a criminal justice system gone rogue.

I was eager to walk the block to the election night party location so I could thank old friends, thank new friends, share a few stories. We had hundreds of volunteers, many of whom I'd never met. I hoped to find some of those folks and thank them, too; it seemed the least I could do. Ben Waxman, our campaign communications chief, scratched that plan. He was another campaign veteran, having worked for years as press secretary for a respected progressive state senator. He schooled me that, for good reasons, politicians don't go to their own election watch parties until the results are in. Going early means the press will capture your face looking angry, frustrated, doubtful, or awkward in the stressed-out and ever-changing environment of a campaign watch party. If your mostly tired, enthusiastic, and imbibing supporters act out, the media will likely get you in the shot. And then there was the other reason not to be there until the outcome was known: We might lose while the press watched . . . and who wants that expression memorialized forever?

That's right: We might lose. It was certain that six of the seven candidates would. I thought about all the reasons, despite our team's heroic efforts and the encouraging moments of the day, that we would probably lose. We started late. I had no political status. The Democratic Party had stayed out of it officially, but had its treacherous ways, as Lisa's first campaign proved, and made no secret of its distaste for progressives and insurgent candidates like me.

Not long before my campaign announcement, the party boss was quoted in *Philadelphia* magazine dismissing progressives as irrelevant and unlikely to vote. We had raised a middling amount of money on our own. But we had a campaign team that was animating reluctant and unlikely voters to come out and vote, mostly because we had an exciting message for outsiders and we had exciting messengers among the activists. Our campaign was getting support from Black Philadelphians, women, and millennials. Where we canvassed, we got more than our share of white working-class and poor white voters. And we had gotten some love from well-educated white people whose knowledge of criminal justice came from *The Philadelphia Inquirer*, the *Daily News*, *The New York Times*. The best news was that our already effective message was amplified by the support of outside PACs during the campaign's last three weeks. On their own, they did mailings and radio and television commercials supporting our campaign. The bad news was that the same PACs had jumped into other winning and losing chief prosecutors' elections much earlier than they did in Philly—often six weeks before election day, according to the information I had gathered on those other candidates, rather than the three weeks here.

In the last three consecutive DA primary election cycles, about 12 percent of all voters had turned out. This dismal number for voter participation was in line with a national decline in voting over the past fifty years. Low voter turnout in Philadelphia was compounded by the fact that our 2017 Philly DA election slate included no candidate for president, governor, U.S. senator, or even Philly mayor.

The Democratic Party's politicians had made things worse by always playing for the middle, trying to position themselves as Republican-lite, as if progressive, populist Democrats weren't a real force in Philly. Mostly, they did so for the worst reason there is: their own incumbency. Who needs more votes you can't predict when you already have control over the ones you can? So the Democratic Party's leadership inadvertently squashed and alienated waves of younger voters and too many voters of color of all ages by its unwavering support of establishment candidates who did little or nothing to address these disenfranchised voters' concerns. The Party of Incumbency was always running toward the middle, dissuading potential new voters from ever voting. Populism was a nope. Progressivism was a nope. Actually pushing racial justice was pointless in their view. What were voters of color going to do? Vote for Republicans? The unfamiliar or transformative was unacceptable.

As a judge, Lisa was still required to keep her distance from electoral politics. The judicial ethics committee's opinions instructed that, if we somehow managed to win the primary, she could not even attend the victory party, because my campaign would be ongoing through the general election. But, if we lost, she could join the party after it became a funeral.

Because my campaign was excluding me from the election party for now, I joined Lisa and her friend at the bar of an elegant vegan restaurant, just a block from my office and a block from the election party location, to wait for the results. There were no televisions for me to watch, which I was told was partly why the place was selected. I didn't know our sons were at the election party getting the election returns and texting Lisa information that she didn't share with me. Expecting a long night, I figured the bar was my post for at least a few hours, good news or bad. Working off that plan, Lisa and I left the bar briefly to plug our car's parking meter so there would be no issue later, when there was news. A car with a D.C. license plate drove past, slowed, and pulled over. The driver waved me over. When I got close, I recognized him right away as a national Working Families Party director who had interviewed me months ago with Brandon, well before WFP brought its full support. He was smiling, excited, cryptic, and had driven a few hours for the watch party. I promised to see him at the party soon, and he drove away, beaming. Lisa said, "He's happy. Seems like he knows something." I didn't allow myself to think more about what that might mean. But I knew he had made a long drive. We plugged the meter and headed back to the bar.

Less than an hour after the polls closed, and long before I expected to see anyone else, my communications wizard, Ben, showed up in the bar. He displayed no emotion but told me I should come with him to our campaign HQ. I asked him what was happening. He told me we needed to go and he would tell me more on the way. I kissed Lisa and headed out the front door. As I headed out, Ben ducked back and said a few words to Lisa that I didn't hear.

On the walk over to HQ, Ben explained that nothing was certain but that we were looking good; victory was likely. I stopped walking. I wasn't sure I'd heard him. I made him repeat it. He did. We walked back into campaign HQ, where several people had already left for the watch party and the people who remained were talking about heading over. Several turned and stopped talking, smiling broadly when I walked in. A cheer went up. Phones were ringing.

We would need good slogans to chant at the victory party, I thought, if there was one. Ben told me to take the phone; another candidate was calling me, possibly to concede. I answered, greeted him, and listened. Even as I replayed his rancorous claims in public forums that I was reckless and unqualified, I couldn't help but feel sorry for him in that moment as he congratulated me and accepted his defeat. A second candidate called and conceded as well. I wondered if I would have been as gracious. As I thanked each of them for their call and tried to soften the moment, it finally sank in. They were conceding. They had accepted what I hadn't yet for fear of disappointment: We really had won.

I hugged and high-fived and shook hands with a few people in HQ. Someone said my boys were already at the party. Core campaign staff walked the two blocks to the party location together, trailed by the faint smell of whiskey. Our party was going to be at Philly's brand-new LGBTQ-friendly independent living senior home. Any doubts that the victory was real ended when I passed the threshold of the automatic doors and was hit with the sound of four hundred people's exuberant cheering, yelling, chanting, and laughing. I walked down a wide, clean hallway swirling with loud, smiling, laughing, mostly young people. To the right was a glass-front conference room full of happy people watching TV screens and socializing. I heard a loud cheer and stopped to look through the plate glass at the television inside, to where they were staring.

It was on the screen. The Associated Press called the DA's race in our favor at 9:07 P.M. Polls had closed at 8:00 P.M.; we won in an hour. We had grabbed more votes than the next two finishers combined. We had turned out fifty thousand additional, unexpected voters, from all parts of the city. Our election was different: 19 percent of all voters cast their votes. It was the highest turnout for a primary in a Philly DA's race in at least twenty years. This 19 percent wasn't nearly as good as it needed to be for an engaged electorate, but it was a big step in the right direction. In one section of West Philadelphia known for its pockets of activism and radicalism that opposed even voting in elections, voter turnout was nearly 70 percent, up from about 30 percent in the last similar election cycle.

Six months earlier, Donald Trump had won all of Pennsylvania by a mere forty thousand votes. And yet here, in this one city, and in an off-year election, we had pushed out so many excited new Black and brown and millennial and unlikely voters that, had they voted the previous fall, they would have changed the outcome of that presidential election. It really was the movement we had hoped would show up. It was something we had wanted to be true so intensely that we had guarded against becoming unrealistic, irrational true believers. But the numbers told the tale: It was true and it was real. I was astonished that we had wished this aspirational dream into reality; I felt like I was floating. Everything slowed down. It was like walking through water in an aquarium.

I looked where we were headed—to the left, through another wall of glass to an outdoor spring garden filled with excited people who were inadvertently trampling flowers (which, of course, we would replace the next day). We passed through more glass doors out into the clear night air of the roofless, starry courtyard. The people behind us were pushing forward in a wave, coming into the garden with new arrivals and local television cameras and reporters. I heard the DJ playing Dead Prez.

The plan was for the stage where I was to speak to be left empty. But it was nearly full, having been invaded by politicians looking for their photos on the cover of the paper the next day, wanting to be in on the win. The least supportive ones seized the stage first. When they couldn't be talked off the stage, others climbed on after them. So many of the volunteers, activists, friends, union leaders, and politicians who had done the most work were either standing at the back of the overflowing stage or couldn't even get up onto it. The crowd roared, and I couldn't stop smiling. I had to stand at the very front of the stage, leaning backward into the surge of people behind me for balance, hoping that at least the heels of my dress shoes wouldn't slip off the edge and drop me into the crowd mid-speech. The DJ played the Clash's "Clampdown" as I found a fixed place to stand and the music came down.

News cameras lit up the night illuminating an expanse of cellphone cameras held overhead. My speech was quick and excited: I expressed my gratitude to all the volunteers and staff who had worked so hard with little or no credit. I heard myself say, "This is not about one person; this will never be about one person." I didn't offer a platform or policy that night; we had done that for ninety-eight days. We were all together, appreciating the moment. Chris Woods, the six-foot-four head of a mostly Black healthcare workers' union that had been instrumental in supporting our campaign, took the microphone and led the crowd in chanting "This is what democracy looks like!" The chant is a standard. It includes everyone and reminds us all of the source of democratic power. It was the perfect chant for the evening.

I thanked and hugged people as I headed back into the thicker air and stuffed hallways of the building, slowly making my way to the street exit—to a cooler, quieter, less populated, and more sober environment on the sidewalk outside. Reporters followed. One asked me about the FOP president's churlish response to our win. I responded: "I hope he has a good night."

For the first time in hours, I saw my sons; they were on the sidewalk socializing a block away. More than anyone there, they knew how unexpected this moment was. My being DA was no long-standing dream, nothing I had stalked my entire life or had even suggested I hoped to do during their childhood, high school, college. None of us saw it coming, which made it all the sweeter as a validation of the unknown possibilities of life. We hugged before they took off for the party and I made my escape from Center City to our three-bedroom "starter home" in the greener Northwest, also home of the Mighty 50th Ward and Marian Tasco, who had shown once more they were the power. In a city where seven of every eight voters register as Democrats, becoming the Democratic nominee meant the general election was already won. Lisa met me on the street corner and we held hands, walking away quietly through the darkness of antique Philadelphia streets to our car, already knowing the outcome of the general election was as good as determined.

We got home but couldn't sleep and didn't feel the exhaustion anymore. The job I'd campaigned for would soon be mine. Our lives were changing for good. We sat at the oak table in our small kitchen talking, laughing, and reliving the day, the night, and the entire campaign. Our boys were home much sooner than expected, telling us of their adventures campaigning and attending the party that day.

The next day, I found out that the campaign workers and volunteers, canvassers, and activists were expelled from the senior center shortly after I left, but would wear out the bars all over Center City and elsewhere until closing time. Some of them didn't find their beds until dawn. The next morning, a political cartoon in the *Inquirer* showed the Frank Rizzo statue lying flat on its back while two young Philadelphians walked past. One said: "What happened?" The other responded: "Larry Krasner got elected district attorney."

Months later, before the general election, I was asked to speak to a well-intentioned, moneyed group of mostly centrist Democratic donors that included law firm partners and high-level executives. Some represented old money. Although overwhelmingly their crowd had been behind my Democratic Party's opponents or agnostic, I viewed the invitation as an opportunity for a little love between the centrist power base of the party and the progressive future DA. Never mind their lack of support and skipping our victory party. The face-to-face meeting also gave Brandon and me the chance to persuade and maybe cultivate donations in the future for other candidates their centrist voters and our progressive voters could get behind. Brandon and I went with a couple of charts and diagrams, knowing we weren't a perfect match with this group but hoping to work together where we could agree.

The donors' meeting was in a vast but minimalist white conference room on the thirtieth floor of a downtown skyscraper. A law firm, of course. We stood in front of the assembled power brokers to tell the story of the campaign, pointing at large boards with colored maps of the city showing the primary election results and the astounding increase from 12 percent to 19 percent voter participation this election cycle. They listened politely.

After a quiet but cordial response to our presentation, one of the donors asked: "It seems like much of your success in the election and what energized your voters had to do with your platform and your message. We have a couple important races coming up statewide where the candidates may need some help. Can you tell us who your consultants were? Who did your polling?"

I stopped myself from smiling, gave a side-eye to Brandon, and said: "Our platform and the message really were the things I thought and believed after thirty years of doing criminal defense and civil rights work. We didn't have any money for consultants or polls at that point even if we had wanted to do them."

The donor who questioned me smiled politely and lightly shook his head as if to say, "Maybe I'll find out who you hired later." Right before we left, the voice of a centrist party patriarch, too ill to attend, boomed from speakers built into the ceiling. He said nice things about our campaign while we were in the room. Right after we left, the patriarch told the donors not to give us any money, according to a friend who texted us from the room. They didn't.

Our primary election was a case study in the popular backlash that forms a movement when a system exercises power against the people it should serve. The people take their power back. It was inevitable in Philly. When the inner circles of politics and the justice system ignored those affected by their decisions— parents of people suffering addiction, communities devastated by the unnecessary disappearance of too many of their young men, employers burdened by excessive supervision of their employees under probation and parole, parents of children in underfunded public schools, victims whose real needs were subordinated to the chief prosecutor's politics—they were spitting in the faces of a family member or friend of virtually every voter. No matter how hard incumbents and their patrons try, no voter suppression tactic can disenfranchise every voter, especially when those voters organize in a movement. The broken old system—and its unmasked hostility to the people who put it into power—is what made our campaign necessary. It's why we won.

# CHAPTER 15

## Changes

*Sign of the times mess with your mind*
*Hurry before it's too late.*

—Prince, "Sign o' the Times"

The May primary was six months before the formality of the general election in November. Swearing-in and taking power came even later; they would start with the New Year. At fifty-six years of age, more than half a year's delay felt to me like wasted time I didn't have. I was eager to start my new job and carry out a movement's plans for what we knew was coming. But I was soon reminded that all plans are contingent, that there's less time than we think. We have to move swiftly, as soon as we can.

Shortly after the primary, a powerful electoral insider whose unfiltered outburst during the primary of "Anyone but Krasner!" and "How can this be happening?" was checking the numbers. He was looking for a way to beat me in the general election. He was wondering if he could do the unthinkable—beat his own majority party's candidate in the general election in a one-party town. No one would even have considered it for a more conventional primary victor, but our win was considered so unlikely by some political insiders that it felt fake. However, when the insider and his insider crew met and looked at the numbers carefully, they gave up. Our primary win was just too strong, especially given the huge increase in voter turnout. Political insiders progressed through the stages of grief and reached acceptance.

But some exasperated haters and a few journalists weren't ready for acceptance just yet. They were wistfully hanging on to the notion that my general election minority party challenger could pull it out somehow. It made the general election a little more suspenseful for some, and motivated me to keep campaigning. For months, I found myself blinking twice to make sure what I saw was really happening. We were getting ready to win a general election. We had already won the primary. But our real challenges were coming from outside of politics.

In August 2017, my father-in-law, Ed Rau, died slowly of congestive heart failure in his late eighties. He said goodbye to family and friends and his beloved golden retrievers, with Lisa and others by his side. My last words with him were by phone. In September, Lisa's groundbreaking feminist aunt, Kate Millett, also died. She was in her eighties, and died in Paris after several years of enduring dementia that had no regard for her brilliant mind or its legacy.

In October, we got the happy news that Mike Lee's healthy baby boy was born. Mike quickly nicknamed cheerful, helpless little Winston "Steppin' Razor" after Peter Tosh's fearsome protagonist who warns, "I'm dangerous, dangerous," just "like a steppin' razor."

In November, a few days before the general election, my younger son, Caleb, just two years out of college, was flying back to Philly from the West Coast. He had helped out and lived through his mother's election battles as a child and a teen. He had just helped out with my primary election six months prior. He was coming again for the general election to help out and to be present for what we knew we had already won.

When Caleb graduated from college with great grades and a degree in "music, science, and technology," he applied for dozens of tech jobs but got none. Without a computer science degree or another, more conventional degree in tech, he was unemployed at first, before taking a job in a coffee shop that barely paid his bills. With typical diligence, he honed his coffee-making skills before finding a tech job for an audio start-up. The job was close to his childhood passion for music, first on keyboards and then in electronic music, and for recording and modifying sounds. Years before, he had recorded the crackling hiss of ice melting and the crunching sound of people walking in dry leaves, and changed the found sounds' speed and tone and timbre until they were unrecognizable. Sometimes he blended the found sounds he collected with electronic tonal music. He performed original music as an electronic DJ and musician at coffee shops, parties, clubs during high school, college, and afterward in San Francisco, sometimes even producing shows with his fellow musicians.

His audio tech job combined his love for music, recording and mixing found sounds, with a fascination with hearing and acoustics that he developed during college. At some point, Caleb learned he has "golden ears." He hears things—squeaks, buzzes, frequencies, echoes, in a recording or a pair of headphones or an audio speaker or an MP3 recording or a vinyl album—that most of us cannot hear. He flew home wearing earbuds he helped build at the start-up. They canceled the droning of the jet's engines while allowing the wearer to hear music, among other things. Flying home, he knew the start-up where he worked was tanking, after its well-funded and seemingly unstoppable rise. He was facing unemployment again, golden ears or not, because his résumé was still more about music than engineering. He was fretting about how long he could last on credit while he tried to land another job and hang on to his apartment and the career he wanted in a pricey city.

After landing in Philly, Caleb helped with the election during the day. When he was done, he quietly disappeared. I spotted him a couple of times, in the dark in some quiet room, his face illuminated by the glow of his laptop monitor and cellphone screens, rewriting a survival budget, absorbing the latest emails and texts from his panicked co-workers, or fielding possible job inquiries coming from larger tech companies looking for talent that knew the start-up was folding.

The night before the general election finally came, we were home. The house was busy until late. We were confident but still working. Lisa was around but more withdrawn than usual, and quiet. So was Caleb. Before I was around, he noticed she had been crying. He got her to tell him what neither of them was going to tell me yet. Lisa's beloved oldest brother, Steve, who was also Caleb's godfather, had just told her he had stage 4 cancer. It was totally unexpected. Doctors said he had only a few painful months to live, at age sixty-two. They decided they would tell me when election day was over; it was a blow I didn't need before the polls closed.

I'd met Steve after suddenly losing a job I wanted in my mid-twenties, a situation parallel to Caleb's now. A Reagan-era spending cut had eliminated my summer job at the Philadelphia U.S. Attorney's Office at the last minute. I was lucky to quickly wrangle a summer job in the Twin Cities, at the Hennepin County public defender's office late in the hiring cycle, which meant I needed short-term housing in a place I'd never been. After Lisa made the introduction, Steve agreed to split his St. Paul apartment with me over the summer.

Steve turned thirty that summer; I was twenty-five. He was an up-and-coming big law attorney in Minneapolis. I was still a kid in law school. Steve's sartorial preparation for big law started in his teens, when he worked in a men's clothing store. He always had, or maybe developed before I knew him, an eye for rich wool suits, cotton shirts, and silk ties and patterns and colors in all of them that somehow brought out the colors in his gray-green eyes, which were almost the same as the shifting colors in Lisa's bluer grays. Women were drawn to him, especially his future bride that summer. As soon as I arrived, he schooled me through buying and tailoring a summer suit I could afford. It was the second suit I had owned, and was below Steve's pricey taste, but he knew it was what I needed.

Some work mornings, Steve risked both our lives by driving us to our Minneapolis offices in his serially dented car. Invariably, he was immaculately dressed. I still remember him at the wheel, steering the windy St. Paul river road, balancing a hot mug of coffee in one cuff-linked hand while holding a lit cigarette in the other, and somehow adjusting the radio while he told stories and laughed his way through them. At least once a commute he punctuated the trip by cursing out another driver with childlike glee, usually after he somehow managed to lower his window. Steve's joyous extroversion meant he drove and maintained eye contact with his passengers, at least the worried ones in the front seat, while talking about his adventures in big law, in college, or in his childhood. The summer he turned thirty, Steve's life was a romp of well-paid hard work and hard play. About once a week he took me along on his night shift, mostly to make mischief in bars where people were fistfighting in the parking lot or to find St. Paul's best greasy cheeseburger at midnight.

We became brothers-in-law. As the years and decades passed, we didn't see each other all the time, but were always laughing the couple of times a year we did, invariably surrounded by family. In his mid-fifties, and after years in corporate law, Steve followed his sister's path and became a judge. Cancer came, but he outdid his oncologist's predicted life expectancy by more than a year. He stayed alive and in the job he loved long enough to lock in benefits so that his wife, Chris, and the kids he adored were completely set. But all of that came later. The day after the general election, Lisa wept when she and Caleb told me about Steve's diagnosis.

Two days after the general election, Nate and Caleb and I were in New York City. We were all dressed up and headed for the memorial service for Lisa's aunt Kate in a huge church that faces Washington Square Park. Lisa had gone ahead earlier to be with Kate's people and to finalize the eulogy she had prepared. When we got to the church, Lisa was onstage, seated with other speakers.

Because Kate had died in September in Paris, the memorial service in the United States came later. Naturally, it was held in Greenwich Village, where Kate had spent most of her years living and writing, working with the leading feminists of her time, socializing with Yoko Ono and John Lennon and other luminaries—actors and writers and such—when she wasn't somewhere else, like her Christmas tree farm, which she bought with book royalties and where she founded a utopian summer community for women artists from everywhere.

Nate and Caleb and I and other family sat in the front rows next to Lisa's mom, Sally, who was Kate's older sister and also had been her protector in many ways. Sally was my protector, too, having loaned me a few bucks to start my law practice in the early 1990s. In her forties, Sally became a family lawyer in Nebraska, a law partner, a savvy businesswoman and small-time investor. As a family lawyer, Sally changed Nebraska law so that a woman could keep her birth name, even after marriage. She helped change state law so that each spouse's pension was shared in divorce, an asset she was denied at divorce after twenty years as a military wife. Sally, too, had raised hell as a feminist, debating Phyllis Schlafly on the Equal Rights Amendment on television and speaking publicly to support the ERA when she wasn't quietly breaking into the men's club of attorneys in Omaha, spending time in the company of radical nuns, or even more qui-

etly helping young women get through difficult times in a conservative place.

Sally and many of the other best hell-raisers on the planet
were in that sanctuary, grayed-out and disguised by time. They
were fierce. Sally, the boys, and I sat, watching veteran feminists
like Gloria Steinem slowly circulate and greet one another under
the gaze of journalists and filmmakers. Sally could still pick out
Kate's colleagues. Some were feminists I knew about. Others had
names I didn't know. Collectively, their sweeping victories advanced movements for equal rights for women, and for LGBTQ
rights, including same-sex marriage, that are the legacies of their
lives' work. Those legacies loomed over their slightly stooped
shoulders in the cavernous heights of the church.

Lisa climbed the elevated stone pulpit and began her eulogy
by remembering Kate through a child's eyes. Kate was fun, an
aunt who sat on the floor and played with her nieces and nephews, yet who always spoke to them like they were adults entirely ready for the world and possessed of ideas that needed to
be heard. Kate led the nephews and nieces in art projects not
unlike the sculptures she made from found objects and sold and
exhibited in galleries or the colorful silk screens she made and
sometimes captioned with calligraphy inspired by the time she
lived in Japan, where she and Yoko Ono became friends before
Yoko was with John. In Kate's sculpture, the two striped legs of
a stool emerged from plaster-filled, worn leather boots. Other
pieces of furniture got arms or heads, as if nothing should be
held down or objectified, not even an object. Lisa eulogized
Kate's brilliant wordplay. Kate believed in the power of words
to heal or to harm. Like her theories of freedom, Kate's style in
writing was more creative than rule-bound. It challenged some
of her editors. Multisyllabic words describing theory butted up
against colloquial words of a syllable or two. Sometimes she
wrote in a stream of consciousness. Kate communicated how
she wanted.

To please family, Lisa left out the story of Kate's wedding gifts to us. They were silk screens Kate had made and brought to the wedding—one for Lisa and one for me. But I knew what Lisa skipped and was smiling as she spoke. Lisa's silk screen spoke to her limitless potential. My silk screen was the outline of a pair of breasts, painted in a calligraphic style in black ink with a brush. Its caption began: "Every young man should have a pair of these at hand . . . on his wedding day."

Aunt Kate, as Lisa called her, emerged from a small Catholic school in St. Paul, Minnesota, where she disrupted by shyly questioning everything. She graduated with honors from the University of Minnesota, Oxford, and Columbia, and later was called a leader of the feminist movement in the 1960s and 1970s, along with her sisters Gloria Steinem, Flo Kennedy, Betty Friedan, and Adrienne Rich, among many others. Her initial prominence came from her Ph.D. thesis at Columbia University, which was turned into the book *Sexual Politics*, an eloquent dissection of male domination and its reflection in literature. Kate's thesis was that some "classic" literature was infected with sexual politics, worded subtly, often beautifully, to program women's subordinate role; the writing's oppressive power was subconscious, nearly invisible. That wonky Ph.D. thesis became a popular bestseller in 1970. Kate's description of patriarchy alone is worth the read. She joined with other members of their movement to use protest to move women's rights and the rights of other oppressed groups forward. Kate fearlessly traveled to Iran at a dangerously repressive time after other leading American feminists backed out because the U.S. government warned it could not protect them. In Iran, Kate was imprisoned while organizing women to fight for their rights.

Kate knew instinctively that becoming the personification of a movement was wrong. She knew the notion of an exceptional leader singlehandedly changing history is nonsense. Movements meet their time; at most, so-called leaders merely help that along.

More likely, the so-called leaders are fungible and contingent, made by their movements and by luck. When *Time* magazine told her she would be on its cover for *Sexual Politics*, she told them to put the movement on the cover and declined to provide a photo or sit for a photo shoot. So *Time* commissioned a stern-looking painted image of her that didn't evoke her famously impish smile and charming, cutting personality. *Time* put that painted image on its cover in 1970. Even when Kate eschewed leadership, feminism's opponents called her a leader to set her up as a target. Her reluctant identification as a leader, coupled with her bisexuality, allowed opponents of feminism to hit her in hopes of fracturing the women's movement. For some in the movement, her difference in sexual orientation, and the difference of others like her, would divide the movement and narrow its immediate goals to those of straight women.

Kate's impact is still felt, but she was abused and marginalized for her difference, and pushed out of academia—where she belonged. Her greatest legacy may be that she was so willing to push feminism forward at the expense of her ego. She pushed feminism forward, then got out of its way.

Fifty years later, looking around at Kate's memorial service, it appeared time was bonding the divides in feminism between straight and gay women, Black and white. Time and a movement had turned ideas that were at first radical and scary into ideas that were commonplace. There was enough room in that church for all of feminism. We were there to celebrate a life, but we knew not to confuse one person's brief life or life's work with the timeless legacy of a movement it served.

Like me in my twenties, Caleb turned out to be lucky in losing his job—because he got hired again quickly, within a month. When his start-up failed in November, big tech declined to buy the company or to pay its founders for the company's ideas. Instead, big tech competed for and hired the company's talent to work on audio technology ideas and projects for them, including some that were similar to the noise-canceling earbuds of the start-up.

Caleb's new job in December kept him in the work he loved in the place where he wanted to make a future, but it meant he would miss the swearing-in ceremony at the beginning of January. He had too few days on the new job to take off more time. As a child and a teen, he had attended both of his mother's swearing-in ceremonies, but I didn't mind. I was still the guy who skipped my college and law school graduations to chase my future. I was even a little jealous that Caleb started his new job in 2017 before I finally got to start mine at the beginning of 2018, after so much delay. Time wasn't waiting for any of us.

After so many changes in my private life reminded me that we are frail, our plans contingent, the illusion of leadership a trap our enemies lay to scuttle the timeless ideas a movement represents, another blow came. This one reminded me again how precious it is to be allowed to do your life's work for the people.

# CHAPTER 16

# Ryden

*I want to fly like an eagle*
*Till I'm free*
*Oh, Lord, through the revolution*
　　　　—Steve Miller Band, "Fly Like an Eagle"

The history of American crime and justice is a history of lives lost and freedom stolen. Coast to coast, America is a blood-red map, pockmarked with jails and prisons built on the dehumanized foundations of empire and slavery and more guns than people. A life's work in public service in criminal justice is about making a future that escapes that ugly history. But that future isn't some abstraction in the distance: It begins with the next crime, ideally handled by people on all sides who have found their calling. At their best, criminal justice workers act in different ways to avoid the next act that harms, to prevent the next victimization, to erase the next unjust year of incarceration. They are winning their good fight because their joy is in fighting with open hearts and brilliant minds to find the truth that points toward accountability and freedom based on justice. At their best, the people who work to reform American criminal justice know that every life is everything. At their best, they are a lot like Ryden.

I was playing poker on a Sunday afternoon when I got the phone call that first told me the news about Ryden Nelson, a hard-core volunteer I met and first knew through the campaign. I had recently written him a glowing recommendation for his law school application. He mailed that application the day before I got the call. On the phone, I heard the words "brain bleed," "coma," "a few days," "not sure." I felt like somebody had hit me with a rock.

Poker club was an octet of old and almost-old men who played monthly, except in the summer. We were in a small farmhouse on an acre of woodsy land within the city limits, gently modernized by Jamie Wyper, its architect owner. Winter sunlight was pouring in the abundant windows; the place was heated by a wood fire in a cast-iron stove. I had been talking to the club's eighty-plus-year-old founder, Armand Mednick, when I got the call. It was around two o'clock, right after the customary ritual of the carefully prepared midday meal complete with appetizers and dessert. You had to be able to cook to play. Wine came with the meal; then came conversation. After-dinner drinks and cigars were available before a couple more hours of poker started.

The club was over fifty years old, still led by Armand, a Belgian Jewish child survivor of the Holocaust. On the run, he contracted tuberculosis. His family concealed him in a Parisian Catholic orphanage under a phony Christian name. He lived there and in a sanatorium, surrounded by doting women, many mothers whose tuberculosis had separated them from their children. Armand lost everyone in his immediate family, and fifty-five people in his extended family died at Buchenwald. Only Armand and a few cousins survived and made their way to America.

Armand spent his life as a potter, sculptor, and teacher of generations of art students in a private school in Northwest Philadelphia. When I got the news about Ryden, at first I couldn't talk. I cleared my throat and explained to Armand why I had to leave immediately. He looked at me with a steady gaze and sat quietly for a moment. I remembered he had lost his son after a terrible accident. He gave me a hug and told me we would see each other soon.

I rushed to the hospital with Lisa, a little unsure of whether I'd be able to find Ryden, be allowed in, or even be welcome in such a crisis. At the hospital, Ryden's dad, Robert, told us Ryden was in a coma. He had suffered a severe brain bleed from a rare and previously undiagnosed arteriovenous malformation (AVM), a vascular anomaly in his brain that had ruptured. Earlier that evening, Ryden and his medical-student girlfriend had hosted a small dinner party for friends. She was visiting from New York over the holidays. When the bleed hit, they were in bed, asleep at first as he began to seize. Her presence and her medical knowledge are likely why Ryden was so quickly hospitalized and survived. Robert said there were real concerns that Ryden had suffered losses to his cognitive functioning; his future was uncertain. Near Ryden's ICU room, about fifteen of his friends, kind and decent young people from all over the United States, were in the waiting room and adjusting to the news.

The name "Ryden" is an anglicized version of Raijin, the Japanese thunder god. Ryden is the only child of his Japanese American mother, Jean, and Anglo father, Robert, who met on a Bay Area Rapid Transit train when she was a student at Berkeley and he was working at a bank. At first, Ryden's maternal grandmother protested her new grandson's name, calling it a yakuza (gangster) name. But Ryden is no gangster.

I first met Ryden early in my campaign at headquarters. A recent Wesleyan University grad, he was a bright, tall, quiet, humble young man wearing a black leather jacket who vaguely reminded me of Keanu Reeves in a more philosophical moment (and without firearms). His day job was union organizing among hotel workers.

Pushing for his beliefs was not new to Ryden. In college, he had been instrumental in ending the few remaining frats, which he viewed as pits of misogyny and boot camps for addiction and bad behavior. While in high school, he was a mainstay writer for the *Daily Urinal*, an independent student publication that derived its name from its early history as a single photocopied sheet of paper posted at eye level above the urinals in the boys' bathrooms. Ryden's muckraking was best remembered in high school for his commentary regarding a prominent donor to the school who also funded anti-gay legislation.

Ryden was all for change, and he was selfless. He found freedom in high school by sticking up for LGBTQ students and making trouble for himself; he wasn't one of them. He found freedom in college sticking up for women and making trouble for himself; he wasn't a woman. He traveled to the Standing Rock Sioux Reservation to support Native American rights; he wasn't indigenous. His first job after college was sticking up for poorly compensated workers who hadn't been to college, many of whom were immigrants. He was a U.S. citizen with a prestigious college degree who could have made a lot more money doing something else. But he felt whole when he was working for other people, not as a concept, but for each one of them and in each of their unique lives. The resistance he got from power only confirmed that what he was doing mattered in ways that were little and big. And Ryden had never been stepped on by the criminal justice system, but he stepped up for our reform campaign.

During our campaign for district attorney, Ryden and his bicycle were our key delivery system for lawn signs and literature. He was a steady presence as a volunteer staffer; his remarkable intelligence, diligence, and ability to work with anyone were obvious and advanced his role in the campaign. He showed he was a quiet leader, equally blessed with charisma and humility. On occasion Ryden joined me at certain campaign events where we had time to talk. His interest in law was apparent. His attachment to the movement for criminal justice reform was clear.

When I worked in New York for homeless people during law school, I spent time with some Catholic Workers, followers of Dorothy Day, who lived together and helped homeless people by pursuing what they cryptically called "the little way." My dumbed-down understanding was that their calling was helping people in need, and their method included being willing to do the humblest, smallest, least noticed tasks: fixing and washing homeless people's feet, like Jesus; washing their clothes. The little way. The Catholic Workers were expressing their own imperfection and their equality with the homeless people they helped while deeply connecting with them by serving their smallest needs. It was beautiful to see. There was no possibility I could discern the bigger picture, except perhaps an organic, multifold increase in the number and capacity of collective Catholic Worker homes. Catholic Workers stayed very close, direct, little, quiet.

And I thought that described what I knew of Ryden then, but it didn't. He had a larger vision, too. Ryden's countless hours of volunteer work on my campaign, like his thoughts about organizing downtrodden laborers, had him exploring a more systemic and sweeping and bigger approach to what people can do for one another, while his one-on-one union organizing remained a more personal and direct and "little" approach to helping others. As a very young man, Ryden was all about the good fight at its most intimate and unsung, but also in its data-driven, somewhat faceless and public aspect. He believed in public service— the giving of himself that connected him to others—in little and big ways and felt its exciting freedom coursing through his veins. People who haven't felt it might look at what he did and misunderstand it as sacrifice. To him it was joy, a gift he received.

When I saw him, weeks after his AVM rupture, Ryden was locked in, unable to speak words or move his arms or legs much. He was continuing to fight to engage the world. His parents had relocated from their home in San Diego to Philadelphia for most of a year for Ryden's rehabilitation while somehow maintaining their jobs back home and paying their bills.

About a year later, he was doing better, but he could not speak. He barely moved his face. His volitional movements were slight. But he was frequently in a chair rather than always in bed, which was good. He blinked. I saw a thumb move, apparently with purpose. It seemed that his eyes often tracked people and sometimes looked with great intensity at the person speaking. He appeared attentive when people visited, which happened a lot. The breathing tube was gone. Four surgeries later, the vascular time bomb in his brain had been defused.

Other people did better than I did; they visited him more frequently. At first, I dreaded it and was ashamed I dreaded it and didn't know exactly why, except that the chaos and unfairness go so deep. It's hard for me not to cry when I visit him, which I didn't want Ryden to have to see. He is about the age of my sons, shiny with promise and talent and potential. The challenges he faces now could have been theirs. He is a victim and a survivor, like so many victims and survivors of crime. But Ryden is unlike others in having no one to blame, no one to want to catch and hold accountable. He is an innocent man unjustly locked in where he doesn't belong, the injustice growing and mounting as time passes.

I hear his speech therapy has helped. It's better. And his family says that they can tell when he is answering yes or no as he blinks his eyes. As I write, he still cannot speak words, but he can make sounds that indicate he agrees or disagrees. A chart of letters has been used, as is often done with people who are locked in, to allow the selection of letters to make words by a blinking code.

On our last visit with Ryden in Philly, his mom showed us photos of Ryden's home in San Diego. The older ranch house is windowless to the street, but it hides and shelters what lies behind it: a wide, sunny grass lawn lightly sloping down toward a sitting area that looks out unobstructed, over its protective railing at the edge of a bluff, above streets and cars and houses to the limitless blue of the Pacific Ocean. I imagine Ryden there, looking outward and free to fly, like Jean-Dominique Bauby described in his biographical account of being locked in, *The Diving Bell and the Butterfly*. Bauby wrote the book by blinking with his working eye to select each letter of the alphabet. It was Bauby's most lasting and important work, even compared with his distinguished career as a journalist and editor.

His family tells me that Ryden blinked his eyes to spell out "Save room for me" when he was visited by some people who work daily for criminal justice reform. It's unsurprising that would be his wish. Our movement will save room for Ryden; he remains in the good fight. He never left.

# CHAPTER 17

# Eleventh Hour

### *Second Interview at the DAO*

*Do things gradually*
*"Do it slow"*
*But bring more tragedy*
　　　　　　—NINA SIMONE, "Mississippi Goddam"

In 2017, the Philadelphia District Attorney's Office was the busiest and biggest law firm of mostly trial lawyers in the city, at three hundred attorneys and three hundred non-lawyer staff. Every day, twenty-four hours a day, the DAO brought new criminal cases against one to two hundred people. Seeking justice in more than forty thousand new cases a year required a pile of discretionary prosecutorial decisions that no chief prosecutor could possibly make or review. The sheer volume of cases and size of big-city prosecutors' offices enable entrenched office culture to try to eat any new reformist policy. Unless it is reined in, organizational resistance and inertia can quietly foil change, one little-noticed decision at a time. The personnel, systems, and policies matter to reformers who are going after change and pushing up against entrenched culture. After winning the May primary, I was hoping to get started early.

Because winning the May primary made our taking office the

following January almost certain, we wanted to begin collaborating immediately with at least some people in the DAO on a smooth transition. That didn't happen. My team and I made overtures to the outgoing administration. But they only invited us to meet in the DAO once, shortly before Thanksgiving. The offer was so belated, it seemed odd. I made sure to bring a witness, my future chief of staff, Arun Prabhakaran.

We were like a couple of grown-up kids walking together before our first day of classes to take a look at a new school. We made our way, excited but cautious, in a determined march at three miles an hour toward what would be our new offices in a few weeks, located directly across the street from City Hall. I joked about the first audible line of the Clash's "Clampdown," which is "What are we gonna do now!?" Although months of work had gone into our transition, setting priorities and making long-term plans, the truth was that we still didn't have a lot of the basic information we needed to operate in the first few days. As we walked, Arun and I gamed out what to say and what to hold back in our meeting.

I'd been in the DA's office many times before to meet with prosecutors on behalf of my clients, to take on the state as its antagonist to get some justice. But now, for the first time, I would enter the office as the DAO's future boss, the DA-elect. The office looked more broken than usual even before we went inside. Plywood covered one of the building's two giant glass windows on the sidewalk, as it had for months, obscuring the gold emblem of the DAO. Standing outside, I didn't know whether the inside would be just as broken.

I pulled the overly heavy glass entry door wide as the wintry wind tried to hold it closed. It felt like this place was already trying to keep us out. Would it always? I went inside and saw that the escalators—which normally carried a constant stream of people to and from the DA's office lobby—were still being rebuilt. I had known for months that new ones were being installed,

but at a glacial pace only an inattentive government would accept. Maybe the problem was money or political capital in this
patronage town. Or maybe it was plain old squalid dysfunction.
Did rebuilding things always take so long inside the DAO?

Because the escalators were down, we had to exit the DAO
lobby to a generic lobby in another part of the building. There
was little signage to tell us or anyone else where to go. Everything seemed to be under construction. Helpful employees assisted us. We were guided up. But what if you were a member of
the public trying to come into the DAO and weren't the future
boss? Despite the fact that the district attorney officially represented "the people," there was nothing people-friendly in the
way the office was laid out for victims, police, and other witnesses, defense attorneys and defendants, or anyone else needing
to find us.

For a moment, I thought maybe the lack of information was
someone's idea of a security feature, a way to make the place impossible to navigate for an active shooter. More likely, it was just
a jacked-up, slapped-together system, like the other clunky, out-
dated systems we suspected might be waiting for us once we
managed to make our way to our new offices.

We climbed in one of several tiny elevators to ride up toward
the top floor and looked at the elevator buttons. Were there two
buttons for the third floor? Looking more closely, I saw the second 3 was rotated 90 degrees. Someone explained it was there to
substitute for a missing "M" for mezzanine. M's were unavailable? The DAO's several floors were scattered throughout the
building, creating a physically fractured office with who knew
what other tenants' space on floors in between. We had a walled-
off piece of the lobby, the mezzanine, and the third, eighth, elev-
enth, twelfth, thirteenth, fourteenth, and eighteenth floors of the
eighteen-story building.

On the eighteenth floor, Arun and I were led past more secure
doors to the chief prosecutor's door, which presumably would

soon be my new office. There was a symbol on the door's name-
plate that looked like three bases of a baseball diamond. It meant
the door was bulletproof, unlike most others throughout the office. Did the DAs who preceded me really think assassination
was imminent? Did my predecessors feel more important thinking that way? Was whoever decided to build the place with a
bulletproof door for the DA trying to make their bones with the
boss? I wondered again if the DAO's inscrutable signage was
purposeful.

The interim DA, an appointed placeholder for Seth Williams
after his forced resignation, greeted me. She was a pleasant
woman I'd known years prior, before she left the DA's office for
corporate work. Unfortunately, during her short term in office,
two high-level supervisors who were lifers in the office remained.
They were sitting next to each other on one side of the conference table. I returned her greeting, disappointed to see the other
two seated there.

These were men I knew and regarded as unrepentant zeal-
ots, standard-bearers for everything broken that I was trying
to fix. Their names had been raised dozens of times by people
who worked in criminal justice who said their immediately
leaving the office was crucial to achieving culture change. One
was dressed in a black shirt with a dark tie: funeral attire, which
was understandable. The other was peering through small
glasses perched on his sharp nose. As I walked into the office
and saw them seated, they looked like a couple of dug-in ticks,
or maybe coiled snakes. We could have shared how we felt
about criminal justice with each other, but it wouldn't have
been good.

The one with the small glasses had already publicly expressed his views on criminal justice reform at the interim DA's
swearing-in ceremony a few months before, a couple of months
after I had won the primary, at a time when everyone knew I
would become the next DA. Out of respect for the interim DA,

I attended and sat in the audience, toward the front of the large courtroom where her swearing-in took place. I was unsure what to expect but still hoping at that point that she would assist in a cooperative transition during the remaining months. The paper program for the swearing-in ceremony said Mr. Small Glasses would be the primary speaker, a very bad sign. When his turn came to speak, he admitted that there were voices claiming prosecutors and prosecution were off course. Then he summarily dismissed them: "The ship doesn't need to be righted." Perhaps he couldn't resist a last-gasp throwdown in a room mostly full of his partisans, people he supervised. Or maybe he wanted to resign with a flourish. To me, it sounded like the old guard's death rattle.

The other one sitting at the table—the one in black—was the architect of what I saw as the office's toxic culture of shrill opposition to nearly everything and everyone that challenged the DAO in appellate and post-trial matters, regardless of merit. I called him "Dr. No." What offended me wasn't just that the positions he took were so universally adversarial and frequently divorced from my opinion of what it meant to seek justice. I was also bothered by his and his minions' bullying, vilifying rants aimed at defendants, at defense lawyers, and at trial judges who dared to disagree with the DAO's positions. That kind of writing was short on law and facts, but long on sensationalism and meanness, an opinion shared with me by several practitioners and judges.

As I stood by the conference room table where they sat, I passed on discussing our differences. We exchanged curt pleasantries. I quickly took in my future office. The office was a big, plain, high-ceilinged shoebox containing what looked like a desk and a conference table bearing seals of the city. The city seals were roughly inlaid in soft wood, coated in shiny marine varnish that glared in the sun. The furniture that bore them reminded me of a careful high schooler's project from shop class in the

1970s. I had seen similar work in the lobby of the State Correctional Institution at Graterford, Pennsylvania, during my defense attorney days while waiting to visit clients in prison. Careful work, mediocre tools, cheap materials, and approximate dimensions. The desk appeared too short, which made me smile. Perhaps some inmate carpenter knew the desk was for a chief prosecutor and had gotten his revenge?

There was also an enormous freestanding trophy case with empty glass shelves spacious enough to serve as a three-layer bunk bed on a submarine. It contained a few mementos of the interim DA's speaking engagements and other events that occupied her days during the few months since she was appointed. The prior DA's undoubtedly larger collection must have been cleared out when he resigned. The glass behemoth sat directly in between windows that looked out to the statue of William Penn, high atop City Hall. I walked over to one of them. Even from what would soon be my eighteenth-floor window, I had to look up to see the statue fully. Then I looked down to see if I could spot Frank's statue, but City Hall blocked the view north of the ground-level bronze Rizzo. I couldn't wave at him or flip him the bird. At least not from here. And at least not while the interim DA was watching.

As the meeting began, I thought about some of the other prosecutors who had occupied it. Its last occupant, Seth Williams, was already sentenced to five years in federal prison. I thought about Seth's predecessor, Lynne Abraham. She signed countless documents here while doting on the pet cats she housed in the office (reportedly their names were Miss Demeanor and Amicus Curiae). I wondered if, during her reign, shipments of cat litter and cat food showed up periodically while her excited cats walked across the desk she used hundreds of times to sign off on seeking the death penalty.

As the meeting continued, the basic documents provided, like employee directories and organizational charts, were obviously

out of date. Arun and I didn't say much, given the meeting's belated timing, given who attended and what their presence said,
and given the apparently useless materials provided. We perceived no real effort to help and wanted to keep our short-term
plans close. We didn't want to share our real concerns. We made
and they agreed to a few non-controversial asks. We thanked
them for their time and left.

My second interview at the DAO was over, except this time I
had already been hired for the job that at least two of the DAO
employees in that room didn't want me to have. The voters hired
me; I stood no chance with those two. And this time the DAO
employees were the ones whose future employment was uncertain.

We left the interim DA's office and took a quick tour. I noticed
that shredders were prevalent as we looked around, including a
high-volume one as big as a small car. It was disturbing. We took
the elevators down and exited. This time, no one would have
wanted a cartoon of my exiting the building. It would have
shown me walking out the door rather than flying and hitting
the sidewalk, papers (albeit useless ones) under control rather
than fluttering around me. Nothing funny there.

For years, I had seen plaques hanging on the walls in the
DAO's main elevator bay that named several years' "best prosecutor." The prominent location guaranteed what the DAO leadership wanted when they gave out the awards—that hundreds of
employees would repeatedly see them and follow their example.
It was my opinion when I visited that the plaques meant the
leadership was deliberately modeling attorneys who won at all
cost. Mostly the plaques recast infamy as glory, naming some of
the most ruthless and unethical trial lawyers. In the Homicide
Unit, a prep room was named after the infamous prosecutor
Roger King, who posted on his office walls the arrest photos of
defendants whose death sentences he had achieved, marked with
an "X" or a diagonal line through their faces. They were paper

trophies from the hunt. His tactics in and out of the courtroom were outrageous. And the convictions and death sentences he obtained were frequently reversed, requiring a retrial where that was even possible.

Prosecutors like that were exactly the ones we had to turn out, the ones whose worst work we had to undo, and whose dirty secrets we had to explore to arrive at justice in the office we would soon be entering. If these prosecutors had committed ethics violations, constitutional violations, or even crimes to convict the innocent, the proof was in that office, and we had to make sure the proof was not destroyed before our administration began its work.

I took no delight in the idea of firing anyone once I was in office. It was waking me up some nights. But 150,000 people had elected a movement that promised reform. If I kept all the old guard around, they would be sure to break the promises my team and I had made. They'd just wait us out—patronizing us to our faces while undermining us daily. We meant to keep our promises. We could not allow them to make us fail.

Given the chance, most of the people I was thinking of discharging would have fired me on day one, without hesitation. Soon enough we would be in office and I would have to finalize the plan for letting go personnel who couldn't help but undermine the office's new platform. We would have to do it all as humanely as circumstances allowed. Mostly I wanted them to be able to move on, preferably to work in a field of law where less was at stake than in prosecution.

Some Philly prosecutors I had gotten to know during my thirty-year career as a defense attorney were as unscrupulous as a prosecutor gets—Dirty Harry in a lawyer's suit—who cared only about winning convictions and maximizing sentences by whatever means. I viewed them as bullies and cheats who were drawn to the position for the same reason dirty cops are drawn to theirs—they find power exciting, and unchecked power even more so. It was their turn to accept responsibility for what they had done. I knew a few of them would lie in wait for me and retaliate whether I separated them or let them stay, because treachery and retribution were in their nature. That danger was real. Many were connected; many had resources.

Others were more professional but were so philosophically opposed to our mission and so impossible to rein in that they would hurt us daily as long as they were on-site. I knew they would have to go once I was in office. Their gravitas and dominant personalities gave them unmerited influence over other employees.

As 2017 drew to a close, I knew there was a long tradition of traditional chief prosecutors coming into office and firing people after their elections. When they did, it was considered normal and okay, regardless of their motivations. Arlen Specter, the last Republican Philly DA, became DA at thirty-five, in 1966, and was rumored to have dispatched every Democrat from his office within a few days of starting his term. That was one approach. Ed Rendell, who became DA at thirty-three, in 1978, required every single attorney in the office to resign first, then to reapply and explain in writing their worth. He told the press he ultimately discharged about 25 percent of personnel after reapplication, no doubt after putting the other 75 percent through sleepless hell in the process.

When I was sworn in as DA at fifty-six, after having known so many assistant district attorneys—some for thirty years—I had an advantage over former DAs Specter and Rendell. Through the decades, I had handled and tried countless cases for the defense that the ADAs in the office were prosecuting. The best ADAs had shown their worth when my client and I were powerless, when they had no idea that I might be their boss. Some ADAs had proved their exceptional talent, professionalism, and moral compass repeatedly. Others were unexceptional but competent and fair. One lied to me and to the judge so often in a case, she couldn't keep straight the last lie she told. Another liked to bully judges who dared to disagree, behaving disrespectfully in court before maligning the judge to journalists, who obligingly wrote uncritical and sensationalist attacks. Both the prosecutor and the press knew the judges under attack were ethically prohibited from responding, but went right ahead. My years in court before becoming DA taught me that some ADAs had abandoned their obligation to represent the people, preferring to protect bad cops, no matter what lies those cops told or what violence those cops did.

But I didn't know all the attorneys in the office well; some I didn't know at all. And I didn't want to promote or fire people without knowing more once I took office. In November and December 2017, I reached out to some people I respected in the DAO, hoping their opinions would bring useful information. Some people I consulted turned out to be trickier than others, and more tribal in their biases. During the transition, I had coffee with an ADA from the Homicide Unit I'd known for years. Almost all the names on his list of best lawyers in the DAO were Irish, just like his. When I asked him to identify the best Black attorneys, he struggled. I mentioned one Black ADA who, ten years into his career, had shown great promise as a trial lawyer. I asked him what he thought of my idea of advancing the Black attorney to the Homicide Unit. He said, "The kid's not ready yet." I found the answer suspicious. During the transition, when I had breakfast or coffee with other ADAs I knew, they told me more of the same. Their tribe was the best. Their biases seemed mostly unconscious, but the pattern became laughably predictable. As they say in Philly, "It's not what you know. It's whoz youz knowz." The Philly DAO was no exception.

For better and for worse, Philly lawyers in general are drawn to their tribes. Especially around the holidays, the segregated nature of the city's attorney clubs comes into relief as each tribe hosts its own party. The profession presumably charged with thinking hard about equality finds itself fractured into separate tribal clubs for people who are Jewish (Louis D. Brandeis Law Society), Irish (Brehon Law Society), Italian (Justinian Society), Black (Barristers' Association), Latinx (Hispanic Bar Association), LGBTQ (GALLOP—Gay and Lesbian Lawyers of Philadelphia), and pretty much any other group that can gather up its own quorum. These clubs understandably came into being initially as groups of outsiders, to promote and protect the careers of their respective waves of entry into the profession from discrimination and exclusion by the dominant clubs that preceded them. They give their own members awards and pass around résumé-building leadership positions. They do good work in the community. They recruit more members from their tribe to join their club. As outsiders, their club becomes part of the solution until they succeed in becoming insiders who mirror the problem for the next wave of outsiders. And so the pattern repeats in a hyper-competitive profession that advocates equality but often seems to do something else.

I guessed it would take years to reduce tribal thinking within the office in a way that got it right. But, for now, one of the first and most looming problems I would face upon taking office would be to discharge a portion of our personnel because it was necessary, and to do so in a way that was tactical yet principled. I didn't want to do it, but I knew I had to, and I had to try to get it right. I learned that lesson the first time I interviewed at the Philadelphia DA's Office: The coach gets to pick the team.

# CHAPTER 18

## Taking Power

### *Swearing In a Movement*

*I give you power*
*Where do you think it all comes from, huh?*
—ARCADE FIRE, featuring Mavis Staples,
"I Give You Power"

Thirty years in my career had taught me some things about criminal justice; ninety-eight days of the primary campaign and everything since had taught me some things about seeing criminal justice in three dimensions. Without meaning to, I had learned a lot—as a lawyer for outsiders and as an outsider candidate. The campaign and the months before being sworn in had been the final semester of that education. I learned that I was never fighting alone, that I was never even just fighting alongside my allies and activists—that all along, because the criminal justice system had directly and indirectly hurt us all, we were all fighting together. It was the lesson I would need to take into elected office when I went from outsider to reluctant insider, just as I had gone from disillusioned voter to reluctant politician. It was the lesson that would remind me how, even on the inside, we can all fight back together.

It was shortly after midnight on January 1, 2018, when I was informally sworn in as Philly's next district attorney at home with Lisa and our older son, Nate. The three of us were dressed down, shoeless but wearing socks. This informal swearing-in seemed like a good idea in case of a New Year's emergency, given the one-day gap between the end of the previous DA's term and my official swearing-in. Luckily, there was a judge in the house. Nate was back from graduate school at the Actors Studio Drama School in New York for the inauguration. He videoed the midnight swearing-in on his cellphone at my request just in case we ever needed to show it had happened. There were several takes. We couldn't stop laughing. It was all so ridiculous, this private ceremony in socks. Nate became our director long enough to video one take that was good enough. We opened champagne, but only after the swearing-in was done, so no one could question the legitimacy of the oath.

On January 2, 2018, we dressed all the way up. We wore socks *and* shoes. I was nervous and went to my closet to pick and re-pick the day's clothing. As I had during the campaign, I figured a box full of change wasn't as scary wrapped in plain paper. This was not the closet of my childhood, when I wore what we could afford. And it wasn't the closet of my years as a private criminal defense attorney, when a flashier look read as credibility in other people's eyes. Now my closet was old-school, American-made gray flannel and navy stuff, a little retro, conservative, plain, and more about a good fit than fashion. Dress shirts fit body type, neck and sleeve. Suits were off the rack but tailored. Clothing is not one-size-fits-all. Who would want that? Shoes fit in different sizes and widths, and are made on different lasts. Even socks and ties come in a few sizes. I checked everything twice. As I eyed my collar and fixed the knot on my tie again in the mirror, I was playing with the idea of what traditional prosecutors might have tried to do in the fashion world: One-size-fits-all clothes that were mandatory to wear? Prison clothes, I suppose.

I was nervous about the swearing-in ceremony and my first

day as DA, but mostly about what disasters we might face in the days ahead, the four-year term ahead, and maybe even more years than that. Almost as soon as we'd won the primary in May 2017, our team began thinking about what haters in the prior administration and their allies outside the office might do in the nearly seven months before we would take office. Although it was a democratic transition, we were anxious to protect the office from sabotage. It wasn't paranoia.

A few months before I took office, I visited a new chief prosecutor in another city. The year before, she had run for DA and had won on a progressive platform. She was the daughter of an old-time politician and had worked briefly in the district attorney's office as a young lawyer before spending a couple of decades in other pursuits, including running a victims' rights organization. As her candidacy gained traction, her incumbent opponent decided to attack her for being a lesbian. It backfired. She won.

After her victory, the hostile old guard asked her to tell them who she intended to retain and who she intended to replace before she took office, so those leaving could look for other jobs. Despite the rancor of the campaign, she felt compassion. So, several weeks before she took office, she provided notice to more than forty people she had decided to separate. Her compassion was not returned. After the notice was received but before she took office, office computer files were wiped and documents were destroyed, all in the midst of an ongoing scandal over bad convictions that would lead to exonerations. The full extent of the damage done by this sabotage may never be known. But crucial evidence was irrevocably lost, and the fact that it was destroyed from within indicated that people in the office had succeeded in hiding some things—and probably meant innocent people would stay in jail forever while the real perpetrators whose cells they occupied went free. When I visited the newly elected DA, she told me she would have charged the ones who did it with crimes if she could, but she had no way to prove exactly who was involved.

Once she took office, she separated forty-some attorneys. When I visited, one of her top staffers privately told me that, in retrospect, they should have fired more people from the start. They ended up dismissing more later. Bitter prosecutors who had received notice they were being terminated told victims that the new DA was their enemy despite her having run a victims' group for years. They shredded and hid and broke what they could before their new boss was even in the door to start the mending.

Philly and the other jurisdiction had some things in common when I visited. Their chief prosecutors' offices were nearly identical in size—about six hundred employees each, roughly half of them lawyers. Both jurisdictions covered around a couple million residents. And the history of disappearing data files in the other jurisdiction already had its foreshadowing in Philadelphia history, although more so in paper files. For years in Philadelphia, there had been instances of prosecutors on the most controversial and most serious cases claiming long after conviction that they could not find their trial file on a person who was serving a sentence of life without parole or facing a death sentence. Defense attorneys darkly joked about Philly prosecutors and their shredders. One of those cases in which the file went missing stands out.

Someone viciously stabbed to death a man who had gone looking for drugs to buy. His brother, a police officer, soon learned about the murder. A young suspect was quickly identified and taken in by police. He wore a white sweatshirt that was spotless, untouched by blood. He had no criminal record. There was no known connection between the two men. No physical evidence or adult witness supported the case. The evidence came from the mouths of two young sibling boys who were interrogated by police in the middle of the night and shortly after the murder without parental involvement or lawyers. The statements police typed when they spoke to the boys indicated the suspect had said something about stabbing someone that night, before the stabbing occurred. There were indications that the police had grabbed the boys off the street before school, and brought them to the trial to testify without notifying their family. The one boy who testified at trial broke down in the middle of his testimony, requiring a break in the proceedings. A detective followed him to the bathroom. After the break, the prosecutor used leading questions and got the boy to confirm the story. On cross-examination by the defendant's attorney, the boy reversed and denied it again. A conviction and sentence of life without the possibility of parole came swiftly for the young man.

More than twenty-five years later, the man remained in jail. Numerous legal challenges had led more than one judge to question the integrity of the conviction based on the children's testimony. As adults, the two child witnesses both recanted, saying they had been coerced by police and the prosecution to say things that were untrue. In another challenge of the conviction, the original prosecutor was required to provide notes and documents from the trial file. She reported that the entire case file was inexplicably missing and could not be located. Whatever secrets it held would never be known. This kind of "missing file" story, usually connected to a particular group of prosecutors and detectives who banded together for years, was all too common. The young man, now in middle age, was eventually released after completing almost thirty years in jail, shortly before I was sworn in.

The DAO data and electronic systems were vulnerable to digital attacks from outsiders as well. We had enemies, some unidentified. Our campaign had been direct at calling out extremists. We had angered a few anti-Semitic and white nationalist trolls after I condemned the desecration of Jewish cemeteries in St. Louis (a cemetery where my father's parents were buried) and the nearly identical cemetery desecration that happened in Philadelphia a few days later. I didn't see anything especially controversial or inflammatory about condemning play Nazis who desecrate Jewish cemeteries, but it turned out white supremacists' supposedly superior skin is pretty thin, so they got brave online. When we won the primary in May, we were also coming off a presidential election manipulated online in unprecedented ways by Russian hackers. And there had been a few high-profile malware extortions of government offices recently—including in Baltimore and smaller cities. My team and I knew the systems in the DAO were not cutting-edge. Hacking was definitely possible—so possible that eighteen months later the Philly court system itself (but thankfully not our office) was hacked and shut down for weeks. We had gotten only tepid cooperation from the prior administration during the transition and had no reason to trust they were protecting the systems we would soon control. Our hope wasn't just to get and preserve the information we needed to run the office day-to-day. It was to prevent sabotage.

My security detail—two Philadelphia detectives I had selected with care, Agnes Torres and Tom Kolenkiewicz—came by the house for the very first time and traveled with Lisa, Nate, me, and other family in the morning darkness and arctic cold the few blocks to distribute tickets and then to Philadelphia's posh, modern classical music venue, the Kimmel Center, a building that looks like a greenhouse had a baby with a spaceship.

Many newly elected officials were being sworn in there that day, mostly judges in black robes looking like a seated choir, spread out across the wide concert stage. Lisa's robe was hanging on a coat rack backstage until the ceremonies began. But the only two elected officials who would speak were the two at the top of the ticket—the DA and then the controller. A movement had elected me, but only I would speak for them, which didn't quite feel right.

Criminal justice reform isn't about any individual. It's about every individual—it's a movement dedicated to taking on a system that has abused all of us, directly and indirectly. I wasn't taking over the district attorney's office. A movement was. And if criminal justice reform was a movement and wasn't about me, then the inaugural address for the movement didn't need much of the politician's favorite word, "I." And the swearing-in ceremony shouldn't be just about me, either. I wasn't being sworn into office; a movement was. That route was safer for a movement's progress. It was also safer for me, moving forward.

I understood the dangers of a movement too closely identified with its supposed leader. For a movement's opponents, a so-called leader is far easier to wreck than the movement itself or the ideas that drive it. Wrecking the leader looks like a win and discourages the movement and its growth, at least for a while. This was clear to me from the history of utopian movements, something I studied in a college history course, and from the lives of so-called activist leaders and their movements in America, which I studied in order to defend them. But I also knew it was true from the history of our extended family. Kate Millett's life, among other things, had taught me that. Her memorial service several weeks earlier had reminded me.

For days, I had been grumbling about the egocentric nature of public swearing-in ceremonies for elected officials, and how contrary to our platform the whole idea seemed. Nate was home from his three-year MFA acting program in New York. He graduated from college with a theater degree and strong academics, but his training in theater and his talent with words, especially spoken words, began long before college. As a toddler, he claimed a neighborhood tree stump where he would air out his lungs for passersby on the sidewalk and squirrels. At thirteen, he seized the stage during a field trip to the Apollo. As he grew older, he excelled in high school theater—slam poetry, hip-hop, college theater, summer stock. He was acting in New York before getting his MFA.

In late 2017, Nate sat quietly thinking for a long time through my talk about the weirdness of my being sworn in alone for a movement. After a while, he said: "If you're all a movement, why shouldn't you all be sworn in? People stand up with you. They raise their hands and get sworn in with you. Why not?" It was perfect if we could get a mostly unfamiliar crowd to follow the plan.

As I did with most of my closing arguments, I chewed on ideas for a short inauguration speech for days but couldn't write it until a few hours before it was time to speak. Starting around six A.M., I spent more time than I had banging out the text on my computer only to discover a printer failure when I tried to print it out. I took out my cellphone and photographed the speech on the computer monitor to capture the text, knowing that emailing the computer file of it to myself and opening that email in the concert hall might fail. The idea of standing in a sleek concert hall before a couple thousand seats without a printed speech was unappealing, even for an old trial lawyer. A photo of the speech would have to do. Past my seven-thirty A.M. deadline, I stepped over my sleeping teenage nephew, one of Steve's sons, who was in town for the swearing-in ceremony and had been sleeping on the floor of the room where I typed out the speech. I took the photo and ran upstairs to shower and change.

Ultimately, the speech had to be about the movement's true north: compassion for every individual directly involved or indirectly affected by criminal justice. That's everyone. Victims need our compassion. So do defendants. And so does everyone uninvolved in a particular criminal case, because their lives are so profoundly affected by it that they stand to gain with a just outcome or lose if the outcome of that criminal case is unjust.

That no one group or side has a monopoly on claiming our compassion is a tricky concept in criminal justice. Sometimes the offender has been victimized before or the victim has offended previously; and, of course, sometimes the ostensible victim lies

and the falsely accused defendant is the one suffering. And sometimes people who think they are uninvolved aren't. The bonfire
of money poorly spent on criminal justice has already burned up
the budget needed to fill the gaps in public education and economic opportunity and futures.


But without the possibility of compassion for everyone, there is
no chance of accurately telling the difference between perpetrator and victim, less of telling where those categories overlap, and
almost no chance of discerning the harm served on everyone else
by a jacked-up mishandling of criminal justice. We are all connected in a web of interdependence and we need to hold on to
that idea: It's only through compassion being available to everyone that things get fixed for victims and perpetrators and all the
rest of us. And it's only through fixing the causes of criminal
behavior that we are all safer. Clergy at swearing-in ceremonies
seem to be a requirement, perhaps a leftover from English traditions before there was a separation between church and state.
For some newly elected officials, perhaps clergy's invocations
and prayers encourage them to approach their new duties with
courage, reverence, and humility. For others, clergy's presence
may just puff up their sense that ascending to higher office con-
nects them to a higher power. As the elected official at the top of
the ticket, I was given the opportunity to suggest some of my
favorite clergy.

Three of the four presiding clergy at the swearing-in were
pro bono ex-clients of mine—Reverends Mark Tyler, Gregory
Holston, and Isaac Miller—for fighting poverty and gun violence, and for sticking up for labor. I defended Reverend Miller
and other clergy when they were arrested for obstructing the
business of an extraordinarily dirty gun shop. Those clergy were
protesting the gun shop's refusal to commit to best practices for
preventing guns from ending up in the hands of criminals. They

sat in, sang hymns, and knelt to pray at the shop. They hoped their protests would be heard and lives would be saved from gun violence. Instead, twelve of them were arrested by Philadelphia police and prosecuted by the DAO on misdemeanor charges. A judge I liked very much had invited her son and his whole middle-school class to come watch the case she was hearing. An attorney I know later told me that he asked her what she was going to do just before she announced her verdict in the case against the clergy. With a grin, he claimed that she said, "I'm not going to hell." Maybe he was joking. But she did find them all not guilty. Reverend Holston and Reverend Tyler had a simpler case. They sat in and sang hymns for organized labor at Philly's airport. Their cases went away, too.

My immediate introduction before being sworn in would come from Reverend Miller, whose Christian radical leanings fit nicely with the idea of swearing in a movement. His church had been the famously progressive Church of the Advocate, where Dr. King once spoke. I selected Miller, the most senior and the only retired member of the clergy, to speak right before me, based partly on the brilliant testimony he delivered at trial when he was a defendant in the gun shop case.

To a silent, captivated audience in the concert hall, Reverend Miller's frequent refrain was "These are ominous times. . . ." His words disappeared into the darkness that blanketed the layered balconies and velvet seats. He methodically linked the moment to our country's slow, wandering march toward justice. Then Miller asked everyone to stand, to raise their right hand, and to get sworn in with me as part of the movement elected to run the Philadelphia District Attorney's Office. After a lifetime in the pulpit, when Miller asked the audience to stand, there wasn't much of a choice. They stood. Lisa, wearing her judicial robe, swore all of us in like she meant it, while Nate held the Bible. I said yes. I kissed her, hugged Nate, thought of Caleb already at his new job while I was starting mine, and shook hands with the reverend. I was officially the DA. And it was time to speak. Taking the podium, I read the text of my speech from my cellphone:

A movement was sworn in today. A movement. A movement for criminal justice reform that has swept Philadelphia and is sweeping the nation. On behalf of that movement, and as nothing more than a technician for that movement, I have taken the oath to discharge the duties of the Philadelphia district attorney. The strange thing is the oath does not say what those duties are. So let's say them now. They are: To seek justice in society; to communicate the truth; to represent the public; to exercise power with restraint, with our roots dug deep in equality. . . .

Let's talk a little bit about our family, because in the City of Brotherly Love and Sisterly Affection, we are all family.

Today there is a little girl in Southwest Philly who wears big glasses. She's a great student and she is going to cure cancer if we let her. Her public school teacher is top-notch, but there are thirty-five kids in a class where there should be twenty. Where is the teacher who would cut the class size in half? The other teacher we need is lost in the cost of a jail cell occupied by a person who has no business in a jail cell. Lost in the cost of a death penalty that is never imposed and is immoral. Today we start the long road toward trading jails (and death row) for schools.

Today there is a young police officer in North Philly who is driving a marked car in the neighborhood where he grew up. He's smart, loves his community, and wants to keep it safe. But when he waves they don't always wave back and they don't tell him as much as he would like because there is a division between his uniform and the neighborhood that never had to be. That was not his doing. Today we start the long road toward trading division between police and the communities they serve for unity and reconciliation. Unity and reconciliation that make us safer.

Today there is a mother in Northeast Philly whose cellphone is always on ring for fear of her son being arrested, or something much worse. He was prescribed pain pills after a work accident several months ago and about the only thing he hasn't lost yet is his life. He is homeless and wasting away from heroin addiction. Today we start the long road toward trading jail cells occupied by people suffering from addiction for treatment and harm reduction.

Today there is a brother of a homicide victim in South Philly whose family can't get justice because the key witness won't come to court for fear of deportation. The witness is afraid of our own federal government. Today we start the long road toward empowering and protecting some of our most vulnerable witnesses and survivors—immigrants who lack legal status—to participate in our criminal justice system as witnesses and survivors because today we trade fear of the federal government for sanctuary.

On these and so many other issues facing the City of Philadelphia, we—this movement—have taken an oath to remember that in the City of Brotherly Love and Sisterly Affection we are all family. We all deserve protection. We all deserve support and help and second chances. We are all this family and we are all this movement. Join us! Thank you.

The acceptance speech was the bookend to the ten-minute campaign announcement; it was my chance in three minutes to wave the flag of the movement that would soon start its work in the new DA's Office. The word "I" showed up only once for a reason. "We" was the point. The people who showed up in the speech I either knew or knew existed—a brilliant schoolgirl, a well-intentioned young Black cop, a mother wracked by her son's addiction, and a brother waiting on justice for his brother's murder. Every one of these people was being hurt by something broken in the criminal justice system we were trying to fix. None of these relatively powerless, diverse outsider characters had been arrested, but they might as well have been by a criminal justice system that was against them, against the people. And every one of their stories ended with a call to action to the largely insider audience in this vast classical music venue: to join our movement, to be family. This was not the small, warm circle of "my people" who had surrounded and supported me during our campaign announcement. This audience was much larger, and mostly unfamiliar political insiders or their allies and people from the criminal courts, with a sprinkling of the same people who attended the announcement and were given one of our small batch of tickets. Somehow, we had gotten insiders and their allies to stand and wait to be sworn in as part of our movement. They were welcome to join us, hopefully for more than the ceremony. Our movement was what we believed. It was what I believed after having been educated three decades as a worker in criminal justice and after having had that education refined in a campaign that connected me to everyone I'd met and some people I'd missed during my career, in every part of the city.

I already knew the Philadelphia District Attorney's Office would look broken when we got there that afternoon. The escalators wouldn't be working. And, on such a frigid, windy day, the excessively heavy front door would try to push us back out, like characters in a cartoon. But, broken or not, we were going inside and we weren't leaving until things got fixed. It was time for the people to turn on the lights.

# EPILOGUE

## Swearing In the Future

*When it go down we woman and man up*
*They say, "Stay down," and we stand up*
—COMMON AND JOHN LEGEND, "Glory"

I was an aging chief prosecutor, fifty-eight years old, holed up in my office, preparing to speak at the swearing-in ceremony for our new attorneys who had just passed the bar exam. The vast majority were just out of law school and had moved to Philadelphia from other states; others were mid-career hires. It was only the second class of attorneys I'd helped swear in, and it was the first class recruited and picked entirely by our administration. They'd had options; they'd accepted our offer, often over better-paying jobs. We chose them; they chose us. In an office of three hundred attorneys, this was a big class of sixty-five. It was just before Thanksgiving week, 2019, roughly seventy-five days after our new attorneys began their post–Labor Day training.

I was alone in my office, preparing my talk. I was staring at a black-and-white photograph in a book. The photo depicted a well-dressed young African American woman being slapped hard in the face by the hand of a man in a suit. The clothing and makeup said 1960s. Her face was a blur as her features contorted and moved with the slap. I was debating whether or not to show such a harsh, shocking image during my remarks—it was offensive, hurtful, like so many photographs prosecutors see in their daily work. But the ceremony wasn't work; it was a celebration. And most people at the ceremony would not be prosecutors accustomed to seeing real violence frozen in time by photography. If I used it, I would need to be clear why seeing the photo at this celebration was so essential.

The image came from one of several big books of photography mostly covering the American civil rights movement that are usually piled like building blocks on the coffee table in front of the sofa in my office. That day the books were in use—littered with brightly colored Post-it notes to identify photographs I wanted to use. Some of the books are specific—one covered the Selma campaign, when marchers crossed the Edmund Pettus Bridge and were beaten down by Alabama state troopers on Bloody Sunday, only to rise again within days. Another features photos of Montgomery's powerful lynching memorial, the National Memorial for Peace and Justice.

The largest and thickest book, *Freedom*, is topically more general: It contains thousands of sepia and black-and-white photographs that cover the entire history of the American civil rights movement and the related history that made it necessary. The book was a gift from my wife a decade earlier that I'd used many times in my work—the source of the photos I had blown up on foam board and used repeatedly as trial exhibits in court to defend protesters who were being prosecuted by the office I now ran. Several of those foam boards, including two depicting the serene and well-dressed portraits of Rosa Parks and Dr. King, were mounted on the wall and over my shoulder, directly behind the sofa where I now sat. They were mug shots from their bus boycott arrests. I hunched over this singular image, the disturbing blur of an arm and face colliding.

Below the black-and-white photograph of the woman being slapped was an explanatory caption: The students and activists were training one another not to react violently to even the most extreme provocation, including actual violence like this hard slap. This kind of training proved useful later when they were sitting at lunch counters while hecklers poured sugar and salt in their hair, when they were pulled off those counter stools, during rough arrests, when prayerful demonstrators were blasted by fire hoses, or when they were attacked by police dogs.

I debated. The image was evocative, emotive, memorable. The slap was real, but it was training to avoid greater violence. An understanding of its context might stick with young attorneys destined for less physical but repeated verbal slaps in some court-rooms from judges and others who are just not ready for change. I stared at the image for a while. Even with the explanation, the image was just too much. How many seconds of shock would pass before its context was sufficiently explained? We didn't need it; we had plenty of other images that made our point but were less disturbing. But the image went with me to the swearing-in cere-mony that day. This was the legacy we were trying to follow. This was our work.

Considerable planning had gone into the ceremony. Because of the new crew's size and the importance of the moment, we needed a big, beautiful room adequate for a few hundred proud friends and family. The class was from all over the country. We decided to livestream and record it for family and friends who were unable to travel from Georgia, California, Chicago, Louisiana, Boston. The class was academically excellent, blessed with extraordinary life experience, diverse; we would try to honor all of that. Names and personal pronouns needed to be correct; we would check those details, practice them more than once, scribble a homemade code of phonetic spellings to help me identify people correctly. Above all else, there would need to be a point to the celebration—a tan-gible point that went beyond personal achievement and went beyond welcome. Weren't we once again swearing in a movement? And isn't a movement fundamentally about public service and sacrifice, the struggle to serve others that fills the people born to do it with joy and freedom?

Our relentless schedule of recruiting and traveling the year before to nearly thirty law schools had brought this energetic class. These hires were not your usual local newbies commonly found among the entering class of big-city prosecutors' offices around the country. They were not a homogeneous group of ex-frat boys, former high school jocks and cheerleaders, and homers who knew one another since childhood in a place where their families had always lived. These lawyers had not arrived on a conveyor belt from one or more local feeder schools that happened to be the office leadership's alma maters. They came from all over and had done everything.

They were heavily from more and different law schools than the usual Philly DAO class hired by prior administrations. More of them were graduates of highly ranked national schools than were hired in other administrations. They were expressive, verbal people, as other administrations' classes had been. But many more in this class used words and phrases from other locales and spoke in regional accents that were clearly different from the language of row-house Philly. They were Blacker and browner.

So many different schools were represented in the class that very few of the new hires were former classmates or had known one another from more than the eight weeks since they arrived, or maybe since they formed a Facebook group before arriving. In a way, they were nearly all outsiders to each other or to Philadelphia or both. But they were also united, just not in all the usual ways of prior administrations.

They were an anti-tribe, and therefore a threat to the worst of tribalism itself. They were idealistic and talented attorneys united by their decision to sacrifice for others, to change, and to be a part of changing history rather than just observing it. Many of them would be future leaders, an arguably unmanageable group of leader types to be managed by an unelectable leader. We were turning into the unlikeliest of utopian communities—inhabiting the structures of power we hoped to restrain. The anti-tribe's mission was to make traditional prosecution obsolete, and we loved it.

An hour before the ceremony's scheduled start, and after a couple of hurried, last-minute revisions and reprintings of the program, it was time to head over. I looked out my eighteenth-floor office window across the street at the gleaming off-white stone chunk that is Philadelphia's City Hall, where the ceremony would take place. I looked up at the giant bronze sculpture of William Penn on top. I checked my watch. As always, from my office window the view of Frank Rizzo's statue was obscured, but others had their eye on it. Within weeks of the ceremony, Frank's bronze back would be graffitied yet again, this time with the word "FASCIST." It happened late one night while Frank's fixed pupils were directed at City Hall's giant Christmas tree, its dormant holiday Ferris wheel and holiday train, its closed ice skating rink, and the closed warming tent that served booze and was sponsored by orthopedic surgeons. That defacement would come later and long before Frank's statue went away.

But, that day, we were starting over. As we crossed the four traffic lanes between us and City Hall, there was no holiday display up just yet. Nothing was sprayed on Frank's back at the moment we entered City Hall, where every Philadelphia adult criminal case was tried until about twenty years ago, when our ballooning criminal justice system outgrew it. The increasing numbers of humans arriving on prison buses for court, increasing numbers of chargeable crimes, increasing cases, increasing mandatory sentences, increasing years of incarceration, and increasing everything else that went with it—judges, prosecutors, defense attorneys, court officers, courtrooms, probation officers—required more space in a newer, bigger building just for criminal cases, initially called the Criminal Justice Center. The criminal justice system outgrew a structure that had been big enough for the prior one hundred years. We were crossing to City Hall. We needed to start over.

I arrived an hour early in a courtroom that seated three hundred. About a dozen seats were already filled. A video screen as big as a Ping-Pong table was elevated high enough in the front of the room to be visible from the back row. Two sets of body-worn microphones were laid out at the podium. One was for the livestream. The recorded version would be a keepsake for the graduates and their friends and family; it might eventually spread through social media as one more statement of the Philly DAO's principles two years in. The second microphone was to amplify my talk when I wandered away from the podium toward the images we would show on the video screen.

I had interviewed nearly all of the new lawyers who were arriving myself, many of them during the prior year. As in most courtrooms in City Hall, the high walls were covered in oil portraits of retired judges—a tradition for retiring judges. Often their tribe of lawyers (the Brehons for an Irish judge; the Justinians for an Italian; the Barristers for a Black judge) will pay for the portrait, or maybe their friends will pay. A few judges reject the arguably ethically hazy appearance of lawyers paying for things for judges (even in retirement) and choose to pay for the portraits themselves, or simply decline to have a portrait done at all.

Most courtrooms' portraits were of white men with waxed mustaches, their high collars protruding up from the collars of their robes. Not so in the space reserved for public events—the ceremonial courtroom, where many of the leadership positions were now held by Black judges and women judges. More recent and more diverse judicial portraits were on the walls of this most public space. Under the oily eyes of judges, our new lawyers were walking in, past where their people would sit, coming inside the heavy oak divider that marks the bar of court. In sport, this would be the playing field. Today their role was to sit in folding chairs and wait for their swearing-in. They were dressed as the new professionals they were becoming, happy and expectant. There were no obvious cliques. And now their people were arriving, although it was hard to know who was with whom.

I suited up with one mic on each lapel. Twisting wires and cigarette-pack-sized transmitters hung from both sides of my belt. With twenty minutes to go before starting time, people were standing around, talking. I got as close as possible to the video screen in order to block what I could of the slides I would show during my talk as I quickly clicked through them with my remote. I was checking, once again, the sequence of images. The gear was working.

The hot coffee I brought with me to loosen up a sore throat was cooling down. In my prior life as a trial attorney, I seldom had a sore throat. But now a hoarse voice or sore throat was almost chronic, possibly the result of so much public speaking and so many workdays full of talking through back-to-back meetings. Maybe the frequent travel around the city and country in all kinds of weather was part of it. Or maybe a sore throat just went with my new job of communicating a movement's new narrative of criminal justice.

Someone told me Judge McKee had arrived. I went back to greet him and talk through the run of show. Theodore McKee is a Black federal appeals judge in his mid-seventies who served as a federal prosecutor and a state court judge in Philly before being appointed to the federal court. He became the chief judge of the Third Circuit Court of Appeals for a while, one notch below the U.S. Supreme Court. He is also the guy I used to see shopping in a grocery store wearing a *Mother Jones* magazine T-shirt. This was the second year he accepted our invitation to preside over our ceremonies. He had worked for decades on the inside in a broken and racist system, wearing different hats. I knew from his talk the prior year that his talk today would be a rousing call to action. I fully expected he would rally the new class to embrace their oaths to seek justice and uphold the Constitution, to reject bias of all types, to elevate equality, to exercise their power with great care, and to uphold the highest ethical standards. It was going to be a good show.

The time came for me to start. I hid my cup of room-temperature coffee on my side of the top edge of the podium. I asked the new class to cheer for their parents, families, partners, and friends who had gotten them there, wherever they might be. I began clicking through the slides of photos from my books, which were broadcast on the big screen. The first slide was an iconic, close-up image of Dr. King, confidently facing the camera and no doubt eloquently speaking behind a small forest of microphones in his suit and tie to an unseen crowd of unknown proportions. It captured how he appeared from the outside, from the perspective of the crowd. It was King's public image, the one that reminds us of another photo of a smiling King dressed in tuxedo and tails to accept his Nobel Prize at a posh ceremony. Long after his death, King's public image would evolve again into a postage stamp and a federal holiday and renamed roadways in city after city.

The second slide was essentially the same event, but viewed from King's side of the podium. Once again, King was speaking to a small forest of microphones; but this time the photographer stood behind him, rather than in the audience's shoes. The shot caught the typewritten text of his speech and scrawled notes handwritten in ballpoint pen, the snaking microphone cables trailing from the microphones and his wrinkled paper cup of water. Beyond all that was the crowd as King saw them, from his spot behind the podium. The shot captured how the outside world appeared from his side, the inside of the movement. King was leaning forward, persuading, energized and straining and pushing against and going over and going around everything that was supposed to be too heavy or too wide or too tall for him to move. The crowd was human: uncertain, certain, rapt, deciding, distracted. The photo of struggle and work from King's side of the podium and the movement was glorious.

The third slide, fourth slide, fifth slide went deeper into what that hourly struggle actually was—grittier shots from inside the movement. Here were King and Ralph Abernathy in unglamorous Elmer Fudd hats with fluffy ear flaps snapped back, trudging along on cold pavement during a march. There they were a little later, sitting uncomfortably in the wintry grass on the backs of their workaday coats and rubbing their suffering feet, retying their boots after miles of walking. Another shot was a close-up of an unidentified swollen pair of marching feet, heavily taped and wrapped.

There was the young, intense, fretful James Forman, Sr. (the Yale professor's father), dressed in overalls, next to King on a campaign against poverty and obviously chewing over some weighty decision no one else in the picture thought was easy, either. Another slide was a photo of King and Ralph Abernathy being pushed from behind, either by police hands or police words, uncharacteristically flustered and dressed in denim shirts and plain pants, clearly having a bad day. In another shot, King was in overalls, head drooping and looking exhausted while standing on a dark church stage at night. The next slide was of neatly groomed young Freedom Riders, white and Black college students mostly in the frame, singing together inside their bus with National Guardsmen outside, visible through the bus windows. The following slide was that bus on fire and billowing thick, opaque smoke, its Freedom Riders outside now, distraught but alive on the berm of the road.

Before Judge McKee spoke and swore in the new ADAs, we took most of an hour to briefly list the accomplishments of every individual lawyer preparing to be sworn in and to project each of their photos on the big screen while we did it. The phonetic scribbles and my rehearsals for pronouncing their names helped me get through, but I still messed up two or three names. The people whose names I mangled spoke up immediately, correcting me in the room full of people; I smiled. These were no robots. They were the kind of people who speak up when something's not right, the ones who are so necessary to a movement. They made sure we all saw them and could say their names just as I hoped and believed they will make sure our criminal justice system sees others and says their names.

Second Thanksgiving—the gathering of our people, the family you choose and that chooses you—came early in 2019. Shortly before regular Thanksgiving, every member of this anti-tribe, my people and our people and their people, watched as the slides on the big screen confirmed the slog of what it means to be inside and part of a movement that matters—the kind of movement that will get you called a troublemaker and worse. They saw the struggling existence that would wear them out, thicken their skin, train them not to respond to the rage of a hostile system by returning rage. They saw its grind of long hours, long distances, and long odds, its pressure and risk and sacrifice and bad days spent fighting the good fight, the fight to find justice for others and knock down the terrible things that get in the way of that mission, even when those terrible things have gone on for a very long time.

They saw that the glory of a great social movement is not the history of its famous so-called leaders, its prizes won, iconic victory photos, or even its posthumous national holiday and postage stamp. The glory of a great social movement is that slog—just being in it, when you are becoming the power that gets it done, becoming the power that is uncomfortable and makes mistakes, becoming the power that ultimately changes you and changes cities and changes politics forever. One by one, they saw their own faces on that same screen as well.

We wished them luck. Judge McKee spoke quietly but with growing force, encouraging and cajoling and challenging these new lawyers to seek out and reject bias, to know their purpose, to keep track of the arcs of their lives, and to live up to their oaths. Then they held up their right hands and took that oath to seek justice—justice that includes everyone, that is as broad as society, that is for the people.

If we and they and our movement are really lucky, they will climb onto our old shoulders and prove that we didn't do enough by doing even more.

# ACKNOWLEDGMENTS

From early on, people have always said that I needed a filter, or at least a good editor. I got a great one for this book: Chris Jackson, the amazing chief of One World, who patiently helped me to build something whole from a parts pile of old stories, breathy rants, and threads of thought on minor fixations like statues, buildings, and music. Thank you, Chris, for your vision, literary craft, and grasp of justice, and your diplomacy when my writing got stupid. And thank you to your endlessly talented, enthusiastic team at One World/Penguin Random House: London King; Ayelet Gruenspecht; Daniel Novack, Esq.; Carla Bruce-Eddings; Lulu Martinez; Craig Adams; Mark Maguire; Greg Mollica; and Mika Kasuga.

An idealistic and futuristic literary agent, Doug Abrams of Idea Architects, got me to Chris Jackson. With the invaluable help of Doug's colleagues Lara Love and Rachel Neumann, the Idea Architects team nudged me to remember and excavate stories from their piles of dust, and to reflect upon them. Thank you all for imagining this book even before I did, for making a science of your business, and for spacewalking with me in the mysterious universe of writing and publishing a first book.

Ty Stiklorius, the powerhouse talent manager (and producer) in charge of Friends at Work got me to Doug Abrams. Thank you, Ty, for your perfect, timely advice and for your selfless support of criminal justice reform in your life and in your work. Even in L.A., you are a favorite daughter of Philly.

Even the idea of writing a book is owed to someone else. That lightbulb was the gift of another ex-Philadelphian, Daniel Denvir. Thanks, Dan, for inspiring me to write and for your incisive journalism in different media, including on criminal justice.

And thank you to all those people in the good fight who are the protagonists of this book. You outsiders, you different kinds of people who joyfully fight for others, are peacefully taking institutional power back from insiders, and are making that power work for everyone. Named and unnamed, you are here and everyone you serve knows who you are.

Thank you to my parents, William and Juanita Frances, for their love and their struggle and what it showed me. And thank you to my wonderfully varied extended family for your kindness and support. To Lisa, Nate, and Caleb, who inhabit this book: I love you. Thank you for listening to most of these stories years ago. Thank you, even then, for letting me know that I needed a good editor. You will always be my dearest companions in life.

# THE *FOR THE PEOPLE* PLAYLIST

Introduction. Elton John, "Philadelphia Freedom"
    Songwriters: Elton John and Bernie Taupin
1. Tracy Chapman, "Talkin' 'bout a Revolution"
2. The National, "Mistaken for Strangers"
    Songwriters: Aaron Brooking Dessner, Bryce David Dessner, and Matthew Donald Berninger
3. Billie Holiday, "Strange Fruit"
    Songwriter: Abel Meeropol
4. Frank Sinatra, "My Way"
    Songwriters: Claude François, Jacques Revaux, and Paul Anka
5. The Clash, "Clampdown"
    Songwriters: Joe Strummer and Mick Jones
6. Bruce Springsteen, "Streets of Philadelphia"
7. Drive-By Truckers, "Never Gonna Change"
    Songwriter: Jason Isbell
8. "Trust in Me" from *The Jungle Book*
    Songwriters: Robert Sherman and Richard Sherman
9. U2, "I Still Haven't Found What I'm Looking For"

Songwriters: Paul Hewson, David Howell Evans, Adam Clayton, and Larry Mullen Jr.

10. David Bowie, "Lazarus"

11. Bob Dylan, "Gotta Serve Somebody"

12. N.W.A, "Straight Outta Compton"
    Songwriters: O'Shea Jackson, Lorenzo Jerald Patterson, Andre Romelle Young, and Eric Lynn Wright

13. The Clash, "Know Your Rights"
    Songwriters: Joe Strummer and Mick Jones

14. The Chambers Brothers, "Time Has Come Today"
    Songwriters: Willie Chambers and Joseph Chambers

15. Prince, "Sign o' the Times"

16. Steve Miller Band, "Fly Like an Eagle"
    Songwriter: Steven Haworth Miller

17. Nina Simone, "Mississippi Goddam"

18. Arcade Fire, featuring Mavis Staples, "I Give You Power"
    Songwriters: Régine Chassagne, Richard R. Parry, Win Butler, Jeremy Gara, William Butler, and Tim Kingsbury

Epilogue. Common and John Legend, "Glory"
    Songwriters: John Roger Stephens and Lonnie Rashid Lynn

# INDEX

# ABOUT THE AUTHOR

LARRY KRASNER spent thirty years as a criminal defense and civil rights attorney before he decided to run for district attorney in Philadelphia. He is currently serving as the twenty-sixth district attorney of Philadelphia. The son of a crime novelist and an evangelical preacher, he navigated from the St. Louis and Philadelphia-area public school systems to the University of Chicago and Stanford Law School. He won the DA race as a political unknown, riding a wave of popular support in 2017. Krasner has frequently said that he considers criminal justice reform to be the civil rights issue of our time. He describes himself, and his fellow progressive prosecutors, as mere technicians for a grassroots movement for criminal justice reform that has been sweeping the nation and electing progressive prosecutors since long before he ran for office. Krasner lives in Philadelphia with Lisa Rau, his wife of more than thirty-one years, a professional mediator and former Philadelphia judge.

ABOUT THE TYPE

This book was set in a Monotype face called Bell. The Englishman John Bell (1745–1831) was responsible for the original cutting of this design. The vocations of Bell were many—bookseller, printer, publisher, typefounder, and journalist, among others. His types were considerably influenced by the delicacy and beauty of the French copperplate engravers. Monotype Bell might also be classified as a delicate and refined rendering of Scotch Roman.